By God's Grace

I Will Get Up Again and Win II

Autum Augusta

Order this book online at www.trafford.com
or email orders@trafford.com

Most Trafford titles are also available at major online book retailers.

© Copyright 2012 Autum Augusta.
All rights reserved. No part of this publication may be reproduced, stored in a retrieval system, or transmitted, in any form or by any means, electronic, mechanical, photocopying, recording, or otherwise, without the written prior permission of the author.

Printed in the United States of America.

ISBN: 978-1-4669-5733-6 (sc)
ISBN: 978-1-4669-5734-3 (e)

Trafford rev. 10/09/2012

North America & international
toll-free: 1 888 232 4444 (USA & Canada)
phone: 250 383 6864 • fax: 812 355 4082

TABLE OF CONTENTS

CHAPTER I

A NEW LIFE

Tim and Lori loaded the U-Haul trailer and the van with their furniture and other belongings, and took the loads to Thomasville. They returned to the old farm again in the van to pick up more things and the two large dogs.

Lori watched as the old house was blocked from view because of the dust rolling up behind the van. She had left so many dreams behind and it was hard to understand why so many dreadful things had happened to her and Tim.

Lori had dreamed of fixing up the old farm, and even building a duck pond west of the house. She had dreamed of having all of her children, and grandchildren, singing together in the music room and having a good time. Now she and Tim were running for their lives.

The house that once was filled with love and laughter is now empty and quiet. Mice run across the dusty floor where once the walls absorbed the bouncing and singing of a young Hispanic girl. If the walls could talk, would they tell a different story than what was in Lori's heart that day? Would they say that Tim was not innocent?

Lori sighed and turned around to face the road. She took another look at the man she had married four years ago.

Tim was forty-four, just one year younger than Lori. He was a new believer in Christ and had probably made some bad decisions, but Lori felt that he was trying to please God. Tim was heavily built. His blonde hair was thinning. His eyes looked in different directions, and he was blind without his thick glasses. Tim was not handsome, but he had made Lori feel loved for the first time in twenty years.

Tim's former family had turned against him and may have had something to do with the nightmare they had just been through.

Lori had grown used to Tim's eyes looking in opposite directions. She still enjoyed the feelings of warmness when Tim took her in his arms. There had been times of terror, but Lori had tried to put these out of her memory.

They had believed God for prosperity, but they had lost almost everything they owned. Storms and drought had robbed them of crops and cattle. They had ended up owing the bank one million and five hundred thousand dollars.

Tim and Lori had to declare bankruptcy. The bank had taken the cattle, land, and Lori's beautiful mobile home that had been paid for when Lori had met Tim. The bank was supposed to leave them a residence after they declared bankruptcy, but the old farm house was on the farmland and was lost with the land. They had been left with nothing except their furniture, a TransVan, and a three-year-old car they had to pay the bank for keeping. Tim's mother was too old to drive so she had given Tim her ten-year-old Oldsmobile.

They had not been able to adopt Rosita, the little Mexican girl that lived with them for a year. Tim had been arrested for child molesting, instead. Lori loved the child as much as if she were her own flesh and blood, and now she would never see Rosita again. She could never believe that Tim had molested Rosita. Lori believed that Rosita had been "set up" to accuse Tim.

The court hearing and lawyers' questions had been as horrible and embarrassing for Rosita as it had been for her and Tim. Rosita had finally said that she couldn't remember what Tim had done to her, and that she wished she was still living with them.

The judge still would not drop the charges against Tim. They did not have enough money to fight to prove Tim's innocence in a jury trial.

Tim had pleaded a Non-CONTENDRA which meant that he admitted to the crime on paper. He had been given one year unsupervised probation, but if he broke the law in any way, he would be sent directly to prison for not less than four years.

Tim and Lori felt that Tim had been "set up" the first time when he was arrested. Now they had to leave the county where they had lived all their lives and live among people they didn't know for Tim's safety. Lori had been forced to leave her teaching job of fifteen years; the job that had kept food on the table through tough times. Now the job was just a part of her past.

It had taken all of Lori's teaching checks to help support Tim's kids the first two years they were married. It had taken all her checks to help farm and take care of cattle. After that the checks had been used to help pay lawyer's fees and keep Tim from going to prison. Now that steady paycheck was gone.

Lori shivered and tried to turn her thoughts around. She tried to think of the exciting new life that she and Tim were driving into. "We can never be defeated as long as we have each other," Lori told herself.

Lori tried to feel happy about the future. She sighed and patted Kato's soft fur. The large coyote looking dog lying beside her stretched out into a more comfortable sleeping position.

Tim had salvaged what he could, including a travel trailer. He sold everything to pay a few months rent on a home in Thomasville. Thomasville had many large, luxury homes for sale. The homes had been on the market for a year or more. Tim and Lori discovered they could rent a large luxury home, and try to help the owners sell it, as cheaply as they could rent a nice apartment.

They had rented a five-thousand square foot home on the side of a mountain. The home had a large double garage, and even a "Maids bell" in the middle of the large dining room floor. Best of all, the whole west side of the house had large windows facing the beautiful mountains. It looked like a giant mural. The east side of the house overlooked the city. The city lights were beautiful at night.

Lori felt tense about the expenses they were facing. But, the vitamin company they were working for promised that their multi-level business would soon be making them a lot of money. They were hoping they could eventually buy the house and not have to move again.

"A penny for your thoughts," Tim said.

"I was just thinking about how beautiful the mountains look from the house, and how pretty the house is," Lori said. Deep down inside she was still thinking about how expensive it was going to be to live in Thomasville and how she was already missing her steady teaching income.

"Don't worry, Lori, everything will work out all right," Tim said for the thousandth time. He smiled and squeezed Lori's hand.

Tim and Lori rode in silence for an hour before Tim stopped the van at a gas station. Lori put leashes on the two dogs and took them for a walk around the food and gas quick stop.

Kato was part coyote, and almost looked like one. He looked out of place in town. Bingo was one of Kato's pups. He was larger than Kato and had soft, black fur, with four white feet.

Tim and Lori were soon on the interstate highway again.

"Lori, you look rather worried," Tim said. "You should be excited about what is ahead and forget what has been in the past," he reminded again.

"I know Tim," Lori replied. "The house we rented is beautiful, but I don't know how we can pay our rent for very long if our business doesn't pick up," she said with a sigh.

"We have two months before we start to worry. If we work hard and run a lot of ads in the paper, we should have enough business to take care of us by then," Tim explained.

"I guess our past finances have been so scary that I worry from habit. I still remember the time you had to go out into a field and "borrow" some butane from a neighbor to keep us warm when we lost our utilities," Lori said. "But, the Lord seemed to always take care of us one way or another."

"And, He still will. If our business doesn't work out, I can find a job and you can teach until our business grows enough that we can work it full time," Tim said.

"It's too late for me to look for a teaching job this year, so the best I can do is try subbing," Lori replied.

"Don't worry, Lori, things will work out," Tim said again. He reached across Kato and hugged Lori's neck.

Lori laid her head back and tried to relax. "Oh, Lord, let me forget the past and I thank you for the future," Lori prayed. She was soon asleep, leaving the driving to Tim.

It was after midnight when they drove up the steep mountain to their new home. The TransVan mini motor home was too tall to park in the garage so Tim parked it on the large curving driveway that led to the garage.

Tim opened the garage with his electric garage opener. He and Lori walked through the garage followed by their two dogs. They walked up the flight of stairs to the main living level. Lori turned at the top of the stairs and looked out through the large glass entrance. The beauty of the city below them almost took her breath away. "It is beautiful here," Lori whispered. "I wonder if it might look a little like this in heaven,"

"That would be good enough for me," Tim answered with a smile. "Our luck just has to change here," he said, giving Lori another hug.

Tim and Lori were soon in bed, in each other's arms, asleep with a large dog sleeping on each side of the bed.

The next day Tim was busy writing up newspaper ads for the health products company. He called them into the two local newspapers. They spent the rest of the day unloading the furniture and putting it in place.

The second day, Lori fixed breakfast and cleaned up the kitchen. After the bed was made, the house didn't need much cleaning and Lori sat down in the office area of the huge kitchen. She decided that she would spend her time writing until she had to help Tim with the business.

Lori wanted to write down what had happened to her and Tim on the farm. She had two reasons to start writing. First, she never wanted to forget the precious times she had had with Rosita. Second, she thought it would be exciting to have her story published someday. People reading her story could be encouraged to be faithful when they went through hard times.

"But, the real reason I'm writing my story is to tell the whole world why I know Tim is innocent of the charges of molesting Rosita," Lori told herself. "And we would have proven it if we hadn't ran out of money,"

By afternoon Tim was receiving calls from people who thought they might be interested in the vitamin company. They were mostly people looking for work. Tim started setting up interviews and planned group meetings in one of the large family rooms downstairs.

On the third day Tim and Lori received a registered letter. Tim signed for it and called Lori into the office while he opened it.

The letter was addressed to the people living at the address of 401 Pine Drive Lane. The letter said: It has been reported to us that you have a motor-home parked on your driveway. It is against the law to have any vehicles parked outside your garage. You must move the motor-home at once or pay an eight-hundred dollar fine and then we will move it at your expense.

"Oh no, what can we do now?" Lori asked.

"Well, for now, we can park it behind the restaurant at the bottom of the mountain. It has a huge parking lot and is should be all right there," Tim answered. "Lori, follow me there so I will have a ride back,"

They soon had the motor home moved to the parking lot at the bottom of the mountain. It seemed like a good place to put it because they could check on it every time they passed the restaurant.

Tim and Lori had two Health Product meetings the first week. When the prospective customers saw the beautiful house that they were living in, they begin to dream of wealth too. Many bought products and several signed up to sell the products.

The second week Tim said, "Lori I want you to start doing the product part of the meetings."

"But, Tim, I'm not a salesperson," Lori protested. "The only thing I know how to do is teach."

"You know the products as well as I do," Tim said. "And, you're good at selling education, so you should be just as good at selling the products that make people feel better!" he shouted.

"But, Tim, it scares me to stand up in front of people and give speeches," Lori said, protesting.

"You have stood in front of your classes and talked for fifteen years, so don't give me those flimsy excuses," Tim shouted. "You WILL do that part of the meeting!" he yelled, and stomped out of the room.

Lori felt confused over Tim's behavior. She had no choice but to help him. She believed in the products and knew she felt better while she was using the products. "I can do it," Lori told herself as she jotted down some notes.

The meeting was made up of mostly black people that had answered the ad. Lori gave her part of the meeting. She gave her personal testimony about how good she felt by using the products. Lori knew she had done a good enough job to make everyone want the products. One lady had a terrible disease and walked on crutches. She needed the products, but the products were too expensive for her to buy on her low, fixed income.

Tim did his part of the meeting. He enjoyed talking about big money. He had always enjoyed talking about big money, but Lori had never noticed it like she did now.

In Tim's presentation, he said, "If one person gets only five other people to sell the products, and each of these five get only five more, and those twenty-five, each get only five more, the first person will be earning several thousand dollars by the third month."

After the meeting, a few people bought a few products. Only one young man was excited about working the business. As he walked to the large, glass entrance of the house, he looked out at the city lights and the stars above the hills. "Yes, sir, my dollars will soon be as many as those lights over there and all around us!" Art exclaimed.

Lori guessed that Art had always been poor and he was excited to see a chance to get all the things he had seen other people have. "Oh, I wish his dreams could come true," Lori told herself. Then she felt a knot in her stomach. "These people think we can make them rich because we live in such a nice place. They think this house is ours and that we have plenty of money; I feel like we are being dishonest with them."

The black people left. Tim and Lori locked the doors and went to bed. Tim was soon asleep on his side of the bed. He had not kissed Lori in a couple of days. Bedtime was no longer a time for snuggling together away from the cares of the day. "Tim must be extra tired trying to start a new business," Lori told herself while trying to go to sleep on her side of the bed.

The next day Jean came in answer to the ad. Jean was in her early forties. She was driving an older Mercedes. Jean was a pretty brunette, but she didn't look happy.

"I'm looking for a chance to make some big money," Jean said. "You see, my husband died and left me quite well off. He had a large insurance policy and other assets," she explained. "I was terribly lonesome after Roy died, and I met this young, handsome man at a friend's party. He seemed to fall in love with me as quickly as I fell in love with him. I couldn't believe that someone in their twenties could be so crazy over me. I was so happy.

John didn't want to get married. He insisted that two people can love each other more by not getting married. As soon as John moved in with me, he quit his job and demanded that I give him money all the time. With his extravagant spending, it didn't take long to deplete what wealth I had. When the money was gone, so was John. I had to admit that he had never loved me, but had only loved my money. I was devastated. I have spent these last few months alone thinking about ending it all. Then I saw your ad in the paper, and I thought if I could make some money, that maybe I can get over what John did to me,"

Lori quickly brought Jean some Kleenex and patted her on the shoulder. "Oh you poor girl, I hope we can help you get back on your feet again," Lori said.

"I'm sorry for the tears. You have been kind to listen and understand," Jean said. "I just hate to cry in front of people. I should have known that John was too good to be true. I found out later that he had dated several younger women while we were living together.

Since John never wanted to get married, there wasn't a thing I could do. Now I'm broke and I have no college degree to help me get a job. If I would have just kept the money, I could have lived comfortable and not have to worry," Jean sobbed. "I'm sorry for crying again,"

"That's all right. Just watch and let me show you what our company can do for you!" Tim exclaimed.

"I'm ready to listen. I can tell by looking around here that you know how to be successful," Jean said.

"I feel like we are living a lie," Lori told herself again.

Jean listened to Tim's presentation and signed up to become a distributor, hoping to soon have her lost money replaced.

"I wish the business made as much money as it claims," Lori told herself. "What you have gone through seems so unfair," she told Jean.

Jean thanked Tim and Lori and trotted off to her car. She looked happy.

The next day a tiny, older woman, in tight fitting jeans, showed up for an interview. Tim explained the products and business to Betty Ruth while Lori listened. Lori was shocked when Tim said, "I'm glad you're interested in the business, but I don't think we have any room for bar flies in our company."

"I do hang around the bars some, but how did you know?" Betty Ruth asked.

"I just know," Tim replied. "Are you willing to change your life style in order to join our company?" he asked.

"I don't think I'll have any problems staying out of the bars," Betty Ruth said. "One of my old boyfriends, who is a truck driver, showed up this week, and I'm not lonely anymore,"

"Aren't you afraid of contacting aids or something?" Tim asked.

"Oh no, he's perfectly safe because he hasn't slept with other women. When he has a need, he just buys the right kind of book or magazine and does his laundry all by himself," Betty Ruth said.

Lori was so embarrassed that she had to leave the room for a few minutes. She knew what Betty Ruth was talking about and it didn't seem to embarrass Betty Ruth, or Tim, to be talking about such things.

"You better be more careful, anyway," Tim warned.

More people were showing up for interviews and training. Tim sent the group into one of the large downstairs family rooms and instructed Lori to show them a video about the company. "I'm going to work with Betty Ruth in our bedroom; we'll have plenty of room and we can use the desk in there," Tim told Lori.

"I don't think that will look very nice," Lori protested.

"That's the best place for me to work with Betty Ruth, so you go on down stairs and start the video," Tim said. "Be ready to stop the video at any time when someone wants to ask a question," "Don't you trust me?" Tim asked with a laugh.

"Sure I do but I just don't think it looks right," Lori replied. She went downstairs, seated everyone, and started the video.

None of the people had asked any questions when Lori heard the front doorbell again. She waited for Tim to answer the door since he was already upstairs. By the third ring, Lori knew Tim was not going to answer the door.

Lori tip-toed out of the room and ran up the stairs to answer the door. There was a handsome, blonde, neatly-dressed man that looked to be about thirty-five.

"Hello, my name is Alan Bloomingale, and I'm here in answer to your ad," the man said.

"Please come in and I'll get my husband to tell you about our company," Lori said. She pointed to one of the living room chairs. "Please sit down and I'll be right back," she instructed.

Lori ran down the long hall that led to her and Tim's bedroom. Lori opened the door and saw Tim at the desk and Betty Ruth sitting on the desk. "Tim, I'm still showing the video downstairs, and there is a Mr. Bloomingale waiting to be interviewed," Lori said.

"I'm not through with Betty Ruth yet, so you'll have to take care of him," Tim shouted.

Lori felt her face burning. Their business depended on these interviews and there was no time for a fight. Lori ran back into the living room. "I'm sorry, Mr. Bloomingale, but my husband is still busy training a new member of our company," Lori explained. "Follow me and maybe you can see the last of the video that I'm showing downstairs,"

Alan Bloomingale followed Lori into the room where the video was almost finished. Lori rewound the video and moved the cart with the VCR and TV into another room. She started the video for Alan, and rushed back into the first room to answer questions from the small group there.

There were eight people in the group. Two of them bought products to try before selling them. Three women were interested, but said they had to talk it over with their husbands first. Three men said they would still look for regular jobs and promised to come to a company meeting.

Lori had just ushered the group to the front door when Mr. Bloomingale came to the top of the stairs. "The video is finished, and I think I'm interested," he said.

Lori led Mr. Bloomingale back downstairs and explained each of the products to him. She was hoping that Tim would come downstairs in time to tell their guest about the money making possibilities. Tim did not show up, so Lori explained the multi-level possibilities of making money. Mr. Bloomingale seemed interested.

"I believe the products are great, but I'm a little skeptical about making so much money," Alan said with a smile. "Nevertheless, I want to give your company a try, so where do I sign up, and how do I get started?" he asked.

"My husband has to sign you up, so I'll go get him," Lori answered. "You can stay here and look over my flip-charts and the products while I'm gone,"

Lori hurried up the stairs again, down the hall, and up to the bedroom door. This time she heard Betty Ruth laughing. Lori thought she should knock first this time. Lori felt her face burning again. She knocked on the door. "Mr. Bloomingale wants to sign up, and we're waiting for you to help him fill out the papers," Lori yelled through the door.

"We're not finished yet, Lori!" Tim yelled. "We need about thirty more minutes," he shouted through the door.

"Maybe I can finish working with Betty Ruth while you sign up Mr. Bloomingale," Lori yelled through the door.

"Keep Mr. Bloomingale busy until we finish here!" Tim ordered through the door.

Lori tried to open the bedroom door, but it was locked. She felt sick at her stomach. The situation brought back horrible memories of when Lori had found out her first husband had been unfaithful to her. She had fallen in love with Hollis and married him when she was seventeen. They had two sons. It was devastating to find out that her sons' father was running around with one of Lori's friends.

Hollis had not wanted a divorce, but he did not want to change the way he was living. Lori could not adjust to an extra woman in her husband's life and she had filed for divorce. Hollis had moved out the day after their twenty-third anniversary. Hollis had married Lori's friend who was eighteen years younger. Lori had been so unhappy until she had met Tim, and now . . . .

Lori shook her head to bring her thinking back to the present. She ran down the stairs to give Mr. Bloomingal some additional information about the products.

"I don't have a job right now, so I have plenty of time for more training," Mr. Bloomingale said with a kindly smile.

It was forty-five minutes before Tim came into the room. Betty Ruth had left. Tim looked neat, but tired. "Sorry I took so long, but I feel that each distributor needs my special training to be successful," Tim said with a smile. It didn't take Tim long to fill out the necessary papers for Mr. Bloomingale to sign.

"Thanks for spending so much time with me," Mr. Bloomingale said as he left the house. "Your wife knows a lot about the company and products,"

It was dinner time. Lori fixed a good meal for Tim, and thought she would discuss his behavior after they had eaten. Tim was always in a better mood with a full stomach. He complimented Lori on the meal, and was so kind and considerate, that Lori forgot about his immodest behavior. "Everything will be all right when we go to bed tonight," Lori told herself.

Lori turned the light off and crawled into bed beside Tim. "Tim, what is a bar-fly?" Lori asked.

"It's a woman that hangs around a bar looking for men to keep her company," Tim explained.

"Oh," Lori replied.

Tim turned over and went to sleep so quickly that he didn't even tell Lori goodnight. Lori had a hard time going to sleep. She felt like she was entering a new, strange world that made her feel uneasy. Lori was frightened by the changes she saw in Tim.

The next morning Lori tried to talk to Tim after breakfast. "Tim, about yesterday and Betty Ruth . . ." Lori started to say.

Tim jumped up out of his chair. "Lori, grab your coat; we're going after the TransVan!" Tim shouted.

"Why right now?" Lori asked.

"I can't explain, but we have to hurry," Tim said.

Lori put on her coat and Tim pulled her down the steps to the garage. He quickly drove to the back of the parking lot next to the restaurant.

"Tim, what is that white flag doing on the handle of the Trans Van?" Lori asked.

"That means that the police are getting ready confiscate the Trans Van because it has been unclaimed," Tim answered. "According to the numbers on the flag, the Trans Van should have been picked up today," Tim explained.

Lori felt her legs grow weak. "You mean we would have lost the Trans Van, and all the money we have in it, and it isn't even paid for yet!" Lori exclaimed.

"That's right," Tim answered. "I talked to your cousin yesterday and he said we could park it in the back of their house," he explained. Tim crawled into the Trans Van and started the engine.

Lori followed Tim to the south side of Thomasville where Tim parked the Trans Van behind her cousin's house next to the alley. She and Tim knocked on the door and told Cousin Ellen that the vehicle was parked on their property.

"Just leave it there as long as you need to," Ellen said with a smile.

Lori tried to talk to Tim about Betty Ruth on the way back home.

"I can't believe that you could be jealous over a woman like that!" Tim said, laughing. "Why would I want something used like her when I have you?" Tim asked teasingly. He gave Lori a hug.

There were two women at the front door when Tim and Lori drove into the garage. Betty Ruth came in later and helped train other new customers and distributors. "See why it was so important for me to train Betty Ruth," Tim said when he saw her working so hard.

Tim's ads were getting a lot of attention. There were a lot of people out of work in Thomasville and needed incomes. Lori felt that Betty Ruth didn't have many groceries at home so she invited her to eat dinner with them. Instead of jealously, Lori felt pity for Betty Ruth.

The next few days were busy. Tim acted like a devoted husband except at bedtime. Lori missed the closeness they had once enjoyed.

One morning Tim said, "Lori, I want you to go back to the old farm and watch our last Milo crop harvested: you can count the truck-loads of grain that go to the elevator." "I want to be sure that the harvesters pay us our share," he said.

"They are our friends, and I'm sure they won't cheat us," Lori replied.

"I have learned not to trust anyone," Tim said.

"Don't you need me here to help with the business?" Lori asked.

"I need you more there counting those truck-loads than I need you here," Tim answered. "I would go, but I can't leave the business right now, besides, you know I would be taking a chance of being arrested if I go back," he explained. "You can stay with your son, Mitch, and visit Mike while you're there, and you can clean out that old, tiny mobile home we bought from the old lady in the Nursing Home before she died," Tim said. "No one is living on the place yet, and the mobile home is one thing the bank hasn't taken; maybe you can clean it out and we can sell it,"

Lori knew it would not do any good to argue with Tim. The next day she loaded some clothes and the dog, Bingo, into the Trans Van and made the six hour trip to Mitch's. She spent her evenings enjoying her son, wife, and small grandson. Each night Lori called Tim and each day she counted the loads of Milo that left for town on the other side of the section of land. She cleaned out the tiny, mobile home, and found that all the fixtures were in need of repair.

The house seemed older now, and Lori had forgotten how the dust burned her skin and made her sneeze. She already missed the view of the mountains as she looked across the flat prairie with no trees.

The harvest lasted a week. Lori ate Thanksgiving dinner with Mitch and the rest of the family before she started back to Thomasville. She made good time, and she and Bingo were back in the city in less than six hours. They were soon traveling up the mountain to their beautiful home.

Tim seemed glad to see Lori. The house was clean, and Tim had oiled all the beautiful woodwork throughout the whole house, including the large staircase. Tim and Lori went to bed in each other's arms for the first time in a long time.

The check for the Milo came in the mail the next week. It was smaller than expected. It seemed like incoming money was always less than what was expected. They were making some money on the products, but they were spending more money to run the business than it was making.

Tim and Lori spent Christmas in the city alone and they ate Christmas dinner at one of the nice restaurants at the bottom of the mountain. Elizabeth, Lori's mother, called that afternoon and Lori talked to some of the other family members during the call.

On New Years Eve, at midnight, Tim and Lori lay in bed and watched fireworks from the highest peak in the near mountain range. They had a "front row seat" looking through the large windows of their bedroom. Although finances were scary, Tim and Lori thought they were enjoying their new rented house, and there always seemed to be just enough money for them to scrape by.

Tim was going through the bills the first of the month. The weather had turned colder, but Tim and Lori hadn't had much time to think about it. "Lori!" Tim shouted.

"What now?" Lori asked running into the dining room where Tim was sitting at the table.

"Look at this!" Tim exclaimed.

Lori looked at the total of the utilities bill. The bill was over $200, not including the telephone bill. Lori was speechless.

"Lori we have to move right away," Tim exclaimed. "We can't afford this,"

"Tim, we can't move because we signed a six-month lease on this house," Lori replied.

"Then we'll have to keep the thermostat at fifty-five degrees," Tim replied. "The house should be warm enough from solar heat when we have people here, but we'll just have to tough it out at night," he explained. "We can't get out of our lease without breaking the law,"

"I'm going to pray and believe that God can get us out of this. And, I'm going to start back to church whether you go with me or not," Lori said.

"You can go if you want to, but I don't know where you're going to get gas money to drive there," Tim replied.

There was gas enough to go to church the next Sunday, but Lori went alone. It was hard since she and Tim used to always go to church together. Lori didn't have any money for the offering so she put in one of her good rings instead.

That afternoon Tim was griping about their finances. "The farm would have been successful if you would have believed in it!" he yelled.

"I did more work on it than you did!" Lori started to yell back, when the telephone rang.

Tim answered the call. "You need to talk to my wife about this," Tim said with a smile, handing the telephone to Lori.

"Mrs. Jones, could we show the house to some prospective buyers this afternoon?" a kind, man's voice said. "We have a couple who looked at the house two years ago, and they want to look at it again,"

"Yes, yes of course," Lori said, trying not to sound too anxious.

"Great, we'll be there within an hour," the man said and hung up.

"Praise the Lord!" Lori said. "This is the first time they have had interested buyers,"

Lori walked with the Realtor as he showed Mr. and Mrs. Cantly the house. She pointed out many great things about the house. The Realtor didn't seem to mind the help.

"When we looked at the house before, it seemed so huge, barren, and empty," Mr. Cantly said. "Now it looks so different with furniture in it, that I think it's the house we're looking for," he said. "How soon can we move in?" he asked.

"I don't know for sure," the Realtor said looking at Lori. "These people have four more months of lease," he explained.

"If you want the house, we'll move as quickly as we can find a place to move into," Lori said.

"You mean that you will be willing to drop the lease?" the Realtor asked.

"Just give us two weeks," Lori replied.

"Great!" Mr. Cantly exclaimed. "Let's go to your office and sign the papers," he said. "Mrs. Jones, it will be a month before we are ready to move into Thomasville so you'll have time to find another house,"

The visitors left. "Praise the Lord!" Tim and Lori both exclaimed.

Tim and Lori did business training in the mornings and looked at houses in the afternoons. They finally found a four-thousand square foot house on a mountain in the south part of the city. The house had four sliding glass doors facing the city and mountains, and a three car garage. The house was built into the side of a hill and the utilities showed to be less than half of the first house.

Cousin Ellen, and her husband Jack, helped Tim and Lori move. The moving was completed in one day and Ellen had even served Domino Pizza for lunch and dinner. Jack had joined the health products company and thought that Tim was his closest friend.

The day after the move, Lori went back to the large house and cleaned. It looked like new when she was finished. Lori looked at the beautiful home on the mesa one last time. This time she wondered what the walls would say if they could talk. She brushed the bad memories from her mind and hurried back to her new home, and to help Tim with his work.

Tim and Lori enjoyed their new surroundings. They had a great view of the city, the mountains, a ski slope to the west, and a pretty lake at the bottom of their small mountain. The upstairs had white carpets. The house had been owned by a doctor who raised dogs in the house. Tim had a cleaning company come in and make the rugs white again. The doctor asked if Tim and Lori would mind if they left their baby-Grande piano there for awhile. Lori enjoyed the piano whenever she had any free time.

The only thing Lori did not like about the house was that all the family rooms were down stairs. There was even a room downstairs with ping-pong and a billiard tables.

The following Saturday morning Tim said, "Lori, look out the window."

Lori looked through the bedroom window facing the front of the house. "Oh no, Tim, it's the people we are buying the TransVan from, and they are driving a new, large motor home," Lori sighed. "They have probably come here to collect all the payments we owe them," Lori went to the door and tried to smile. "Peggy and Richard, it's so nice to see you; come on in," she said.

"We were here in Thomasville visiting our son," Richard explained. "We went to our grandson's high-school graduation yesterday, and we thought we would stop by and see you on our way back home,"

"I hope we're not intruding," Peggy added.

"Oh no," Lori replied. She led her guests into the large living-room where they shook hands with Tim and sit down. Lori went into the kitchen to fix some refreshments and coffee.

"We moved from Kansas to Arizona and like it much better," Peggy said.

Peggy and Richard were so friendly that Tim invited them to spend the night. The next morning at breakfast, Richard said, "Tim, you're several months behind on Trans Van payments."

"Yes I know, but it's taking more time for us to get back on our feet financially than we thought it would," Tim explained.

"Would you like for us to take the Trans Van back?" Richard asked kindly.

"Yes, if you don't mind," Tim answered.

"We can tear up our agreement papers and I guess you have just rented the Trans Van for nine months," Richard explained.

The two friends shook hands. Peggy was driving the Trans Van and Richard was driving their new motor home when the couple left for a ten-hour journey back to their new home in the Arizona desert.

In the following weeks, the health products company business almost stopped. Tim became depressed and spent most of his time sitting in a large chair in the dark family room downstairs. He only came upstairs for meals and bedtime. When Lori tried to go downstairs to cheer him, Tim shouted, "Get out of here; I want to be left alone!"

Tim's eyes had never bothered Lori before, but now they seem to penetrate into her innermost being.

Lori backed out of the room. She fixed Tim's evening meal and called him upstairs. Tim ate in silence, staring at her.

"Tim, you need to find a job because our company isn't making any money and I don't know how we're going to pay our bills and buy groceries," Lori said.

"I'm not well!" Tim shouted. "You're the one with the education, so you're the one that should be looking for work!"

Lori ran into the smallest bedroom. She closed and locked the door. Lori fell across the bed and cried until she heard Tim going to bed. When she thought he was asleep, she tiptoed into the room and went to bed. It seemed harder and harder to forget troubles and go to sleep on her side of the bed.

CHAPTER II

IS IT REAL?

Lori tried to keep busy and away from Tim. She cooked the meals and kept the house clean. She enjoyed playing the Baby-Grande and working on her story. In the warm afternoons, Lori took the dogs and walked around the area of a nearby mountain. These were times she could get out of the house and relax and talk to the Lord.

Lori and Tim had another argument. Tim stayed in the dark family room. Lori returned to the small bedroom to cry. Two hours later she was still sobbing when she heard Tim shouting through the bedroom door.

"It's time for supper! Where's my meal?" Tim shouted.

Lori pulled her trembling body up from the bed and went into the large kitchen. She took the last package of meat from the freezer and put it in the microwave oven to defrost. Lori had a complete meal for Tim, including the three vegetables Tim always demanded, in forty-five minutes.

Lori went to the top of the stairs and called Tim. Tim came up the stairs and into the kitchen without even looking at her. They ate in silence, and Tim went back downstairs. Lori cleaned up the kitchen and went to bed. Tim did not come in until late. He did not say anything and they tried to sleep without touching each other.

The next morning Lori fixed breakfast. Tim still didn't feel like talking. After Lori had straightened up the house, she put on some of her best clothes and drove downtown.

Lori applied at all the schools for a teaching job. "We don't need any teachers, but we do need substitutes," every school secretary told her. One school secretary said, "You might as well give up finding a teaching job; the school districts can only hire black teachers until we catch up on our government quota.

Lori filled out the necessary papers to sub. She returned to the other districts and filled out subbing papers there too. "I should be called for plenty of days of subbing since I'm a certified teacher," Lori told herself. She had never lived in a large city before and was not familiar with Thomasville. One of the school districts had fifty-one different schools that could call her to sub. Lori bought a city map. She went home and drew a circle around each school and the streets to take to get there.

A raging winter storm hit Thomasville the next morning. It was snowing and blowing. Lori could not see the houses across the street because of the storm. She had just crawled out of bed when the telephone rang. Lori was called to drive in the storm, across the large city, to an unfamiliar school to sub.

"Tim, I need the good car to go to work," Lori said.

"I need the good car; you'll have to drive the old car today," Tim shouted.

"But, Tim, it's not running right," Lori protested.

"I might have to go somewhere for the company today, and I must be driving a nicer car to be successful," Tim yelled. "Can't you understand that!" he shouted.

Lori held her tears and ran to the garage. "Oh Lord, please help me," she prayed. Lori turned the key. The Oldsmobile spurted and shook as Lori backed out of the garage.

Lori felt like her heart was in her throat while she drove across the icy streets of the city. She was praying that the old car would get her there and back. The roads were slick, but the old car was heavy enough to keep it from sliding if Lori drove slowly. Her heart was pounding as she drove through heavy morning traffic. She found Washington Elementary School and found a place to park. Lori was thankful for her snow boots when she walked the distance to the large building.

Lori spent the day working with thirty rebellious, sixth graders. They knew most of the tricks to play on subs. She had no lesson plans and had to guess what the kids were supposed to do that day. Lori was tired, and her nerves were shot by the time she fought the storm back home. The car was still sputtering, but it had gotten her to work and back home safely. "It will be so nice to kick off my boots and relax," Lori told herself as she closed the garage door.

Tim was sitting in his large chair in the dim-lit family room. "It's about time you got home!" he shouted.

Lori didn't answer but ran up the stairs to the main level of the house. She walked into the kitchen to fix some hot chocolate. Lori moaned when she looked around the kitchen. There were dirty dishes, and pots and pans, everywhere. The stove had food all over it. Lori knew that Tim had gone to a lot of extra work to make such a mess. She wondered how many times he had eaten during the day.

"Where's my supper!" Tim shouted almost as soon as Lori had entered the kitchen.

Lori started the evening meal before she cleaned up the kitchen. Tim came in to eat without talking, and then went back downstairs. It was almost midnight when Lori had the kitchen cleaned up and went to bed. Tim was already in bed and snoring. Again, Lori felt very alone as she tried to go to sleep.

Lori was called to sub about two days a week. Most of the time she was called during bad weather, but there was enough money for groceries. Tim was always in a bad mood when she came home, and he never let her use the newer car. Lori decided that she would just drive the old Oldsmobile until it completely quit running.

One evening Tim was in a better mood when Lori came home. "Ellen and Jack have asked us to go to the Health Club with them tonight," Tim said as soon as Lori came through the door. For once he was not yelling.

"That sounds great!" Lori exclaimed. She fixed a light dinner early. Tim and Lori picked up Lori's cousins at seven o'clock. "It's fun to have someone to talk to that isn't yelling," Lori told herself as she and Ellen visited in the back seat.

The four adults enjoyed swimming in the large pool. Lori had finished swimming another lap and joined the others sitting on the edge of the pool. She heard Tim bragging about their business and how he and Lori were able to live in such a fine house on the mountain.

"But, it's taking a little longer than I thought to get everything going, Jack, and I wonder if you could loan us two-thousand dollars to get us over the hump; we can pay you back real soon," Tim was saying.

Lori felt sick. She never knew just how they were going to pay the rent, but to borrow from a relative just to live in an expensive house was wrong. "Should I tell Jack not to lend us the money, or be a submissive wife and support Tim?" Lori was asking herself. She was afraid that Jack and Ellen would never be paid back, yet she said nothing.

Lori remembered the third month they were in Thomasville, Tim had forced her to borrow two-thousand dollars from her mother. Elizabeth had sent the money, but there had been tears over the telephone when Lori had called her, and tears on her letter containing the money. Now he was borrowing from another relative.

As soon as they all were dressed, Jack took out his checkbook and wrote Tim a two-thousand dollar check. Tim took the money with ease and a half-hearted, "Thank you,"

Lori was beginning to see a side of Tim she had never seen before. Tim had the ability to make people believe almost anything. Jack was completely convinced that the business would soon be making big money, and that the loan was just a small jester of faith.

Jack had worked several years for a cement company. He worked hard for what he had. Ellen was busy raising four kids, including a set of twins. She also worked several months a year for an income tax company. Lori felt ashamed over the loan as they drove into their luxurious garage that night. She knew all she could do was pray that they would soon be able to pay back the money.

Tim and Lori had an unlisted telephone number. Somehow, some people had found their number, and Tim received several telephone calls from people that were looking for a place to borrow big money. Tim decided that he would try to make a commission by helping people find loans. When that didn't work out, he started to spend his time in the dark family room again. Tim didn't want Lori around most of the time.

Subbing was hard work and the transportation was scary, but it was nice to get out of the house and not be yelled at. Lori was sill taking walks on the mountain with the dogs when the weather was warm enough and she had the time.

Tim had finally decided to look for a job. He was looking at the want ads in the paper one day when the telephone rang. Tim was afraid it might be a bill collector so he shouted for Lori to answer the phone.

"Hello," Lori said.

"Hello, Lori, this is Ann, Tim's sister in Illinois," the voice said.

"Hi Ann, how are you, and how is Tim's mother doing since she came to live with you?" Lori asked.

"Not so good," Ann answered. "Oh, mother is doing fine, but she is causing so much trouble between me and my husband that if she stays, we'll end up in a divorce. Mother is always telling Wilson how to run his business and he has had enough," "Lori, you must take her off our hands, even just for a little while so we can put our lives back together," she begged. "We have had her ever since Daddy Andy died, and now it's your turn to take care of her for awhile,"

"But, Ann, we don't even have enough money for just the two of us to live on," Lori protested. "You and Wilson have plenty of money."

"You must take her," Ann said. "My son, and his family, is already on their way bringing her to you. They should be in Thomasville around three tomorrow afternoon. Tell Tim hello for us," Ann said and hung up.

"Who was on the phone?" Tim yelled up the stairs.

"It was Ann, and you're mother is coming to live with us," Lori said. "You're nephew, and family, is bringing her and they will be here tomorrow," Lori explained. "Oh Tim, how on earth are we going to be able to even buy groceries to feed your mother, and our company while they are here?" Lori whaled.

"I think it's great that mom and Jarin and his family are coming," Tim said, and continued to look over the job ads in the paper.

"I have a little cash," Tim said. "Let's go downtown and buy groceries in case you have to work tomorrow," he said. Tim chose expensive food items while Lori tried to be economical with the things she put in the shopping cart.

It was almost dark when Jarin pulled into the driveway in their motor home. Jarin's three young boys jumped out of the vehicle and ran into the house. Sarah told Lori hello, but she was very happy to see Tim.

"Are you taking care of yourself?" Sarah asked Tim. "You don't look very well," she said.

Tim commented that he had felt better, and shook hands with the rest of the relatives.

"Boy, you sure live in a pretty place," Jarin said.

Tim began immediately to lie about their financial situation.

Jarin youngsters were full of life, but Lori had plenty of things for them to do to keep them busy. Lori had always liked Kim, Jarin's wife. Despite the situation, Lori enjoyed their company. Jarin and his family left the next day, so there weren't so many meals to fix.

The following day Tim and Lori took Sarah around Thomasville and showed her the area. They visited some stores, and Lori was shocked when Sarah started asking Tim to buy her certain things.

On the way home, Lori said, "Sarah, you have more money than we have, so why don't you buy yourself the things you want instead of asking Tim and me to buy them for you?"

"I don't have any money!" Sarah shouted.

"I know you have a steady Social Security check, and that is more than we have coming in right now," Lori replied. "I remember when Tim and I paid all your utility bills when you were living in my mobile home before Daddy Andy died; you said you didn't have any money. We found out later that you had your Social Security check plus an oil check that no one knew about. When we cleaned up the house before the bank took it, I found twenty-four new dresses that had never been worn. I also found a new sewing machine, microwave, and many other new things. We were paying your bills at the very time we were going bankrupt," Lori said.

Sarah started to cry. "I don't have any money, or home, or anything!" she sobbed.

"Lori, don't you ever talk to my mother that way again!" Tim shouted. "Our home is her home, and it won't hurt us to buy her things once in awhile," he yelled. "You don't have to be so selfish!"

When Tim drove into the garage, Lori hurried up to the main level to get supper and to be alone. She called Tim and Sarah to supper, but they didn't answer her. Lori walked down the stairs and heard Sarah talking.

"Son, don't try to find a job," Sarah was saying. "You aren't well, and if you start to work, you'll die, and I won't have anyone,"

"Tim has to find work, and supper is ready," Lori said in desperation.

"No he doesn't!" Sarah shouted as she followed Tim up the stairs.

Sarah and Tim visited during the meal, but Lori didn't feel like talking. She was glad they went back downstairs to leave her to clean up the kitchen alone.

The next morning Tim didn't feel like getting out of bed. "I have a terrible headache!" he exclaimed.

Tim's face was red and Lori knew that his blood pressure had gone up. There was no money to take him to the doctor, and no insurance. Lori brought Tim two aspirins and started breakfast when the telephone rang. She was needed to sub in a school in the north part of the city. It was, at least, a way of escape.

"Don't worry, dear, I'll take care of Tim for you today," Sarah said in a sweet voice.

Lori found the school. She also found out that one of the students had tripped the regular teacher. The teacher had fallen and broken her toe. That was why Lori had been called to sub so late in the morning.

There were two fifth grade classes and two sixth grade classes in one large open room. Lori estimated there were at least one-hundred, and twenty students in the large room. Each class was in a separate corner. The students were going anywhere they wanted and talking. There were no lesson plans, and the room was in chaos.

Lori rushed over to the other sixth grade teacher and asked about lesson plans. "I don't have any idea what she was planning on doing today," the man said.

Lori looked through the books and asked the students on what page their last lesson had been on in each subject. No one seemed to have any idea. Lori had the students to do some sentence writing for English and Spelling, and gave the students certain problems to work from a Math book she found. "I expect you to finish these simple assignments by the end of the day," Lori said.

"My dad will get you for making us work so hard," one blonde girl shouted.

"You can't talk to a teacher that way, young lady," Lori replied.

"I can talk to you any way I please, and my dad is going to get you!" the girl shouted.

"Sit down, be quiet, and do your work," Lori demanded.

"I don't have to, and you can't make me!" the girl shouted.

"All right young lady, you're going to the principal's office with me," Lori said. She took the girl and pulled her down the hall and into the principal's office. She reported the student's behavior and left the room. Lori could barely hear the noise of her class above the noise of the other three classes when she returned to the large room. "Whoever invented this open school concept didn't know much about teaching," Lori said to herself as she tried to get her group back to work.

The rebellious girl returned with the same attitude. By the end of the day, most of the students had completed the assignments so Lori read to the students a few chapters out of a story she had written. The story was about a pet raccoon that Mike had raised when he was twelve-years-old. The students loved the story and thought Lori was a hero for writing it. They respected her and were well-behaved for the rest of the day. Lori used her story several times after that when she had no lesson plans to follow.

Lori was glad when the day was over, but she did not look forward to going home. She wished she could drive around a little first to relax, but she had to conserve every gallon of gas in her old Oldsmobile. She came home to a house more messed up than ever. Tim had been well enough to eat, and cook, but not well enough to even put the dishes in the sink. That evening Tim and Sarah visited as though Lori was not even present. Lori heard Sarah telling Tim several times that he was too sick to work.

Tim seemed to feel worse and worse. The atmosphere in the house was so bad that Lori could be working on something and feel cold chills going up and down her spine. She always knew it was Sarah staring at her although she never heard the older lady come in into the room.

After a few weeks, Lori could not take the circumstances any longer. In desperation, she called Ann. "Ann, if you can't take Sarah back, I'm leaving Tim," Lori said. "I can't take this any longer!"

"Wilson and I are getting along a little better," Ann replied. "We might be able to keep her again, for awhile," she said. "I don't know what Tim would do if you left him."

"Thanks," Lori replied. "We'll put Sarah on the plane that comes directly to St. Louis on the Thursday flight, that is if we can find enough money to buy her a ticket."

"Mom has enough money to buy her own ticket," Ann said. "But, you'll have to force her to use her own money."

The next day Lori subbed again. This time it was in a school close to the air base. The students were well-behaved and Lori enjoyed the day. When she came out of the building, she noticed that every one was looking up into the sky. Lori looked up. She saw a 747 Jet circling over their part of the city and there was a space shuttle tied to the planes back. The sight took her breathe away.

That night Tim and Lori took Sarah to the air base where they drove close by the two air crafts. "I bet you can remember seeing the first cars, mom." Tim said. "Was it as exciting as looking at the space shuttle?" he asked.

"I think so," Sarah replied.

Tim was forced to get money from Sarah to buy her airline ticket. Sarah had never been on an air plane and she was frightened. Lori almost felt sorry for her.

"I will take care of you myself," a pretty air-line hostess said. "We'll be sure you reach your destination safely and have your relatives pick you up at the air port." She took Sarah by the hand and led her up the steps to the large plane. Sarah was smiling when she waved good-bye to Tim and Lori as the plane took off.

Tim seemed relieved to have Sarah going back to Ann's. He gave Lori the first hug in a long time.

"Maybe things will get better now," Lori told herself over and over while Tim was driving back to their number II house on the mountain.

Chapter III

Am I Dreaming?

Tim seemed happy for a few days, but his blood pressure did not go down and he became cranky again.

Although Lori's subbing brought in enough money to buy groceries and pay utilities, she was continually worrying about the rent and other expenses. They were already two months behind on the rent. Several Realtors showed the house, but no one seemed to be interested. One day when Tim and Lori were not at home, the owners came into the house and had the business telephone removed. This completely stopped the health product business.

It seemed almost funny living in a fancy house in a fancy neighborhood and not having any money. Tim still wanted to be left alone and dreamed of his "Pie in the Sky" business.

Tim expected Lori to do everything for him, because he "was sick". He was never too sick to eat, but there was no love expressed. Lori felt unloved and used.

The days Lori came home from subbing, she always found the house in a mess, and the kitchen full of dirty dishes. It looked like Tim had eaten all day long.

Lori was lying on the bed one day, sobbing. Tim had gone down town for something. Lori was almost asleep when she heard the door bell ringing. She looked out the upstairs window and saw a new, white

Cadillac parked on the driveway. It did not look like the kind of vehicle a bill collector would drive. Lori wiped the tears from her face and answered the door.

The man standing at the door was very tall. Lori guessed him to be close to seven feet. She looked up into the face of the handsome stranger. His smile looked familiar. Lori quickly thought about her high school days. Then she thought she recognized him. He was a guy Lori had dated in high school before she started going with Hollis, her first husband.

The young man had been so heart-broken when Lori quit dating him that he had even quit school. He had told Lori that he would always love her. After he left school, he had become a heavy weight boxer in the army.

"Oh Lori, I'm so glad to see you. I'm serving God, and I have money enough to give you anything you need." the handsome man said. "I've never stopped loving you and I've come back for you."

Lori looked up into the clear blue eyes of what she thought to be her former friend. Jess was much taller than she remembered. The boyish features had developed into a handsome face. Jess's hair was a darker blonde with patches of white at the temples.

"I'm terribly unhappy," Lori said with a sigh, "but, I can't go away with you. I still love Tim and, although I've gone through one, I don't believe in divorce, Besides, I couldn't leave Tim in the condition he's in, even if I wanted to,"

"Lori, I love you and I want to help you, but I don't know how," Jess said. "Please tell me what I can do to get you out of this mess so we can be together. Every woman deserves to have security, and Tim has never given you that."

Lori was surprised that Jess seemed to know all about her life. "Oh Jess, I have made such a mess of my life," Lori sobbed. "But, I don't want to ask you, or anyone else, for help."

"Lori, I have enough wealth and yearly income that, well, if I can't have you, I can still help you; I can find happiness in that," Jess replied.

"This has to be a good dream for a change, so I might as well ask for the things we need," Lori told herself. "I have a hard time believing that this is really happening, but if you insist, could you please see that Tim has a steady income?" Lori said.

"I'd love to, so how much do you need?" Jess asked.

"Well, Tim's a heavy spender so would two-thousand dollars a month be too much to ask?" Lori answered with a prayer.

"I'll put that amount in your bank account each month, but you still need to encourage Tim to go to work as long as he can see well enough," Jess replied.

"You even know that Tim's gradually going blind from his eye surgeries years ago!" Lori exclaimed.

"Yes, I know, but he still has some good years left," Jess answered.

Lori wanted to throw herself into Jess's arms and go with him, but instead, she said thank you and closed the door. The past rushed through her mind and she wished she was a teenager again, and could make some different choices. She cried the rest of the afternoon. Lori did not expect Jess to send the money. "Why should he?" she asked herself.

Lori was surprised when the money in the bank never ran out. Tim did not keep very good records of their checks, but eventually, their debts were paid off. Tim remained unemployed and looking for his "Pie in the sky". He was still cranky. Lori still took her walks in the forest just to get out of the house. She did not have to face the trials of subbing anymore. They had better cars to drive.

Lori still felt unloved. One day she was walking through the forest with the dogs when she looked up and saw Jess standing on the mountain path. His handsome smile penetrated through her very soul. She felt weak.

"I have come back for you," Jess said simply.

Lori fell into Jess's arms and felt a love and security she had never felt before. Jess led her through the trees and up to a large, new motor home, with a new vehicle attached to the back. Jess lifted Lori up into the passenger side and together they drove down the mountain.

"I must leave Tim a note to let him know that I'm not coming home again, and leave the dogs," Lori said.

Jess handed Lori a piece of paper and a writing pen.

Lori wrote:

> Dear Tim,
>
> I'm leaving you. I still love you, but I know you no longer love me. I can't take your rejection and insecurity any longer. Please don't try to find me. May you find your peace with the Lord.
>
> Lori

Lori put the letter in the mailbox at the front of the house. She did not want to take time to go back into the house in case Tim might come home and make her change her mind. With what Jess had promised her, she could not think of anything important enough to take with her. They traveled down the rest of the mountain and out of sight.

"Lori, is there something I can do to help your boys?" Jess asked, as he drove through Thomasville.

"Well, if you need tax write-offs, I'm sure they can also use steady incomes," Lori replied. She still felt like this was too good to be true.

Do you want me to make the same arrangements for them as I did for Tim?" Jess asked.

"That would be great!" Lori exclaimed.

"It is done," Jess replied. He reached over and took Lori's hand in his huge hand and squeezed it. Jess drove through beautiful mountain areas until he pulled into a large driveway in front of the most beautiful home, in the most beautiful setting, Lori had ever seen.

Lori followed Jess into the house and Jess showed Lori every area of this beautiful home. There were several bedrooms, family rooms, a kitchen with every convenience, and an indoor swimming pool. There was a weight room and tennis court. Lori could not think of one thing that the home did not have, but most important, it had love.

"Jess, may I ask you something?" Lori said.

"Yes my love," Jess answered. He took Lori into his arms and hugged her.

"Jess, why do you want me?" Lori asked. "You are handsome and rich, and you could have about any pretty, young woman you want. Why have you chosen me, an older, heavy woman, who has passed her days of being pretty?" Lori asked.

"You have always been beautiful to me, and are still beautiful to me," Jess answered. "I have loved you all this time. I've constantly dreamed that you would be mine someday."

"I'm still concerned about Tim," Lori said.

"If I can prove to you that he is happier since you are with me, will you be satisfied?" Jess asked.

"Yes, but how can you do that?" Lori asked.

"Follow me," Jess answered. He took Lori by the hand and led her into a room that looked like an office on the second floor of the mansion. Jess turned on a machine that looked something like a TV.

Lori gasped as she watched Tim reading the letter she had just left him. He was smiling. She watched him leave the house and go to a young friend's place. He was asking the young lady for a date when Jess turned off the machine.

"I hate to hurt you like that, sweetheart," Jess whispered. "But, I didn't want you to worry. It's time for you to rest now, darling." He led Lori to a beautiful bedroom and kissed her goodnight.

Lori had never felt so peaceful and happy.

The next morning Jess called an attorney that came to the mansion and had Lori to sign divorce papers. "You need to give Tim his freedom before he is tied up with someone else," Jess explained.

Lori signed the papers.

"It will be three months before the divorce is final," the lawyer said. "I'll take the papers to Tim to sign so the time can start right away."

Lori's days were filled with fun things with Jess. They went swimming every day, worked out in the weight room, and played tennis. There were many mountain walks. With all the fresh fruit and vegetables to eat, and exercise, Lori lost the extra weight she wanted to lose. Jess took her to town to shop for new clothes. It was fun to buy pretty clothes again instead of the clothes heavier women wear. But, the most fun time was the time Lori and Jess spent studying the Bible. The days just flew by. Soon the divorce time was finished and Jess and Lori were married in the beautiful mountain setting. Lori's entire family was watching and smiling.

Jess and Lori were now one in spirit. The intimacy they shared was far greater than any physical intimacy Lori had ever experienced in either one of her other marriages. When Lori felt Jess's large arms around her, she felt peace, security, and happiness beyond description.

Lori often asked, "Why me?" She enjoyed all the things money could buy, but she also found Jess's commitment to God very comforting. Jess had a comical side, and many nights Lori went to sleep laughing. She could not believe that such ecstasy was possible. Jess was so handsome, loving, understanding, and dedicated.

When Lori's mother was sick, Jess somehow arranged for Elizabeth to be well again. There was no end to what Jess was doing for her and her family.

Lori was enjoying her happiness one day, when she asked Jess, "Who are you, anyway? I know you are not who I thought you were."

Jess smiled at Lori and said, "I am your Lord."

"Lori, get out of that bed and get my breakfast!" Tim was shouting.

Lori opened her eyes and felt terrified. It had all been a dream. She was still in her unhappy prison, but as long as Tim could not control her mind, there was still hope.

Lori jumped out of bed and ran into the large kitchen to start Tim's breakfast. She took time to enjoy the morning view from each window. An early autumn snow had fallen and covered the higher elevations of mountains. The skiers were already sliding down the small slope to the southwest of the house. There were still a few small sail boats on the lake below where it was still summer. "What a beautiful place to live," Lori said to herself. Then the fears of their state of poverty gripped at her heart.

Lori soon had a large breakfast of pancakes, scrambled eggs, and bacon ready and called Tim up from his dark seclusion downstairs.

Tim climbed the stairs slowly and sat down at the table. He said nothing. Tim started to devour his breakfast. He stared at her constantly. Tim's thick glasses magnified his eyes and made Lori feel uncomfortable.

They ate in silence. Eating seemed to be one of the few things they still enjoyed. They were both heavier than they had ever been. Tim finished his breakfast and returned to his darkness downstairs.

"I promised myself that I would never get in this predicament again when I divorced Hollis," Lori said to herself. "I said I would only marry a Christian this time." "What's wrong with me?" Lori asked herself.

Tim had been very religious when they first married, and he had even started a new church. Now, Tim had stopped going to church, and he did not want Lori to go either. Lori had no money to give to the Lord, and Tim had not wanted to tithe even when they had money. How could things have changed so fast?

Despite Tim's indifference, Lori had managed to have enough gas in the car to drive to church every Sunday morning. She had no money for offerings, so she put more of her jewelry in the offering plate at church. The Lord could not bless them financially unless they gave Him something to multiply. Tim was angry when he noticed the silver ring he had given Lori was missing from her finger.

Lori cleaned up the kitchen, made the bed, and straightened up the large upstairs. As she worked, she thought about the wonderful dream. "Was I really asleep, or had it been a daydream?" Lori asked herself. "Is it sacrilegious to think about Jesus that way?" Lori wondered. She tried to reason out her dream.

"I was in high-school when I accepted Jesus as my Savior, so that part fits," Lori reasoned.

"I know Jesus loves me and wants to do everything he can for me, and I know I need to put him first," Lori told herself. "I also know God cares what happens to me and to my family, and that he owns the cattle on a thousand hills. I know that the intimacy we can have with the Lord is greater than physical intimacy."

Lori heard Tim stomping up the stairs. She knew he was angry again. Tim rushed into the living-room where Lori was playing the Baby-Grande piano. Tim had the morning mail in his hands.

"Lori, they have just raised our rent from eight-hundred to a thousand dollars a month!" Tim shouted. "We're going to have to move again; that money I borrowed from Jack is almost gone," he said.

"It's scary living here anyway," Lori replied. "I'll be glad to move into something cheaper if we can find it."

"I like living here, and if you'd have enough faith, we could be prosperous!" Tim shouted. "I had enough faith, but you weren't in agreement and that is why we lost a million and a half dollars while we were farming and ranching! You're supposed to be the religious one and you couldn't even believe God for making our operation successful!" Tim shouted. "This is your fault!"

"But, it was your idea to borrow all that money from the bank," Lori protested. "I knew it wouldn't work even when you persuaded the bankers that it would. You wouldn't work! Many days I came home from working in the field all day to find you lying in front of the air conditioner! You forced me to put my mobile home, that was paid for when I met you, as collateral. You even talked one preacher into asking me to go forward in church and agree in prayer that we would get the million dollar loan."

"I was sick and couldn't work!" Tim shouted.

Lori ran into the bedroom and closed the door. She flopped across the bed and cried. "How could I have gotten myself into such a mess?" "Am I judging Tim unfairly?" Lori asked herself. "Maybe he hadn't been well and couldn't help what happened to us," Lori tried to convince herself.

The telephone rang. Lori did not answer it. She did not want to talk to anyone.

"Lori, your son, Mike is on the phone," Tim called from downstairs.

Lori took a drink of Pepsi to clear her voice before she answered.

"Hello, mom, I was just wondering if you guys are going to be there around Christmas?" Mike asked. I have a few days off and thought I would come and visit you," he said.

"That sounds great!" Lori answered.

"I'll be there Christmas Eve about noon, and I don't have to be back home for three days," Mike explained.

Lori ran downstairs to tell Tim that Mike was coming.

"I know, I was listening," Tim said with a smile. He had always liked Lori's sons. "I think you should call your mother and step-dad, Mitch and his family, and your sister, Elaine and her family, and see if they can all come here for Christmas," Tim said.

"But Tim, we don't have money enough to feed them," Lori protested.

"I have a little cash for groceries, and we can worry about moving after Christmas," he replied.

Lori made the calls. Mitch and his family had other plans, but the rest of the family planned to come for Christmas. Tim found the money to buy two large hams and a large turkey. He fixed the meats and trimmings while Lori made pumpkin and pecan pies.

Lori's step father, Arther, decided that he had too many cattle to feed. He brought Elizabeth to Tim and Lori's house and started the six-hour trip right back to feed and water cattle. Elizabeth was disappointed that Arther could not stay, but she was determined to have a good time anyway.

Mike was the second one to arrive. He was so thin that Lori hardly recognized him. "I don't know if a bachelor's life is good for you or not," Lori said. She gave Mike a hug. Elaine, Barry, and Lori's niece, Cheri, came in right after Mike. The family had a lot of fun eating, playing games, singing, shopping, and enjoy the large house and view, not to mention exchanging gifts.

Elizabeth was extra funny one evening and started jumping up and down on the bed she was sharing with Cheri. Elizabeth had face-cream on her face and her night-shirt on. Cheri kept saying, "Grandma,

Grandma!" Lori ran and found her old camera and took Elizabeth's picture and other pictures. Everyone had a good time and Tim was as kind as he had been when he and Lori were first married.

Christmas was soon over and everyone went home. Arther drove the six-hour trip to pick up Elizabeth and drove right back.

After the family left, Tim returned to his dark corner. Lori was feeling lonely when the telephone rang. It was Mitch's wife, Staci.

"How was your Christmas?" Staci asked.

"Wonderful, if only you guys could have been here," Lori answered.

"I have good news for you anyway," Staci said.

"I always like good news, dear," Lori replied.

"I'm pregnant," Staci said. "You're going to be a grandmother again," she explained, excitedly.

"Wonderful!" Lori exclaimed. "How far along are you" she asked.

"Two weeks," Staci answered.

Lori had to laugh. "I guess since you're a nurse, I know you know for sure," she said.

"There is no doubt," Staci replied. "Love ya, and good-bye," she said and hung up the phone.

Lori was so happy she bounded down the stairs to tell Tim. She couldn't tell if Tim was happy over the news or not.

That afternoon, the telephone rang again. Lori did not feel like answering it. Tim finally answered the phone on the fourth ring. "Hello," he said.

"Hello, Mr. Jones; this is Vance Jackson," a man's voice said. "I was at one of your vitamin company meeting several months ago, and I was impressed with your salesmanship qualities. I have just taken over a new mobile telephone company and I wonder if you'd like to come to work for me as a mobile telephone salesman, strictly commission of course," Vance Jackson said.

"I might be interested," Tim replied.

"I also have a need for a secretary and wondered if your wife would be interested in that position," Mr. Jackson added.

"She'll take the job," Tim replied. "When and where do you want us to meet you?" he asked.

"I have just rented a new office, in a new office building at 716 Mountain Road, and I would like for you to be there at eight o'clock in the morning," Vance Jackson said.

"That is at the foot of the mountain where we live, and only about two miles from here," Tim replied.

"Yes, I know; see you tomorrow," Vance Jackson said.

Tim and Lori started to work the next morning. Mr. Jackson showed them around the office, left some orders, and was gone for the rest of the day.

Lori was paid very little, but it was better than substitute teaching once in awhile. Lori would have enjoyed her secretary work, if it had not been for Tim's demands.

"I want you to use that telephone book and call every business in the city and try to set up appointments for me to demonstrate the mobile telephone," Tim ordered.

"But, Tim, I've never done anything like that before," Lori protested.

"You will do as you're told, and besides, if this job doesn't work out, you might be sleeping in the street," Tim shouted.

Lori made calls all morning while Tim sit and read the newspaper. She felt embarrassed butting into someone's morning and trying to sell them something. Out of fifty calls, five businesses said they would work in a time for a demonstration the next day. "I've made so many phone calls that my neck is stiff and hurting," Lori said. "You aren't busy, so why don't you make some calls."

"It's not impressive if I make the calls. Besides, you're a lot better on the telephone than I am," Tim answered, stretching out in one of the large office chairs. "Your neck will get used to the telephone work, and after all, demonstrating the telephones is a lot more work than what you're doing."

Lori still did not consider herself a salesperson. The calling made her so nervous that she often had stomach aches. She felt like she was intruding into people's lives. Most of the people she called were nice, and she learned how to leave good messages on answering machines. A few guys kept Lori on the phone for several minutes just to have someone to talk to. They wanted someone they didn't know to listen to their problems. Very few phones were sold compared to the number of calls Lori made in Thomasville and the surrounding areas. Most people wanted to wait for something they called Cellular 1 that would reach across the nation from coast to coast.

Mr. Jackson never came into the office before 10:30. He was a stuntman driver and had been in such movies as "The Dukes of Hazard" and many car advertisements. Vance Jackson also worked as a male model. He put keeping his body in shape above the business of the mobile telephone company.

Tim became acquainted with the company boss above Vance. He arranged for the boss to come to the office when Vance did not know he was coming. As Tim had planned, Vance was fired and Tim was hired as the new manager of the office, but his salary was still on a commission.

During the first month, Tim sold several telephone units and made close to three-thousand dollars.

Lori had been busy with her secretary work and making phone calls all day. Tim had been gone since early morning. Lori heard Tim drive up and park in front of the office.

"Lori, come out here, I want to show you something," Tim yelled as he came through the door.

Lori followed Tim through the front door and moaned when she saw a new, expensive, New Yorker parked near the door. "Oh no, Tim, you shouldn't have . . ." Lori said weakly.

"Isn't she a beaut?" Tim asked excitedly.

Lori crawled into the automobile and felt the red velvet seats. It was a beautiful car. "Tim, how did you manage this?" she asked.

"I talked to a banker downtown. He said he had heard of me and about the large farming and ranching operation I used to have," Tim started to explain. "He said he thought I would be successful again, and he loaned us the money for the car."

"It was too late for Lori to protest. All the papers had already been signed.

Sales were drastically down the next two months. Tim sold Lori's car for enough money to make two payments on the New Yorker. Lori was back to driving the old Oldsmobile. Tim enjoyed demonstrating the telephone in the new car. "Maybe he needs it for business," Lori tried to convince herself.

Mike called again. "Hi mom, I quit my job and I'm moving to Thomasville," he said. "I'm going to try to get a job in a music store so I can continue my studies on the guitar," Mike explained. "I was wondering if I could stay with you until I get a place of my own," he said.

"Tim and I both will be glad to have you here," Lori replied.

"Mom, I'm bringing a friend, that's all right, isn't it?" Mike asked.

"Sure, we have plenty of room," Lori said. "Is your friend anyone I know?" she asked.

"Yes, you taught her in school," Mike replied. "I call her PJ," he said.

"Oh, I remember her," Lori said and hung up. The thought of Mike having a girlfriend hadn't even been in Lori's mind. She remembered PJ. She had been a student Lori had really enjoyed teaching. PJ had thought a lot of Mike since she had been in the fifth grade. Mike had never asked PJ for a date and she ended up getting married right out of high school. If Lori remembered right, PJ had a baby girl and was still married. "Oh Lord, help me to do what's right," Lori prayed.

Lori told Tim about Mike's phone call. "It doesn't surprise me any," Tim said. He was excited about Mike coming and treated Lori with more compassion.

It was late Monday evening when Mike and PJ came in. Mike had gained some weight and looked better than he had for a long time. He seemed happy. PJ seemed to still have her crush on Mike.

Mike and Tim visited downstairs while PJ helped Lori fix supper. "How have you been all these years?" Lori asked.

My only happiness has been my little girl," PJ answered. "My husband doesn't love me, but he won't let me have my baby unless I stay with him. He has made me go to a hospital for the mentally ill, and there's nothing wrong with me. I love Mike, but I don't know how long I can go without my baby."

"PJ, you're husband must love you or he wouldn't want you to stay with him," Lori replied.

"I know he doesn't love me, and I don't know why he won't let me have my baby," PJ answered.

The next day Mike and PJ drove around the city looking for work. By evening, Mike had not found a job, but PJ had several large homes lined up for cleaning. PJ looked real cute leaving for work Wednesday morning. She had on denims and a red bandanna over her hair. PJ was carrying a broom, a mop and bucket. Mike took PJ to work and spent the day looking for a job. He finally found a part-time job working in a hardware store.

The second week, Mike and PJ found a small apartment and moved Mike's furniture into it. The third week, one of PJ's brothers came to live with them. One Sunday morning, Mike called.

"Mom, would it be all right with you if I came over for a few days; it's getting crowded around here and I need some time alone," Mike said.

"Sure," Lori answered.

Lori had planned to go to church, but she felt like she was needed at home to talk to Mike. Mike came in with his guitar and a suitcase and took them to the downstairs bedroom. Lori left him to himself, but she enjoyed the music coming from the bedroom. It had been a long time since she had heard Mike's music.

In the middle of the afternoon, Mike ran up the stairs. "Mom, I have to get back to the apartment right away," he said.

"What's the hurry?" Lori asked.

"I don't know, I just have to get back there," Mike said. He ran down the stairs and out to his pickup truck. Lori heard him driving away. An hour later she heard the pickup truck pulling up to the house again.

Mike ran up the steps. "PJ has left me," he moaned. Mike handed Lori the note PJ had left.

"I can't be away from my little girl any longer. Sorry things didn't work out, Love PJ," the note read.

"I don't know what to do," Mike said. He ran back to the bedroom and slammed the door.

Tim waited awhile before he knocked on the bedroom door. "Mike, may I come in?" he asked.

There was a period of silence before Mike said, "Yes."

"Mike, what you need is the help of the Lord," Tim said. "I think you should go to church with Lori and me tonight and let the Lord touch you."

Lori knew it was what Mike needed, but she was shocked that Tim would even mention it.

"I guess it won't hurt, I have nothing else to do," Mike replied.

"It is so nice going to a night service after all this time," Lori said to herself as she rode in the back seat of the New Yorker. Tim and Mike were visiting in the front seat. They heard a powerful message that night and Mike went forward for prayer.

"Please pray for me and my girlfriend," Mike said. "Pray that she will be strong no matter what happens."

After pastor Rick laid hands on Mike and prayed, the associate pasture took him into another room and counseled with Mike for over an hour. When the two men came back, Mike seemed to be at peace and was ready to go home. "I like that guy; he talks my language," Mike said on the way home.

Mike and Lori stayed up almost all night. Lori listened to Mike talk. All of his former ideas had been changed, and he had peace. The following week, Mitch helped Mike move back to his old home close to the old farm where Tim and Lori had lived.

Lori received one letter from PJ. She was in a mental hospital. PJ said she was laying out plans for her life on how to live for God, and keep her self confidence. She said when she was released, she was going to be with her husband and baby.

CHAPTER IV

MOVING TIME AGAIN

Mobile telephone sales were still slow. Tim and Lori could not keep up with the expensive rent. They found a cheaper place in a different area of Thomasville. The house was a large, three-story with a balcony overlooking the mountains from the master bedroom, another balcony off the family room facing the mountains, and a large patio leading from the open basement family room. There was a great view of the mountains from every level of the house.

This time when Lori went back to clean up the house on the mountain, she knew all the history that had taken place the year and a half they had lived there. It had been eighteen months of despair and heart ache. It seemed almost impossible that such terrible memories could take place in such beautiful surroundings.

Tim seemed to be more satisfied for awhile. The mobile telephone company was forced out of business by the Cellular I company. Tim and Lori were without jobs and soon behind on their rent again.

Lori sold all the clothes that were too small for her in an effort to help with expenses. After only three months of living in the three-story house, they were forced to move into a smaller house in the northern part of Thomasville. There was not much cleaning to do in this large house after the move. Lori realized that she had felt like a prisoner the three months of living there.

School was out for the summer and Lori had no where to sub for that small income. Tim still felt that he was too sick to go out and find a job.

Lori sold her beloved piano that she had bought the first year she had started teaching twenty years ago. It brought only enough money for two months rent. The next month Lori sold her trampoline, her last form of exercise. She did not know how Tim was keeping the New Yorker, and she was still driving the old Oldsmobile. Finally, Lori had to sell her electric guitar and the accordion that her folks had given her when she was in high school. She still had the large accordion that Tim's family had given her for as long as she was in the Jones family.

"Lori, we need money again, I was thinking that you might sell some of your furniture," Tim said.

"I have already sold so many things that meant a lot to me!" Lori shouted. "Why don't you sell some of your things?" Lori asked.

"Because my things are more valuable that your things and I wouldn't get enough out of them," Tim shouted.

"Tim, you just have to get another job!" Lori shouted. She ran into the bedroom to cry again.

Tim joined another multi-level vitamin company and pushed Lori into helping him with meetings. Many times no one showed up. Tim and Lori had to pay the expenses of the hotel meeting rooms, and the uneaten refreshments. Lori felt like crying one night when she had to pour a large amount of expensive coffee down the sink in the large meeting room. She could almost see dollar signs going down the drain in the steam. Sometimes, the refreshments became their groceries. The business was faltering when Jack Thomas joined the company.

Jack had a Master's Degree in Nutrition and did a great job of introducing people to the products. He was six-foot, three-inches tall, with blonde hair and a thick blonde mustache. Tim, Lori, and other people thought Jack looked just like the handsome model on the Marlboro cigarette advertisement.

Tim decided to try the next meeting at the house. Lori put all their chairs in the downstairs family room and fixed refreshments. Eight people showed up. Jack presented the products part of the meeting and turned the meeting over to Tim to explain the money-making prospects.

During a meeting the next week, Lori heard the telephone ringing and ran upstairs to answer it so it would not disturb the meeting.

"Is Jack there?" a woman's voice asked.

"Yes, I'll get him for you," Lori answered. She motioned for Jack to come upstairs to answer the phone.

Jack took the telephone. He said "Yes" and Okay" and hung up. He called downstairs to Tim. "I have to go home now because I have a sick girl," Jack explained.

Lori thought that the girl must be terribly sick since all three of Jack's daughters were old enough to be in high-school. She helped Tim close the meeting and sell a few products. After all the guests had left, Tim and Lori counted their money. As usual, there was not enough to meet their needs. "Tim, you just have to get a job in order for us to survive," Lori said. "I can't sub until school starts again," she tried to explain.

"I don't have an education, and I'm almost blind," Tim replied. Some people have trouble adjusting to the way I look," he said. "I'm doing the best I can," Tim said. "I'm going bed."

Lori cleaned up the downstairs and carried the chairs back to the living room and other rooms. She again wished for the times that she and Tim had gone to sleep every night in each others arms. Lori knew she could not put up with this insecurity and rejection much longer. Lori forced her tired body up the stairs and into bed. She slept on the edge of the bed away from Tim because he never wanted her to touch him. "Where had their marriage gone wrong?" Lori asked herself again.

"Good morning, Jack," Lori said when she answered the front door the next morning. "How is your sick girl?" she asked.

"I need to tell you and Tim about it," Jack said.

Lori followed Jack into the living room where Tim was sitting reading the morning paper. Tim nodded for Jack to sit in one of the large living room chairs and Lori sit in another one.

"I guess I did have a sick girl last night," Jack begain. "But, it's much more complicated than that," he said. "My oldest daughter has been arguing with my wife. I've tried to convince June that Ruthy isn't a bad girl. I don't have any trouble getting along with her. Anyway, last night they had another argument and Ruthy picked up a large kitchen knife and tried to stab her mother. She missed, thank God," Jack said.

"Ruthy ran into the bathroom and locked the door. June couldn't get her out so she called the police. The police couldn't get her out because our bathroom is on the second floor, so they had June to call me. I talked to her a long time and she finally unlocked the door. June is at work now and Ruthy is at home, so I thought it would be safe for me to come over and tell you about it. I don't know what I'm going to do tonight," Jack said. A sob shook his tall body.

"Things will work out," Tim and Lori both said.

"I know they will because I've prayed about it, but I need to be home when June gets off work to keep peace," Jack said. "I'm sorry, but I won't be able to help with the evening meetings until we get things worked out," he explained.

Jack worked with Lori and Tim during the day and Lori took Jack's part of the meetings at night for two weeks. The following Monday, Jack came to help Tim with the ads, etc. He looked troubled. Jack sat down in the living room and said, "June has asked me for a divorce." "I know it's for the best; she hasn't been happy with me for a long time," he said, trying to smile. Jack left to go home early that afternoon.

Jack did not come to work the next day. On Wednesday he came in about ten o'clock. "Well, I'm a free man now; I can date; I can go anywhere I please, and do anything I please, ain't I a lucky man," Jack said. He forced loud laughter, and then his countenance changed. Jack threw his arms around Tim's neck and cried like a baby. "I have to go through this to give my Ruthy a good place to live," he said after he had gained control of his emotions. "I have to go now and find a place for Ruthy and me to live," Jack explained.

Tim and Lori did not hear from Jack for several days. Tim happened to be downtown one afternoon when Jack came over. "I have a small apartment for me and my girl," he said with a forced grin.

Lori stopped cleaning house and poured two cups of coffee. She sat down at the dining room table across from Jack.

Jack talked about his new life and a former pasture's wife he was now dating. "Our pasture gave some classes on divorce, and then he divorced his wife for a younger woman in the church," he said. "They are now married and living in Florida. I'm dating his ex-wife, and she is a wonderful woman, and Ruthy likes her."

"How strange, Lori replied. "I thought those classes were to help people in the church that were already divorced," she said.

"Jack, I can't live with Tim any longer," Lori said. "He won't work and we are always broke. He doesn't seem to want me around most of the time, and he demands more of me than I can give. We have some friends, from back home, coming to visit us. I plan to leave with them, but don't tell Tim. I don't want him to know until the time I leave in case he'll try to talk me out of it."

"I understand, and I can't blame you," Jack replied.

"My life has been so miserable with Tim that sometimes I wish I would have stayed with my first husband and tried to adjust to his mistress," Lori said. "I think that's what the Lord would have liked for me to do rather than breaking up our home."

"Oh Lori, God loves you too much to ask you to do something like that," Jack replied. "Don't punish yourself for what you had to do, and don't punish yourself for what you feel you have to do now,"

Lori fell across Jack's chest and sobbed. After she had gained her composure, Lori gave Jack a big hug. "Thanks for being such a good, understanding friend," she said.

"Thank you for being an understanding friend, too. Keep your chin up, and good luck," he said as he told Lori good-bye.

That afternoon Lori was still waiting for Tim to come home. She enjoyed the quietness, but wondered why he had been gone so long when the telephone started ringing. "It must be Tim calling from the mobile telephone," Lori told herself.

"Hello," Lori said.

"Hello, I want to join your company," a man's voice said. "May I come right over?" he asked.

Normally Lori would have been excited with business picking up, but something told her to be careful. "He must be calling from our newspaper ad," Lori told herself. "You have to wait until you come to one of our meetings," she replied.

"I want to come now," the stranger said.

"My husband will have to talk to you and he's busy right now," Lori said.

"I want to come and see you right now," the stranger said again." I have seen you before and I love your breasts."

"You don't want to see me; I'm just an old grandma," Lori replied. She felt her face burning.

"Age doesn't make any difference," the man said.

"You don't want to see me and you don't know where I live," Lori replied.

"Yes, I know where you live; I've been there before," the man said. "I need you!" the man whispered. Lori heard heavy breathing over the telephone. "I'll be there in a little while," the man said through heavy breaths and hung up the phone.

Lori was terrified. She called Tim's mobile telephone number. "Praise the Lord!" Lori exclaimed when Tim answered. "Tim, come home right now, I'm in danger!"

"I'm on my way home now, so tell me why you're in danger," Tim replied.

Lori told Tim about the conversation she had just had with the strange man over the telephone. "He said he was on his way over here and he's in bad shape," Lori tried to explain.

"I think I know who it is," Tim said. "At our last meeting I had one of our new sales persons give the products part of my meeting while you were working with some people upstairs," he explained. "A man in the group made the same remark about Jenny's breasts. Jenny was so nervous about doing her first presentation that she never heard what the man said. The man seemed to be all right, but I was glad he didn't join the company; I hate to have someone in the company that talks like that anyway. I'm pulling into our driveway right now,"

For once, Lori was glad to see Tim. Nothing happened that evening, but Lori felt fear all night long. "I know the man had sexual needs, and that he was going to get them filled one way or another," Lori tried to explain to Tim.

Tim just laughed at Lori's fear. The next morning he was reading the Thomasville newspaper. "Lori, you might want to listen to this," Tim said.

Lori came into the living room and sit down to listen.

Tim read: There was a triple murder in Thomasville early this morning in Wellington Place, a nice neighborhood. Ms. Margaret Hilton, who worked for the law-firm of Smith and Smith, was found murdered, along with her twelve year old son and fourteen year old daughter. The two females had been sexually assaulted. Ms. Hilton's boyfriend has been questioned and released. The authorities are wondering how three murders could take place in the morning with no neighbors hearing anything, and there are no leads at this time.

"That's awful!" Lori exclaimed. "I know the murderer is the one I talked to on the telephone yesterday. "And, he knows where we live!" Lori exclaimed.

"Oh I don't think you'll be in any danger," Tim said with a laugh.

"I don't think it's a laughing matter!" Lori shouted. She went back to her daily work. "Oh Lord, please protect us," she prayed.

The paper had short reports on the murder in every issue for several days. There were still no suspects. Lori finally called the police headquarters and asked for the detective that was handling the case. She told the detective what had happened. "We don't have the man's name, but my husband could identify him," Lori said.

"I'm sorry about your obscene telephone call, miss, but I'm sure it has nothing to do with our case," the detective said.

"But, you don't have any other leads, and he could strike again if you don't find him," Lori argued.

"I'm sure you're not in any danger, and your phone call has nothing to do with the murder," the man said again and hung up.

"Well, I've done what I could," Lori told herself.

CHAPTER V

SOME BIG DECISIONS

Violet and Sam had been some of the few friends that stood by Tim and Lori when Tim had been arrested on charges of child molesting. They arrived on Friday night to spend the weekend with Tim and Lori.

Tim pretended that he and Lori had plenty of money and took their guests out to an expensive restaurant to eat. Lori listened to Tim's bragging all evening long. Later that evening, while the men were visiting in the downstairs family room, Lori took Violet upstairs so they could talk.

"Violet, I'm leaving Tim, and I wonder if you guys could give me a ride back home and leave me at my mother's place?" Lori asked.

"I understand, but what are you going to do with all your furniture and things?" Violet asked.

"I don't know." Lori replied. "I'll stay at Mother's and try to get my thinking straight, then I'll send someone here to get my things, I guess."

Tim took their guests to church and pretended that he was used to going. Then they went out to eat again. After the meal was over, the four friends sit at their table a little longer to visit.

"We need to start home, now," Violet said. She looked at Lori.

"Tim, I'm leaving you," Lori said. "We're going back to the house to pick up some of my clothes. I don't imagine you care, but don't try to talk me out of it, because my mind is made up." Lori felt like a dead person getting ready to fall off a cliff. Her whole body felt numb.

"I thought this was going to happen," Tim replied.

Lori crawled into Violet's car so she would not be alone with Tim on the way back to the house. She already had her suitcases packed so it did not take long to put them into Violet and Sam's car. "Good-bye Tim," Lori said as she crawled into the back seat of the new, tan Oldsmobile.

Tim did not say anything. Lori looked up into the face she had once loved. Tim was crying. The tears were stacking up at the bottom of his thick eyeglasses. Lori turned to look the other way. She tried to act happy during the six-hour drive to her mother's and was glad when darkness came and her friends could not see her crying in the back seat of the car.

"Lori, it's so good to see you; we didn't know you were coming," Elizabeth said. "Where is Tim?" she asked.

"I left him," Lori answered. "It's all right if I live here for awhile, isn't it Mother?" Lori asked.

"I'm not surprised about you leaving Tim," Elizabeth replied. "You're always welcome here, dear," she said, giving Lori a big hug.

Lori went to bed in one of the guest bedrooms. She felt more relaxed than she had felt for a long time. The next day she helped Elizabeth around the house. By the end of the week, Arthur, Lori's step father, had hired her to drive a tractor pulling a tank of water to water his cattle. She hauled several tanks-full the first day to the cattle that were in a large pasture of buffalo grass.

The second day, Lori fell off the back of the tractor. Her leg was cut badly when she fell and was bleeding more than it was hurting for the first few minutes. Lori took the scarf she was wearing over her hair and tied it around her upper leg above the wound. The bleeding slowed down, but her leg started to hurt. It hurt so badly that she lay on the ground for a few minutes and gritted her teeth. "Oh Lord, this is the only job I have so help me get through it," Lori prayed. "God, if my folks find out how badly I'm hurt, they won't let me do this anymore," she said.

Lori crawled upon the tractor and started after another load of water. No one was living on the ranch where Lori filled the tank. It was thirty miles to the nearest doctor, and Lori had no money to go to the doctor anyway. She kept working. It was very painful to crawl down from the tractor each time to fill, or empty the tank, but by evening, most of the stiffness was gone.

Elizabeth was concerned over Lori's injury, but Lori convinced her that it didn't hurt and she enjoyed hauling the water every day. Lori had always enjoyed being outdoors.

During the following days, after Lori finished hauling water, she visited with relatives and enjoyed the presence of loving people again. There was no word from Tim.

"Lori, there's an ad in the county newspaper for a teacher in Lucas," Arthur said, handing the paper to Lori.

Lori picked up the telephone and called the school she had attended her first twelve years.

"Yes, we're still looking for a teacher," the superintendent said. "Could you meet with the school-board Thursday night?" he asked.

"I'll be glad to; what time?" Lori responded.

The school-board was made up of people Lori had known all her life. The meeting was formal and Lori was asked a lot of questions. "We hear that you have just left Tim Jones," one school-board member said. "We were wondering if there is a slight chance that you might go back to him."

Lori remembered when she had almost lost her last teaching job because of Tim's reputation for child molesting. Lucas was only ten miles from her old school. Lori guessed that all the school-board members, here in this meeting too, thought that Tim was guilty. "I have no intention of ever going back," Lori replied.

"We'll let you know when we decide," The superintendent said. He escorted Lori to the door and called the next person waiting to be interviewed.

The superintendent called the next morning and said, "We decided to hire you; you can come in and sign your contract whenever it is convenient for you,"

Lori was so happy. It would be nice to have enough income to live on again.

The next week Lori went to a four-day Church Camp meeting with her aunt and cousin. It took them two hours to get there. The campground was in a beautiful canyon that dropped off from the flat prairie. The three ladies registered and found bunk beds close together.

"We're so glad that you left Tim," Cousin Pam said.

"I don't think your health would have lasted much longer with all the stress he put you through," Aunt Martha added.

"Isn't it fun to get together, and visit, and go to church," Pam said, giving Lori a big hug. "Let's go over to the dining hall and get in line for dinner." Pam walked to the door of the sleeping barracks. "Oh no, Lori, look outside!" she exclaimed.

Lori ran to the door. Tim was standing on the path between the barracks and the dining hall. There was no way to go around him. Lori felt sick. She walked down the path feeling like she had been hypnotized. Tim took her by the hand and led her to the dining hall. Lori walked beside Tim because she did not want to protest and cause an ugly scene in this tranquil place.

Tim acted confident and pretended that they were still happily married. The meal was soon over and Tim asked, "Lori, can I talk to you for a moment, outside?"

"I have said all I want to say, so please go away," Lori whispered while smiling at everyone.

"Would you rather talk in here in front of everyone?" Tim asked with a confident smile.

Lori followed Tim with the feeling of helplessness like she had done a thousand times before. "Maybe I can find a way to get rid of him," Lori was telling herself.

It was now dark. As soon as they were a few yards from the dining room door, Tim took Lori into his arms and kissed her. "I want you to come back, Lori," Tim said. "I have a job selling General Motor vehicles, and you won't have to worry about expenses anymore. I need you, Lori. I want to go to the church camp meetings the one day I'm here, and maybe I can get close to God again."

"I have a new life and I don't want to come back," Lori replied.

"I think I can change your mind," Tim said. He sounded confident. Tim took Lori's hand and led her into the church meeting. He took advantage of the situation and sit with his arm around Lori during the meeting.

Tim's touch made cold shivers go up and down Lori's spine. She felt like she was being smothered by a stranger. As soon as the meeting was over, Lori ran to the women's barracks, the only place she could get away from Tim. Pam and Aunt Martha were right behind her.

"Lori, will you never be safe?" Aunt Martha asked.

"I feel like he's looking in our windows right now," Pam said. "He's always made me feel uncomfortable."

There were four ladies standing together at the front of the barracks. They were talking when one of them yelled over to where Lori, Pam, and Aunt Martha were sitting on their bunks. "You shouldn't talk about someone like that!" the lady shouted. "Christians don't say things like that about other people; I've just gotten real close to God and I know!"

"The nerve of some people," Pam said as she crawled into bed.

Lori had a hard time going to sleep. She wished she had a car of her own so she could make another escape. Lori used the back door of the dining hall the next morning and sit down at a crowded table so Tim could not sit close to her.

"Lori Jones, may I talk to you?" a dark-skinned man asked, as Lori was leaving the dining hall after breakfast.

Lori quickly started walking toward the barracks.

The man caught up with Lori and walked beside her. "I'm a pastor and one of the speakers for the camp meeting," the man said. "Your husband has asked me to talk to you because you have left him," he said. "Would you mind telling me why you left him; he seems to really love you."

"I'm not sure he loves me," Lori tried to explain. "I've lost everything I had since I married him and he wouldn't try to support me. These last seven years have been a nightmare, and the only way I can keep my sanity is to stay away from him. The only thing I have left is my teaching retirement and the inheritance I'll receive when my mother dies, and he wants that too. He's continually borrowing money from my relatives and forcing me to borrow from them."

"God doesn't like divorce," the pastor said. "Will you be willing to let me help you people work out your differences?" he asked.

Tim ran up beside Lori before she could answer. "I don't see what's wrong with wanting an inheritance or borrowing money from people who have plenty," Tim explained.

"That's the wrong way to look at it," the pastor said. "Every woman has the need to feel secure." "Have you ever given her security," the pasture asked.

"I've done my best, and I love her," Tim replied, squeezing Lori's hand.

Lori knew Tim was, again, doing a "sale's job" on someone. She ran back to her barracks and got ready for the next service.

After the church service, Lori and her relatives hurried back to the barracks to rest and avoid meeting Tim. "Lori, do you know what I think you should do?" Pam asked. "I think you should draw up a contract for Tim to sign before you ever go back to him." She opened up her tablet and handed it to Lori. "Write down everything you want Tim to change and make a place for both of you to sign it," Pam said.

Lori started to write. #l: Always keep a job and have money enough for rent, utilities, and groceries. #2: Never borrow any money from friends or relatives. #3: Never buy anything without first getting your wife's consent. #4: Don't blame your wife for your failures. #5: Go to church with your wife. #6. Treat your wife as your equal. "I think I could live with that," Lori said and took the list to the pastor.

Tim refused to sign the contract. He showed his temper as he spun the New Yorker around and raced out of the campground.

Lori was relieved. She enjoyed the rest of the camp-meeting and returned to her mother's. Lori ordered a book on how to get a divorce without a lawyer. She wondered how she could afford a decent car and a place of her own, even with her teaching job.

Lori and Elizabeth had just come into the house from a walk when the telephone rang. "Lori, someone wants to talk to you," Elizabeth said after listening for a minute.

"Lori, this is Pastor Rick in Thomasville. Tim has been coming to me for counseling. He wants you to come back and he promises to come for counseling with you after you move back to Thomasville," pasture Rick said.

"I don't want to come back," Lori explained. "I'm getting my life put back together again. I have a good job now. I never know how sincere Tim is when he wants something. I just don't want to come back."

"Lori, do you have Biblical grounds for leaving Tim?" Pastor Rick asked.

"Not that I know of, if you're talking about another woman in his life," Lori answered.

"Pray about it, Lori. I think God would like for you to give Tim another chance," Pastor Rick said.

"Thanks for taking time from your busy schedule to call me. I know you have a thousand people to pastor and you're awfully busy. I'll pray about it," Lori said and hung up.

Lori knew Tim could change drastically after he got his own way. She was afraid. She thought about the Bible giving only infidelity as a basis for divorce, and not always then, either. Lori prayed and mailed Tim the contract to see if he would sign it. It came back signed the next day. Lori wanted to be in the Lord's will so she called Tim to come and get her. Lori had to break her promise and notify the school board that she could not fill the teaching job.

Tim came the next weekend in a state of arrogance. He could not keep his hands to himself even before they left Elizabeth's.

Tim was like a maniac as soon as they were home. Lori would not have minded the love, but she felt like she was being used and not loved, again. Lori looked forward to Tim leaving for work every day.

Tim went with Lori for counseling, but he told Pastor Rick that everything was fine. He said the only trouble they had was that he couldn't afford to support Lori in the way she wanted to live. Tim told so many lies that Lori refused to go to counseling the third time. "Pastor Rick is too busy to listen to your lies," Lori told Tim.

Tim and Lori moved out of the bi-level house and into an upstairs apartment. They had to give the dogs away, but the apartment was three-hundred dollars a month cheaper than the house had been. The apartment complex had a recreation area including an outdoor swimming pool, indoor pool, and Jacuzzi. Lori decided that she was going to lose some weight and made a goal of swimming fifty laps every day.

Two weeks later, Tim came home from work early.

"What are you doing home so early," Lori asked.

"I quit my job; I want to know if you're serious about standing by me no matter what happens," Tim explained.

"But you signed that contract!" Lori exclaimed.

"A couple doesn't need a contract to stay together," Tim said. "And, don't answer the door because the police are trying to serve back child support on me."

"But, the twins are twenty years old, and out of school," Lori moaned. "Why do you have to support them now?" she asked.

"They say I have to support them until they're twenty-one," Tim answered. "Just do what I tell you and don't answer the door!"

Lori was shaking as she put on her swimming suit. At least swimming her laps would give her a chance to get away from Tim and his shouting. She carefully looked out over the apartment complex from their upstairs window. There were no strangers who looked like they might be carrying some sheriff's papers. Lori ran to the indoor pool for her exercises.

All Tim wanted to do was to sit around the apartment, have his physical needs filled, his stomach filled, and blame Lori for all their problems.

Lori was so terribly nervous after Tim quit working that she thought she was going to die. One day she had been busy buying a few groceries. She had a little change left in her purse. Lori found herself stopping by a gas station and buying a package of cigarettes. She lit one up immediately. She felt more relaxed as she started back to a habit that she had quit thirty years earlier.

CHAPTER VI

MORE EDUCATION

Although Tim wasn't working, he seemed to be gone a lot. Lori thanked the Lord for these times of getting away from all the stress Tim put her under. She was afraid to answer the telephone, but yet she did not want to be cut off completely from her family. Tim was out one evening when the phone rang. Lori gritted her teeth, prayed that it wasn't a bill collector, and answered the phone.

"Mom, this is Mike. I'm in my truck coming into Thomasville," Lori's youngest son said. "I just wanted to know if you were home, and thought I'd spend the night with you."

"We'll be glad to see you," Lori replied.

"Mom, where can I park my truck close to the apartments?" Mike asked.

"There is an open, undeveloped area just east of us, and I think it will be all right if you park there for just overnight," Lori answered.

Lori was excited. She checked the linens on the spare bed, and made some pumpkin pies. Tim came home and was glad that Mike was coming by.

When it was time for Mike to be there, Lori went outside and stood at the front entrance of the complex to show him where to park his huge, gas truck. She waited an hour before she saw the only truck for miles coming down the busy road. Lori motioned for Mike to pass the complex and showed him where to park.

Mike climbed out of the truck. "Mom, you've lost some weight, you look real nice," he said.

"Thank you, I'm exercising a lot," Lori said proudly. "And, I've started smoking," Lori said, feeling ashamed.

"I guess I can't criticize you since I smoke too," Mike said, giving Lori a hug.

Tim acted like everything was all right while Mike was there. Lori hated to see Mike leave the next morning. "Come back again real soon, son," Lori said as she and Tim waved good-bye. They watched Mike warm up the truck, turn it around, and take the highway south. Tim lost his smile almost immediately.

School started, but Lori was not called to sub like she had been the year before. The only school that called her the first two weeks was a small Christian school located close to the apartment complex. The school was having a lot of problems because they had allowed students to enroll that had been kicked out of the regular public schools.

Lori called Elizabeth one morning. "Mother, could I borrow daddy's old pickup for a few months?" Lori asked. "I'm just two miles from a university and I think I'll start working on my Master's Degree in Special Education. I think I can wait to pay the tuition until the end of the semester and maybe there will be enough money from the estate crop check to cover it. It seems to be the only way I'm going to find a teaching job, but I don't have any transportation since the old Oldsmobile quit running," she said.

"I think your father would be pleased to let the pickup be used for that, if he were still alive," Elizabeth replied. "But, how are you going to get it to Thomasville?" she asked.

"First I need to call the university to see if I can still enroll since classes have already started, then maybe I can get Tim to drive me down there for it," Lori replied.

Lori called the university. "You must enroll right away, and the tuition will be due the last day of Fall Semester classes," the registrar said.

That weekend Tim took Lori the six-hour trip to Elizabeth's and she drove the red and white Chivvy back to Thomasville. Lori went to the university early Monday morning and signed up for fifteen hours of classes. She used the money Elizabeth had given her to buy the needed books. All the graduate classes were at night, so Lori started her classes that evening. She would be spending four hours in class four evenings a week for five months.

Lori had trouble finding the right room in a strange building. She finally found the room that had the same number above the door as was on her schedule papers. She took a deep sigh and walked into the room.

The room was crowded and the professor was getting ready for his lecture. Lori quickly walked to the front of the room. "Dr. Snead, I'm just now staring class and . . . ." she said.

"#$^*%^$. Didn't anyone tell you the classes started two weeks ago, woman?" Dr. Snead shouted.

That was not the encouragement Lori needed at that moment. "Yes, but the University let me enroll late, and I need a Synopsis for this class," Lori tried to explain.

"I don't have any more, you'll have to find one on your own!" Dr. Snead shouted.

Lori was embarrassed and found a seat in the back of the room.

"Since this class is studying current issues in education, I'm going to have special guests for each class meeting that are on opposing views of current issues; this way, you students can decide which side you agree with; your tests will be essays written on the issues and why you decided on one side or the other," Dr. Snead was saying. "It takes a very good paper to get credit in this class."

After class, Lori asked one of the other students if she could borrow their Synopsis and make herself a copy. The lady was glad to help Lori out. Lori found one of the copying machines in the hall. The nickels it took to run off the four sheets took every bit of change Lori had left in her purse.

In spite of its terrifying beginning, Current Issues of Education turned out to be Lori's favorite class.

Things were still difficult at home. Tim thought of Lori classes as fun, and demanded as much from her as always. He was always angry when she had to take time away from him to study, even-though he demanded that she go into the third bedroom and close the door whenever she wanted to smoke.

Lori also took four other classes including Behavioral Psychology. Lori had an A, B, and B—in four of her classes, but she failed her first month's weekly test in Behavioral Psychology. The class was an upper class number which meant that before a student took the class, they needed to take another easier class to get ready for the BP class.

Dr. Shaffer had just had Adonis surgery before school started and he could not talk very loud. The room was hot, and some of the students kept a fan running in the back of the room. It was impossible for Lori to hear Dr. Schaffer most of the time. When she could hear, it was difficult to know what he was talking about.

In one class Lori thought she knew all the terms, but she had made the lowest test grade in the class. Lori was thankful that she still had a B—in the class. Anything less than a B was like failing in graduate school.

"Lori, I think you should drop this class," Dr. Schaffer said after grading the tests one day. "Your test grades are so low that there is no way you can pass this course. You should have taken an easier course in the same area to prepare you for this one. If you drop out now, you won't have a failing grade on your transcript. You can take the class again next year when you're more prepared for it," Dr. Shaffer explained. "You know that nothing but an A or B will count on a Master's anyway, and you're not even passing."

"I can't drop out. I've borrowed money to be here, and I need to get my degree as quickly as I can. I'll just have to work harder and do extra work if I have to," Lori replied.

"I'll help you if I can; just call me anytime," Dr. Shaffer said as he walked beside Lori down the hall.

"Oh Lord, please help me," Lori said in such fear that made her stomach hurt. She hurried on to her next class which lasted until about 10:30 p.m. Lori stayed after class to talk to the professor about some assignments. The huge building was deserted when she descended the three flights of stairs leading to an exit door.

Lori opened one of the large double doors and stepped outside. It was so foggy that Lori could hardly see her hand in front of her face. The campus lights only gave an eerie glow in the white fog. Lori took careful steps and tried to remember where there were steps and sidewalks. The air was so still that her breathing sounded terribly loud.

Suddenly, Lori heard a man's footsteps behind her. She thought about the creepy movies like "Weir Wolf". She thought about the tales she had read about serial killers that preyed upon women. Lori knew that rape and killing were not unusual in Thomasville, since the city had an air base, army base, colleges, and all types of people coming in. Besides, there had been a female student murdered on the campus a week ago and the killer had not been found yet.

"Oh Lord, please protect me," Lori whispered. She tried to walk faster but she could hear the foot steps getting closer and closer. Lori gasped for air as she turned to face the person. A tall, huge, handsome man stepped close enough to be seen.

"This sure is a spooky place around here this evening, isn't it," the young man said. "I just came from the Engineer Class Building, and I'm trying to get to my car in this thick fog. Would you mind if I walked with you until we reach the parking lot? You never know what might happen to a person in a situation like this.

Lori could tell that the young man was frightened, but she tried not to laugh. "Who would attack a large, young man like that?" she asked herself. "No I don't mind," she answered.

The man walked beside Lori until they reached the parking lot. "I think my car is in this direction," Lori said. The man wasn't there. Lori believed years later that she had seen an angel since there had been another woman murdered close to the Engineer building that night.

Lori was relieved when she found her faithful red and white pickup in the large parking lot. The fog did not seem so heavy now and she was able to travel slowly the two miles home.

Tim was in a terrible mood as usual when Lori came in. "What took you so long to get home?" he asked. "Don't you care what happens to me?"

"Tim, I'm going through some tough times and I could use a little encouragement," Lori replied. "My classes are terribly hard and I have to study twice as much for each class as I spend in the classroom."

"You'd do a lot better if you quit smoking," Tim shouted.

"Tim, you need to keep your voice down so the people in the next apartment can't hear us," Lori replied. She went into the third bedroom that had become her study room and tried to settle down from the events of the day. She wished she could stop smoking, but it seemed to calm her nerves. "I'll stop when things get better," Lori promised herself.

Lori studied several hours during the days, but she took time to swim her fifty laps every afternoon before she went to class. Along with housework and cooking, Lori was always stressed for time. The Christian school was still calling her to sub once in awhile.

Lori had just come into the school to learn that she would be teaching fifth and sixth grade that day. She covered the lesson plans and had time to chat with the students before they went home. Lori asked the different kids about their home situations and had a discussion on family values.

The school called Lori to teach the next day. One of the sixth grade girls came up to her and said, "I want to thank you Mrs. Jones for what you did yesterday."

"What did I do yesterday?" Lori asked.

"Well, me and some other girls had made plans to run away from our homes last night, but when you talked to us yesterday, we changed our minds," the girl explained and walked on into class.

"I'm glad I'm a help to someone," Lori sighed.

Lori had just come in from swimming one afternoon and getting ready to study. She shivered when she heard Tim come in. Tim opened the double doors leading to "Lori's room". "You should be happy, Lori, I've just been hired to sell Ford vehicles right across the street from where I used to work. At least one of us will be working."

"I'm proud of you, but please don't quit," Lori answered.

The following weeks were much easier for Lori since Tim was gone a lot of the time. He even worked many evenings and did not get so angry because Lori was not at home.

Lori had to do some field work for Dr. Shaffer's class. This meant that she could not sub for several weeks because she would be working with a handicapped student in a school of her choice. Lori heard Dr. Sanders speak in Dr. Snead's class. He had just opened a school for students that were too dangerous to be in other schools. It was a "one more chance place" before the student was put in an institution.

After class, Lori had asked Dr. Sanders if she could work with one of his students in his school.

"I think that would be a good idea," Dr. Sanders replied. "Why don't you visit our school for a day or two and decide what student you would like to work with."

Lori visited the school the next day. It was different than any school she had ever seen. The teachers locked their wallets, purses, and all valuables in the school safe before they went to class. "You can be putting your life in danger if you ever touch one of these kids," Dr. Sanders had told Lori.

Dr. Sander's school employed two man teachers and ten woman teachers. "The students are not as likely to become violent with a female teacher," Dr. Sanders had explained.

Lori chose an attractive woman teacher, Mrs. Hutches, and asked if she could follow her for the day and learn about the school. "I will appreciate your help," the teacher replied.

Each student was given three grades during each class. One grade was for behavior, one grade for effort, and one grade for achievement. At the end of the day, the students could turn in their good grades for a penny a grade. The school operated a store where the students could buy candy and trinkets with their money. The students were also allowed a ten-minute smoke break between each class. Most of the kids smoked, but all of them seemed to need the time outside. One girl was large pregnant. The rest of the kids treated her special.

Lori followed Mrs. Hutches into another room for another class. "Oh dear, what do you smell in here?" she asked Lori.

Lori sniffed the air. "It smells like pure Colombian to me, and not coffee either," she replied.

"I know that's what it is," Mrs. Hutches replied. "I have to report this to Dr. Sanders."

Lori watched the class until Mrs. Hutches returned. There was one student that Lori felt compassion for. She decided he was the one she wanted to work with to write her field papers for Dr. Shaffer's class.

Ronny was very black. He was sixteen, about six and a half feet tall, and quite heavy.

Lori told Dr. Sanders that she had chosen Ronny. "Are you sure; he'll be a challenge," Dr. Sanders replied.

"He should give me plenty to write about for my papers," Lori said with a grin.

"We'll tell him in the morning," Dr. Sanders said.

The next morning Lori walked up to Ronny. "I'm in school just like you are and I'm doing homework for my teacher," she explained. "My teacher wants me to work with a student and write things about it, and I have chosen you to work with." Lori was not prepared for Ronny's response.

Ronny look down at Lori and begin to laugh. He laughed so loudly he could be heard all over the building. Ronny started running through the whole classroom building. He ran back up to Lori, and started laughing again. Ronny ran through the whole building again. Lori could hear his heavy footsteps going through each classroom. The whole school was looking at Lori now. Lori did not move, but waited for Ronny to return. When Ronny ran, full speed, up to her the second time, Lori said, "That's enough for now Ronny, follow me to this classroom."

To Lori's surprise, Ronny followed her to the classroom she had pointed to.

Lori had looked over Ronny's grades the afternoon before. His records showed him to be reading on a second grade level. His first class was American History. "Ronny, I don't have a book, so you'll have to read to me instead of me reading to you," Lori said.

Ronny opened his book and begin to read. Lori was shocked that he missed very few words out of a high-school History book. Suddenly Ronny realized what he was doing. "Here, you do it, I can't read!" Ronny exclaimed and jammed the History book into Lori's stomach so hard she could hardly breathe. Lori tried not to laugh, but begin to read. She demanded that Ronny listen to her as quietly as she had listened to him read.

Ronny was a challenge, but Lori enjoyed working with the young giant. He seemed to be a child that had never felt much love. One class gave a dinner honoring foods from other countries. Each student was assigned to bring some type of foreign food. Lori did not think Ronny would bring anything, so she fixed some guacamole dip and chips. Ronny was happy that someone was paying that much attention to him, but he refused to eat any of the dip. "I don't eat green food," he said loudly.

The police were almost daily visitors to the school. Usually it was an arrest for possession of drugs, or bad conduct. Once, one student tried to kill another student, and another day, a student tried to kill himself. Several weapons were confiscated from the students while Lori was there.

Two boys were expelled from school one day. They did not want to leave and Dr. Sanders got close to them and stared at them until they left. The boys ran out onto the main highway that passed the school. As usual, the highway was filled with fast city traffic. The boys jumped between the cars, not caring if they were killed or not. One of the boys was yelling, "Get out of my face, Sanders!" as he ran through the traffic.

Lori watched until the boys reached the other side of the highway without being hurt. "Praise the Lord!" she said under her breath.

Everyone was eating lunch one day when a former student came in. The tall, nice-looking, well-dressed young man walked up to Dr. Sanders and said, "I want to thank you for helping me in this school."

"You look great," Dr. Sanders said. "What are you doing now days?" he asked.

"I'm confiscating cars that people are behind on their payments for a collection company," the young man answered. "It's a good paying job." The young man sat down and visited with the doctor for a few minutes.

When the young man left, Dr. Sanders started laughing. "I guess Jim got his training while he was attending school here, all right," he said. "He was arrested and sent to reform school for hot wiring cars, stealing them, and driving them to a large organization in the state capital."

Lori had to laugh too.

Lori worked with Ronny for four weeks. She tested him and drew scales to show his progress. Lori wrote a ten-page assignment on her work with Ronny for Behavioral Psychology. "Dr. Shaffer, may I work with another students for another assignment to help my grade," she asked her professor.

"I think that's a good idea," Dr. Shaffer said.

Dr. Snead's class was a lot of fun. He had the class meeting on Halloween at his house. The special guests were dressed up like pirates, and the class had to search the whole two-story house to find the "treasure" that contained the things needed for the class. The students searched the up-stairs, and main floor. They finally ended up searching the dark basement of the old house. Lori felt cobwebs sliding over her face as she followed some students from room to room. The students entered an almost dark room with two ugly monsters standing on each side of a gold-looking chest.

"You found us, so we have to give the treasure to you!" one monster shouted. Everyone jumped and then started laughing. The important class papers were handed out and everyone was served creepy refreshment. There were chocolate cakes baked in flower pots with gummy worms in it, and a good desert that looked like dog food and was served from dog food sacks.

Lori, for once, had a lot of fun. One of the important papers that were in the treasure chest was her first essay paper. She received an A-, and there were several positive comments on the paper from Dr. Snead.

Lori visited an elementary school located close to the apartment complex. It was important for her to conserve the gas in her pickup. She spent the first day helping Mrs. Happy with her Special Ed. students.

Mrs. Happy was a teacher about ready for retirement. She was a good teacher that loved her students. Lori had not made up her mind what student she wanted to work with when Mrs. Happy said, "Mrs. Jones, would you mind working with David, my little third grader. He is a discipline problem, and I haven't been able to help him much. I have a lot of test to give him because he won't be coming to this school after this semester; we have staffed him to be put in a school for just Special Education students."

Lori followed David from class to class the next day to become familiar with each of his classes and the child. David had two ways of meeting each of his classes. He would, either put himself in the furthermost corner from the teacher and try not to be noticed, or he would act out and be sent to the principal's office. Lori had never seen a student thrown out of music class before. Even if David was trying not to be noticed by the teacher, he was constantly harassing other students. None of the other students liked David or wanted to be around him.

Lori gave David the State Standard Tests the first two days she worked with him. He seemed to always get "lost" on his way to Lori's table, and he barely scored on any test.

"Mrs. Happy, I only have three more weeks to work with David," Lori said that afternoon. "He's going to fail every test, and He's not trying." "Would you mind if I stopped testing him and tried to teach him something the short time I'm here?" Lori asked.

"I'll appreciate anything you can do for David," Mrs. Happy replied. "Just do what you think is best."

Lori had just been studying about Language Experience Learning. She thought it might help David. Lori "found" David when he was late for class the next morning. "Come with me, David; we're going to do something fun today, and no more testing," she said. Lori seated David at her work table and asked, "David, what do you like to do when you can do anything you want to do?"

David looked at Lori a minute and said, "I like to play little league football."

"You're a football player!" Lori exclaimed.

"Yeah, my team is called the Bears," David said.

"What are the names of the teams you play?" Lori asked with interest.

"We play the Tigers, the Lions, and the Bob Cats," David said importantly. The child was excited and begin to talk. "I play in the backfield, that is I get to carry the football once in awhile," David said.

"Yes, I know, my sons also played football; our whole family loved it," Lori replied.

"You did!" David exclaimed. "Well, we have this great big kid that plays in front of me, and we call him Refrigerator," David explained. He was soon telling Lori all about the players on his team and the coach.

"David, I would like to have a story about your football team," Lori said. "Would you help me write one so that I can take it with me?" she asked.

David started writing things down. When David did not know how to spell a word, Lori helped him sound it out. "We have to spell our words like other people do or other people can't read what we have written," she explained. She also explained that a period is used when we are finished with a thought, and a comma is used when we want to pause.

Lori and David went to the library and checked out two books about football and spent part of the day reading. When it was time for Math, Lori asked, "David, if the quarterback throws the ball 12 yards to a receiver, and that receiver runs the ball 14 yards before he is tackled, how many yards has the team moved the ball?"

David quickly came up with 26 yards.

"Great, David!" Lori exclaimed. "Did you know you could add double numbers?" she asked.

David was surprised at what he had done. "But I can't subtract," he said.

"David, if the quarterback was standing on the 40 yard line, and he ran backwards 10 yards to throw the ball and was tackled there, what yard line would he be on?" Lori asked.

"The 30 yard line," David answered.

"David, that is subtraction," Lori said.

David had enjoyed the day until Lori told him she had some homework for him.

David put his head down on his chest and pouted.

"David, I want you to bring me a picture of you and your football team to school with you tomorrow," Lori ordered.

David said a quick yes and bounced happily out of the room.

The next day David brought two pictures and showed them to his class. It made him a little more of a hero.

"David, I'd like to help you write a letter to your favorite professional football player," Lori said. "I'll see if I can find the right address for you so you can mail it to him," she said.

David wrote a full-page letter to John Elway, his favorite football player. Lori was surprised, and David was elated when he received a letter by from John a week later.

David was so proud of his letters and stories that he showed them to everyone. Mrs. Happy was so proud and surprised over David's progress. David told Lori how proud his parents were over his letters. He told Lori that his parents were divorced, but he usually spent the weekends with his father. David also had two older sisters that had families of their own.

Lori and David took the stories and letters to the copier, and "published" David's work. It was some of the most fun days Lori had spent in school, and she was getting plenty of material for Dr. Shaffer's class.

David always ran to Lori's table, anxious to start another school day. He was no longer a discipline problem in his other classes and he was almost caught up with the other third graders.

One morning, David did not show up for class. Lori went to look for her "lost" student. No one had seen David that morning. She checked with the bus driver, and found that David had ridden the bus that morning. He had to be somewhere in the school building. Lori was walking across the gym from the bus garage when she decided to look behind a large section of bleachers. She saw a dark object pushed into the top crevice of the top deck. It was David. He was curled up in a tiny ball, crying.

"David, what's the matter?" Lori asked.

"They are pushing me out of this school today, and I have to go to a school where I don't know anyone," David sobbed.

"Come on to class and I'll see what I can do about it," Lori replied. She pulled up the defeated little boy and half carried him to her working table. "Will you work on your new story while I go and talk to Mrs. Happy?" Lori asked.

David pulled the half-finished story from his folder and looked at it without saying anything.

"Thank you," Lori said and went to talk to Mrs. Happy.

"I'm sorry, Mrs. Jones, there's not a thing we can do now, David has already been staffed into the Special Ed. school," Mrs. Happy said. "I would not have let this happen if I would have known he would do so well with some special help, but it is too late now. I don't think he needs to go there, but it is too late now."

Lori went back to talk to David. "David, you might like your new school better than you do this one; the kids here haven't been very nice to you."

David did not answer.

"David, you're getting real smart and maybe there is a boy in this new school that you can help the way I've been able to help you," Lori said.

David was still quiet. He had large tears rolling down his cheeks. Lori felt like crying too. "David, you're a good kid, and I know you will do well in your new school, and make some great friends," Lori said. "This is our last day together, so let's make it a fun-learning day, and you finish all the things you want to do before we say good-bye."

David worked for Lori, but the fun was gone. He was a different student than he had been the day before. The day was finally over. David hugged Lori good-bye. Lori watched the precious little boy walk away facing a great big challenge. She knew what it was like to face big challenges.

Lori hurried home and finished her research paper for Dr. Shaffer.

Dr. Snead had the Christmas class at his house too. There were fifty students in the class, but Dr. Snead had plenty of food and fun for everyone. It was a great time for the class's last meeting. Dr. Snead handed back the final essay test papers.

Lori was almost afraid to unfold hers. She looked at it and smiled. She had made an A+, with more positive comments. Dr. Snead had turned out to be a marvelous teacher. No wonder his classes were always filled. Lori felt like she had learned more in his class than any class she had ever had. But, the next day was when she was to turn in her last papers to Dr. Shaffer. Lori had made two Bs and two A s in her other classes.

Dr. Schaffer had his last class in his house. It was a new home situated on a high hill overlooking Thomasville. It was a pleasant meeting, but Lori was nervous wondering if she was going to pass or not.

"I'm not through grading your reports yet, so I will send them to you in the mail," Dr. Shaffer said.

Lori was hoping not to have to wait to see her grade, but she should receive it in two days.

Lori ran to the little building, that housed the post office boxes for the residents of the apartment complex, everyday looking for the grain check from her dad's estate. The milo harvest had been over for several weeks and the grain had been sold. Still, there was no check. Lori finished her last two class meetings one evening and the universities last classes were the next day. There was still no grain check.

"Oh Lord, please don't let me lose all this hard work," Lori had prayed over and over. She had already borrowed money for books and gas from Elizabeth and she was not going to borrow more.

Lori checked the mail again the last day, and there still was no check. "Maybe the check would not be enough to cover the tuition anyway," Lori said. She leaned against the wall of the small building and cried once more. "Please, help me Heavenly Father," she prayed. Lori was walking out the door when she heard someone calling her.

"Mrs. Jones, I think this should have been in your mailbox," the lady said.

Lori took the envelope. It was from an elevator company back home. She ripped open the envelope. Her tuition was one-thousand dollars. The check was made out to her for $1020.00. Lori had just enough time to get to the bank, cash the check, and take it to the university. She jumped into her red and white pickup and drove the speed limit to the bank. Lori had to stand in line in the bank. She only had ten minutes to drive the four miles and run up two flights of stairs before the university office closed for the weekend.

Lori ran up the two flights of stairs. She looked up and the window, with bars facing the classroom hall, was closed. The room was dark. Lori knocked on the other door. It was a few minutes before she heard someone unlocking the door. "I need to give you this money," Lori said weakly. "Can you take it this late?" she asked.

"I guess we can make an exception," the lady said. She wrote out a receipt and gave it to Lori. "You should pay your bills a little early!" the lady snapped.

"If you only knew how much I wish I could," Lori whispered under her breath. She skipped down the stairs. Everything seemed so much brighter than it had been just a few minutes before.

It was the following week that Lori received a manila envelope from Dr. Shaffer. Her hands were trembling as she carefully opened the package. There was a note covering her grade. "I didn't think you had a chance of getting a grade from this class, but I was so impressed with your field work and reports, that I think you deserve a B-. Congratulations, Mrs. Jones," the note said. Lori sat down and cried for joy.

Lori knew it would take thirty more graduate hours to finish her mater's degree, but maybe these fifteen, hard-earned, hours would help her get a teaching job, or at least steady subbing. There was no money to go to school the next semester.

Lori drove off of the university parking lot for the last time. She stopped by a gas station and bought five dollars worth of gas. "At least I'll have fifteen dollars left from the check to buy a few groceries before Tim gets home," Lori said to herself. The young man gave Lori a five dollar bill for change.

"I gave you a twenty-dollar bill and only bought five dollars worth of gas," Lori explained to the young attendant.

"I'm sorry mam, but you only gave me a ten dollar bill," the young man said.

"I gave you a twenty because that was all the money I had in my purse!" Lori exclaimed. "I want the rest of my change!" she shouted.

"Mam, I know you gave me a ten dollar bill," the young man said again. "See here in my money drawer, see I don't have any twenties in my drawer."

Lori looked in the drawer and did not see any twenties. "I know I gave you a twenty, and you must have slipped it somewhere else when you picked up the five to give me back!" Lori screamed. "I need that extra money for groceries!" she shouted.

"Mam, do you take me for a fool, and think you could talk me out of an extra ten dollars?" the young man asked. "You can contact my manager and you'll find out I have a good reputation," he said. "I think you were trying to rip me off!" he yelled.

Lori did not know what to do. She drove back home feeling like she had been robbed. Lori wrote the head of the company, but never got her ten dollars back.

CHAPTER VII

LORI LEARNS THE TRUTH

Tim was working on a commission. "Maybe he will sell a car today and we can go grocery shopping anyway," Lori whispered, "It seems like I just jump out of the frying pan into the fire, sometimes."

Tim sold a car that day and there was money to meet some bills. They found enough money to buy the gas to take the red and white Chivvy pickup back to Elizabeth and Lori had another chance to visit with her mother and sons.

"Lori, they have an old station wagon on the used car lot; it has low mileage and seems to be in good condition," Tim said one day. "I want you to drive it a few miles and see if it would be a good old car for you to have."

"But, Tim, where will we get the money to pay for it?" Lori asked.

"The company is only asking eight-hundred dollars for it, and my banker will loan you the money," Tim replied.

It scared Lori to owe more money, but she did need a vehicle. They probably would not be able to find another one priced that low. Lori took the station wagon for a test drive. She liked the car and Tim made the deal.

Mike called again. "Mom, I quit my truck driving job again; my back just hurts too much to keep driving the big truck," Mike said. "I'm coming to Thomasville in a couple of days and wonder if I could stay with guys again until I get a place of my own."

"Mike, I might as well be honest with you, Tim and I both love having you around, but we hardly have enough money to buy groceries even just for the two of us," Lori answered.

"That's all right, I have a little money and I can help you with expenses," Mike said.

"I hate to ask you to do that," Lori replied.

"You furnish the bed and I'll furnish the food," Mike said. "What's wrong with that?" he asked.

"Nothing, I guess; see you soon," Lori said and hung up.

Tim was always glad to see Mike. Mike looked for a job during the days, and went swimming with Lori in the evenings. One evening, Tim did not have to work and decided to go swimming with Lori and Mike. They were all in the indoor pool. Tim was standing in the shallow end and Lori and Mike were swimming laps in the deeper part.

"Tim, are you sure you don't want to try to swim?" Lori asked.

"I never learned to swim and I'm too old to learn now," Tim answered. "You and Mike go ahead and go back to the deep end. I'll just wait for you." Tim suddenly looked past Mike and Lori. His eyes grew even larger. "Lori, look at what just came in," he said.

Both Lori and Mike looked toward the front door of the swimming pool room. A beautiful young lady had walked into the room and was walking down the cement area beside the pool. There was something strange about her. The lady turned her back to the pool and removed her robe. Lori gasped when she saw that the lady did not have a swimming top on. The lady slowly turned toward the pool.

"It's a man!" Tim exclaimed. "Things like that just make me sick."

The person looked like a woman, but she had the chest of a man. The man jumped into the pool without even removing his long, dangling ear-rings. He smoothly swam through the water and stood up beside Tim. The man started talking to Tim while smiling and blinking his long eye lashes.

Tim walked quickly through the water over closer to where Lori and Mike were standing. The man followed Tim and kept smiling.

"See you guys at the apartment," Tim shouted. He swished his way to the side of the pool, crawled out, grabbed his towel, and ran for the door.

Lori and Mike were laughing, but they were relieved that the strange man did not follow Tim out of the building. Instead, he came back and dove into the deep end of the pool.

Tim was in bed, asleep when Mike and Lori came in that evening.

Mike could not find a job. Tim soon talked Mike into going into the multi-level business with him. Tim quit his job at the Ford place. He talked Mike into paying for an office downtown, and paying for a large supply of products. Tim demanded that Lori be the secretary of their new company.

The office was in a newly remodeled building. There was a large "boss" office in back of a secretary desk, and a smaller office next to Lori's area. Tim took the large office and set up the smaller office for Mike.

"I'm going to teach you how to be a top-notch salesman," Tim told Mike several times.

Tim advertised in the newspaper and a few people came in to see the products and business opportunities. Meetings were scheduled twice a week. Lori again introduced the products, and Tim told people of the fantastic money making part of the business. Mike helped, listened, and learned.

The night meetings were not successful until a new family came to the meeting. Sam had been a farmer in Oregon. His wife, Sharon, was a nurse. Connie was eighteen. She had finished high school and was now working and saving her money to go to college. She wanted to be a nurse, too. Rebecca was fifteen. Able was thirteen, and Amber and Ashley were eight.

Sam and Sharon were home schooling their children. Rebecca looked more like twenty-one than fifteen. She was gifted and did not have to study to pass the high school test that the state required of home schooled children.

Sam was a hard worker. Sharon knew a lot about health. Rebecca had plenty of time to be at the office every day to help Lori with the secretary work. The Caldrons brought several new people to the meetings.

Lori thought she was still under too much strain to stop smoking. There was a lot of stress working at the office all day, fixing the meals at home, and doing the laundry, etc. Tim and Mike could sit down and rest after work, but Lori had a full day's work waiting for her when she came in from work. And, it would have been hard to quit smoking with Mike still smoking.

The second week Rebecca took over the office so Lori could go home early for once. "It has been so long since I've gone swimming, I think I'll enjoy doing my laps before I have to get supper for Mike and Tim," Lori told herself.

Lori checked the apartment complex before she ran over to the indoor pool building. She had done only half of her swimming laps when she noticed she had become terribly tired. "I must be out of shape already," she whispered as she gasped for breath.

Lori was determined to do her fifty laps to get back into shape. She could hardly pull herself out of the pool when she was finished. Lori noticed that her body was aching when she came into the apartment. "I shouldn't be so stiff and sore like this so quickly," Lori told herself. She noticed that her chest hurt every time she smoked that evening.

Lori sat in the living room and tried to relax. She was so depressed. "Tim has talked Mike out of his whole life-savings, and the business isn't working," Lori was thinking. "If it hadn't been for me, Tim would have never known Mike and been able to ruin his life," she told herself. "Oh, God, I wish I was dead," Lori said aloud. "I have ruined my own life and now I'm ruining my family's," she sobbed. "I need for my life to end before I do more damage to other people."

Lori drug herself around and fixed Mike and Tim's supper. They were too busy talking about the business to notice how tired she was. "How did it feel to get off early today to rest," Tim even said.

Lori did not feel like answering him. "I wish I could rest at the end of the day when I feel so tired," she whispered.

"Tim, I don't feel well today," Lori said when she woke up that morning. "Do you think Rebecca can handle the office and let me rest today; maybe I'll feel better tomorrow," she said.

"Sure, she does a great job," Tim answered. "I guess Mike and me can fix our breakfast this one morning."

Lori felt guilty about staying in bed. She managed to get up and fix Tim and Mike some cereal and toast. Lori did not tell Mike that she was not feeling well.

Lori was alone that day and felt worse that afternoon than she had felt that morning. She felt like she was freezing and finally had to go to bed.

"Mom, you don't look so good; do you want us to take you to the doctor?" Mike was asking.

Lori raised her head up and put forth the effort to answer. "We don't have any money or insurance!" Lori heard a voice shouting. "Was that voice Tim's????" Lori asked herself.

"No son, I'll be all right," Lori managed to whisper.

"Okay, but let us know if you don't start feeling better," Mike said. His voice trailed off into the distance.

Lori forced her eyes open. There was no one else in the bedroom. Her body ached so much that she wanted to die. It hurt so much to breathe that she wanted to stop breathing. "Had Mike really been there or had she been dreaming?" Lori wondered. Who's voice had been yelling about money and insurance?" Lori asked herself. It sounded more like her own voice, or was someone else in the house?" Lori wondered. "Were Mike and Tim still at work?"

The next time Lori opened her eyes, she was not in the bedroom. She looked around. Lori was in a reddish-orange cave. Lori was stumbling over the black rocks on the floor of the cave. The rocks were wet and slick, and she fell several times. Each time her body hit the black rocks, it hurt her and caused her to cough. The cough made her hurt even more.

Lori's feet felt cold. She looked down and saw that reddish water was staring to fill the cave. It had already covered her feet. "I must find a way out of here, and soon," Lori shouted.

Lori felt the cold water covering her ankles, then her knees felt cold from the murky liquid. She found it more and more difficult to breathe. The nasty water was now up to her waist. Lori was fighting for every breath now as the oxygen was forced out of the cave.

The water was now making her breasts very cold. Lori felt the freezing liquid going up her neck. She stood on the tip of her toes and held her head sideways against the top of the cave to gulp in the last bit of air. Lori hurt so badly that it took all her strength to breathe in her last breath of air.

Lori realized that she had her head pushed sideways against the ceiling of the slimy cave. She counted to three. Before another wave completely covered her nose and mouth, she gasped for one last breath. "I didn't now it hurt so much to die!" Lori shouted into the cave. Lori took her last breath. She felt herself being swept away into the orange, slimy tide. Her body was going down, down, down.

"No!" Lori shouted. "Satan, I'm not going to die! You can't kill me! I don't want to die! I want to live to see my grandsons grow up! In the name of Jesus, I'm going to live and get well! In the name of Jesus, you can't drown me in my own lungs, or crush me on the nicotine rocks below!"

"Mom, are you all right?" Mike's voice came roaring through the cave.

Lori tried to answer, but she could not open her eyes or talk.

"I think she's worse. I think we should take her to the doctor, Tim. I have money enough to pay for it," Mike said.

Lori felt cold air hitting her face. She felt herself being carried down the stairs outside the apartment before she lost consciousness again.

The next thing Lori knew, she was laying on a small cot in a medical emergency room. The doctor came in and examined both lungs. He called a nurse in to run some blood tests.

The doctor left the room and went into the waiting room to talk to Tim and Mike. "She has pneumonia in both lungs and infection in her blood," the doctor said. "She needs to be in the hospital with antibiotics and under oxygen," he explained.

"We don't have insurance," Tim explained.

"We'll do what's best for her," Mike replied.

"I'm going to give her some antibodies. You take her home and keep her in bed. Open all the windows in the bedroom, but keep her warm with blankets. Pour gallons of Gator Aid down her. Let me know tomorrow morning if her fever is down," the doctor said. "If you can't keep her fever down, then she must go to the hospital. Keep me posted every twelve hours. And, even if she does live through this, she won't live much longer if she continues to smoke."

A nurse came in and gave Lori two shots. Lori was hurting so badly that she did not know if she was glad to be alive or not. She felt like she was going to faint again and wished that she could.

Tim and Mike carried Lori back to the car. When the cold air hit Lori's face this time, she begin to convulse and shake uncontrollably. The men drove Lori back to the apartment and carried her back up the stairs. They put her back in bed and opened the two bedroom windows. Mike rushed to the store to buy some Gator Aid while Tim brought in all the blankets he could find.

Lori was so sick that the hours dragged by. "Why can't someone put me out of my misery?" she wondered. Lori was thankful when she finally felt herself slipping into a deep sleep.

Mike helped Lori sit up and drink the Gator Aid. He gave her aspirin every four hours. Lori's fever gradually went down. The pain in her body begin to be less unbearable. By the end of the week, Tim and Mike thought Lori was well enough for both of them to go back to work. Lori was left alone at the apartment. She had several sick spells and felt that no one cared about her.

"What day is it?" Lori asked Mike.

"It's January 23," Mike answered.

Lori started to cry. "Oh Mike, every year I've wanted to be with you on your birthday. You were here with us this year, and I slept through your birthday two days ago, and I didn't even get to bake you a birthday cake," Lori said, sobbing.

"There will be other years, mom," Mike replied. "Do you know what is happening today?" he asked.

"No," Lori answered.

"The astronauts are going into space today. They are taking a school teacher with them," Mike explained. "Do you think you're strong enough to come into the living room and watch the 'Blast Off'?" he asked. "I thought you might be especially interested since you're a teacher," Mike said.

Lori drug herself into the living room by hanging onto Mike and resting her body on pieces of furniture along the way. She plopped down on the couch in front of the TV. Lori was trying to breathe better while she listened to the countdown. She heard: 10-9-8-7-6-5-4-3-2-1-Blast off.

"I've never seen rockets look like that on other take offs; they must be using some kind of new fuel," Lori said.

The TV showed the crowd cheering at the launching pad. Then there were screams of horror as the whole world watched pieces of the giant air ship re-enter the earth's atmosphere and burn like sparklers on the fourth of July.

"The space shuttle has just exploded!" an announcer shouted. "The crew has been blown up in the very sight of their families!" he yelled.

Lori had been fighting depressions. Now she felt a deep one coming on. "I want to go back to bed," Lori said, sobbing.

Mike and Tim helped Lori back to bed. Lori covered up her head and tried to put the terrible, exploding scene from her mind. She finally cried herself to sleep.

Lori woke up about eight the next morning. Mike and Tim were already at the office. Lori felt very weak and tired. She forced herself into the kitchen and fixed two pieces of toast and a large glass of Gator Aid. The simple tasks made her so tired that she had to rest for several minutes before she had the strength to eat. Lori had just finished her toast when she heard footsteps coming up the stairs to the apartment.

Mike unlocked the door and said, "Good morning."

"What are you doing here this time of day?" Lori asked, trying to smile and cover up how weak she felt.

Mike poured himself a cup of coffee and sit down at the table across from Lori. "Mom, I'm just not cut out to be a salesman. I'm going back home and see if I can start driving the gas truck again. I think you're going to be all right, and there's nothing to hold me here now," he said. "Besides, Tim is always just a phone call away if you need someone."

"If you're sure that's what you want to do, then do it, but I hate to see you leave right now since you have put all your money into the business," Lori replied.

"I'm sure this is what I want to do," Mike answered. "I'm going to help Tim for the rest of the week before I go back to my old job. My back seems to be stronger now, and maybe it won't hurt me to drive the truck again."

Before the week was over, Tim said, "Lori, it's been a week since the doctor said you were doing better. I want you back at work in the office Monday morning."

"But, Tim, I don't feel strong enough to even get dressed, yet; please let me rest a few more days," Lori replied.

"Sam and Sharon are keeping Rebecca home for schooling. She probably won't be back in the office for at least two weeks," Tim shouted. "I need you at the office as soon as Mike leaves. You can build up your strength by working."

On Thursday Lori forced herself to fix a little supper for the two men in her life. She had to spend as much time resting as she did working.

Tim and Mike came home from the office and went to the two separate bathrooms to wash their hands for supper. Mike came back into the living room and sit down in one of the large chairs next to the fireplace. Tim was still in the bathroom on the other side of the Master bedroom.

The door bell rang. Mike forgot that they were not supposed to answer the door. He forgot to look through the peak hole in the door before he opened the door.

Lori was finishing the evening meal when she heard Mike talking to someone. She walked into the living room to see who Mike was talking to.

"Are you Mrs. Tim Jones?" a young man, with long blonde hair and beard, asked.

"Yes," Lori answered weakly.

"Then these are for you!" the man shouted. He shoved a stack of papers into Lori's face and knocked her down to the floor. The man was laughing loudly as he ran down the stairs from the apartment.

"Are you okay, mom?" Mike asked.

As soon as Lori was able to nod her head yes, Mike was running down the stairs after the intruder. "I'll teach you to push my mother around," Mike shouted as he pursued the tall skinny man.

Tim came running out of the bedroom and down the stairs to catch Mike.

Lori heard loud arguing at the bottom of the stairs. "Oh Lord, help Mike not to get into trouble," she prayed. Lori heard a car start and spin its wheels as it left the apartment parking lot. She grabbed the arm of a chair and pulled herself up into it. Lori was gasping for air when Mike and Tim came back into the apartment.

"I'm sorry, mom, I forgot," Mike said. "I was ready to 'clean his plow' when Tim pulled me off of him."

Tim picked up the papers and begin to curse. "Just as I thought. It's for child support for the twenty year old twins," he said.

"I still can't understand why you have to pay child support on them now that they are adults. They have been out of school two or three years now. They are probably more able to earn a living than you are with your sight problem," Lori said, almost in tears.

"It's the dumb law. I'm supposed to pay on both of them until they are twenty-one, like I tried to tell you before," Tim answered.

"I'm sorry, mom," Mike said again.

"Well, at least, we won't have to be afraid to answer the door now," Lori said, trying to laugh.

It was close to ten o'clock by the time Lori finished cleaning up the kitchen. "If Mike and Tim knew how bad I feel, I'm sure they would help me," Lori told herself. She went right to bed and left Mike and Tim talking in the living room.

Mike left Thomasville after the office closed on Friday. Lori felt depressed as she and Tim waved good-bye when the blue pickup left the apartment complex.

"Remember, I want you in the office full-time starting Monday," Tim said gruffly when they walked back to the apartment.

On Saturday, Tim and Lori took Vance Jackson, who had just joined the company, to the state capital for an in-service class covering the company's new products. Tim and Vance laughed at Lori as they waited for her to pull herself up a flight of stairs. She was working hard to keep breathing.

"If they knew how close I am to fainting, they would probably be more understanding," Lori told herself. Lori felt so embarrassed and depressed that she excused her self to go to the women's rest room. As soon as Lori was in the rest room, she took out a pack of cigarettes she had hidden in her purse. It hurt her lungs terribly to smoke, but it seemed to relax her. She threw half of the cigarette away and joined Tim and Vance for a long day of meetings.

Lori was glad when the tiring meetings were over. She slept in the back seat of the car all the way home.

Lori struggled through her work for the rest of the weekend by resting for five minutes after working for five minutes. Tim expected three good meals a day and did not help with any of the work. He spent the rest of the weekend ignoring Lori, reading the newspaper and watching TV.

Monday morning Lori got up early and fixed Tim's breakfast. Tim went on to the office while Lori cleaned up the apartment. Lori felt very tired as she dressed for a days work and combed her hair. She descended the stairs and had to rest sitting in the car to get strength enough to drive. "I just have to get to work and help make the business successful so Mike will get his money back," Lori whispered. She drove slowly through the fast early morning, Thomasville traffic. Her body ached to go back to bed for another week of added rest.

Lori finally made it up the two flights of stairs leading to the office by clinging to the railing and pulling her acing body up the stairs with the strength of her arms, one step at a time. Her legs just seemed too weak to lift her body up the stairs. Lori pulled herself into the women's rest-room and fell to the floor. Again, she felt the need to light up another cigarette and bear the pain in her lungs. Lori fell into her secretary's chair and laid her head on the desk.

Tim came out from his inner office. "I want you to start calling people for the meeting we are having tomorrow night," he said. "You don't have time to lazy around!" Tim shouted. He grabbed the daily Thomasville newspaper, walked back into his office, and slammed the door.

"Well, I won't have to walk, or exercise much to do that, at least," Lori told herself. She did find it very tiring to concentrate enough to give the people she called all the important information, and write down their names.

Tim left the office at noon to pick up something to eat. He seemed to be gone for a long time before he returned with some sandwiches. Rebecca was with Tim when they came into the office. They were laughing and having a lot of fun.

"Could Rebecca take my job for this afternoon so I can go home and rest?" Lori asked Tim.

"You stay where you are; you don't need to rest. All you've been doing is just sitting there!" Tim snapped. "I have to train Rebecca on the new products this afternoon, and we can't be disturbed!"

Rebecca giggled and followed Tim into the large office.

Lori heard the door close and lock. She struggled through the afternoon. Tim and Rebecca had just come out of the office when Sam came in to pick up Rebecca before closing time.

Lori had to stop for some groceries on her way home. She was so weak that she had to stop in the grocery store several times and breathe hard just to keep from passing out, yet she lit up another cigarette before she pulled out of the parking lot. "I'm going to quit when things aren't so hard," Lori told herself again.

Lori pulled herself and her sack up the steps to the apartment and managed to unlock the door. She dropped her groceries on the floor and fell into a large lounge chair. The room was spinning around her. She was not aware of her surroundings until she heard Tim stomping up the steps.

"What's for supper?' Tim shouted. "I'm hungry!" he yelled.

Lori pulled herself into the kitchen and opened a can of soup. She put the soup on the range and sit down to rest in one of the kitchen chairs. She knew Tim was angry by the way he was flipping through the pages of the newspaper. "Oh Lord, give me strength for one more day," Lori prayed.

Again, it was past ten o'clock when Lori finished working in the kitchen. Lori dragged herself into the small bedroom and lit up another cigarette. It hurt her lungs, but she thought it would help her sleep better. Lori was glad that Tim was still watching TV. She dragged herself into the master bedroom and got ready for bed. It almost took more strength than Lori had to pull her clothes off of her aching body. She fell into bed and was asleep before Tim came to bed.

Rebecca did not come to work anymore that week.

Lori was just as tired and weak that weekend as she had been the weekend before. On Monday morning, it seemed even more difficult to pull herself up the stairs than it had been on Friday.

Lori met Sam in the hall. "I have to go downtown on business, but I'll be back later to help around the office," he told Lori.

"Thanks, we can use your help," Lori replied.

Rebecca and Tim were in the inner office. Lori heard them talking and laughing. Lori was alone and called her doctor. "Dr. Lang, this is Lori Jones," she said. "Doctor, why am I still so tired, and why am I still having trouble breathing?" Lori asked. "I'm having a terrible time coming up the steps that lead to our office," she explained.

"Mrs. Jones, I have not given you permission to even be out of bed yet!" the doctor shouted. "You should spend two more weeks in bed, and then only get up for short periods of time for another two weeks! You should not be doing any work, and you shouldn't be going up any flights of stairs for a long time!"

"I'm sorry doctor, but that's just not possible," Lori answered.

"I should have put you in the hospital, and if you don't do what I say, you can have a relapse and be sicker than you were when you came to my office the first time," the doctor tried to explain.

"Thank you, doctor, I'll try to take care of myself," Lori said and hung up. She wished she had not made the call. She wished she could go home and go to bed. Lori felt so tired and was thankful that Rebecca was there to help her with her work.

It was two hours before Tim and Rebecca came out of the inner office. Rebecca took over the telephone calls and did a great job. She saved Lori a lot of work during the rest of the day.

Lori made it through another week with Sam and Rebecca's help.

That Sunday was Tim and Lori' eighth wedding anniversary. "What would you like to do on your anniversary, tomorrow?" Tim asked Lori as they left the office Saturday afternoon. He seemed little more friendly and that was something Lori could gain strength from.

"I'd like to go to church, then on a picnic in the mountains, and then rest all evening," Lori answered. "We can wear warm clothes and enjoy the beautiful outdoors. I think resting in the fresh air of the mountains might help my breathing."

Lori was shocked when Tim said, "Then that's what we will do."

Lori packed some sandwiches, chips, and desert into an old cooler box they had brought from the farm. Tim carried the cooler to the car and they drove across town to church. It had been several months since Tim had gone to church with Lori, and this made the day special.

After church, Tim drove the station wagon up into the foothills of the Rocky Mountains. They found a pretty spot close to a mountain stream. Lori put out their lunch on the end gate of the station wagon and she and Tim sit on each side of the end gate to eat.

The area was so pretty that Lori enjoyed looking in every direction. She breathed deeply the fresh air. Tim tried to sit and enjoy his time with Lori, but he was too restless. Lori knew he was not enjoying the beautiful scenery and was anxious to get back to the city. "Tim would probably enjoy watching TV more than this," Lori told herself. She suggested that they go back to the city. They soon put everything back into the car and started back out of the mountains.

They had traveled about ten miles when Lori said, Tim, you have used all of Mike's money, and the business still hasn't made any money. "I don't know how Sam and his family are surviving. But, as for us, you're going to have to get another job, or I'm going to have to leave Thomasville and move to where I can get a teaching job. I can't live the rest of my life in fear of being kicked out into the street."

"Lori, I love you and I don't want you to leave me again," Tim replied. He picked up Lori's hand and held it firmly as he drove back to the city. "Don't you still love me?" Tim finally asked.

Lori did not answer. She felt so tired and confused. Large tears rolled down her cheeks and dropped into her lap.

Tim parked the station wagon close to the apartment. He helped Lori out of the car and up the stairs. Tim opened the door for her and closed the door behind her. He led her to the bedroom and laid her on the bed and tried to make her comfortable.

Tim was back to his terrible attitude when he went to the office Monday. Lori went an hour later. She found it just as hard as ever to get up the stairs and breathe at the same time.

Sam did not come to the office and Rebecca went with Tim to buy some pizza for lunch. They were gone for over an hour. Lori heard them bouncing up the stairs. Rebecca was giggling. They left two pieces of pizza on Lori's desk and went back into Tim's office. "I'm going to be training Rebecca, and I don't want disturbed," Tim said again. He closed and locked his office door.

Tim and Rebecca came out of the office at two o'clock. "Lori, you don't look well. Would you like for me to answer the telephone for you so you can go home early?" Rebecca asked.

"Oh yes!" Lori exclaimed. She was soon in the station wagon and on her way home when she remembered she needed to stop and get a few groceries. Lori smoked on the way to the grocery store. She was so sick by the time she got back to the car that she laid down in the back seat of the station wagon and rested for thirty minutes. She finally made it on home. Lori rested again before she struggled up the stairs with the groceries. Lori fell into a chair and rested before she put up the groceries. She rested again before she started the evening meal.

Tim came in. "Why isn't supper ready?" he asked. "I'm hungry!" he shouted. "You came home early so you have no excuse!"

Lori did not answer. She tried to hurry with the rest of the meal. She finally dropped into a living room chair. "Tim, I don't feel well, can't you take over?" she asked.

"I'm tired, and I don't feel well either," Tim snapped. He took off his shoes and reclined in the other lounge chair.

Lori almost had dinner ready when the doorbell rang. Tim answered the door. It was Sam and Rebecca. "We were wondering if we could stay here until my older daughter gets off work," Sam said. "It will save us a thirty-mile trip home and back, if you don't mind," he explained.

"Sure, and you might as well stay for supper," Tim said with a smile. "Lori, set the table for two more," Tim yelled into the kitchen. Tim was not tired anymore.

Lori could not believe that Tim had invited Sam and Rebecca for supper. She thought Rebecca might help her, but the fifteen-year-old curled up in a large, brown chair in the living room and listened to the two men talking, instead.

Lori seemed to be walking in a trance by this time. She tried to do everything automatically rather than trying to think. She made a tossed salad and took some desert out of the freezer to make the meal stretch further.

Lori was almost finished when Rebecca came into the kitchen. "Can I help?" she asked.

"You can set the table while I finish the desert, if you want to," Lori said. She set out the two extra place settings.

"I wish I didn't have to go home tonight," Rebecca said. "I have just started my period and I'm having stomach cramps. It hurts worse when I get out into the cold, and it is so cold tonight," the girl explained. "I just wish I had a warm place to curl up and try to feel better."

Lori felt sorry for Rebecca. During dinner, Lori asked Sam if Rebecca could spend the night. "We have an extra bedroom and it might help her to feel better," Lori said.

"I'll have to call her mother and ask her if it's all right," Sam replied. He picked up the telephone from the end table next to the divan and dialed. "Sharon doesn't think it's a good idea, but I don't see what it would hurt if it's okay with you," Sam said.

"We'd love to keep her," Tim said.

Lori agreed by nodding her head yes. "Lord, give me more strength," Lori was praying.

Tim and Sam were visiting and waiting for Sam's daughter to get off work. Lori put Rebecca to bed. She covered up the girl and brought her a heating pad to put on her stomach. "Goodnight, Rebecca," Lori said and closed the door. "She is such a pretty girl," Lori told herself.

Lori went back into the living room to excuse herself. She was tired and weak and anxious to get to bed. Lori soon fell into a deep, troubled sleep.

A noise woke up Lori. She looked around. It was almost daylight. Lori realized that the noise that had awakened her was the sound of someone coming through their bedroom door. I wonder if Rebecca is feeling worse, was Lori's first thought. Lori turned over toward the door. She saw Tim slip back through the door from the main hall. He did not have on any clothes. Tim quietly slipped back into bed and was soon snoring.

I must be dreaming, Lori was thinking. She turned over and tried to go back to sleep. Something seemed terribly wrong, but Lori could not figure out what it was.

Rebecca got up early and went to the office with Tim. Lori cleaned up the breakfast dishes and the apartment before she drove to the office. She did not feel much better than she had the day before. She was smoking more and more even though it was painful. Lori hoped Tim would not need her since Rebecca was back to help, but Tim ordered Lori to watch the front office while he did more training with Rebecca in the inner office.

Lori was hoping to be able to rest on Saturday, but Tim demanded that she go to the state capital again with him and Vance. "These are special meetings given by the company's president from California," Tim shouted when Lori asked to stay home.

Tim and Vance laughed at Lori again when she was so slow getting up the stairs. "You're really out of shape," Tim said, laughing.

Lori was so hurt over Tim's lack of understanding that she excused herself again, and went into the ladies rest-room to smoke another cigarette. "I know these will probably kill me, but I want to feel numb from all the hurt Tim is putting me through," Lori told herself again.

The following week, Tim spent a lot more time with Rebecca, training her to do part of the meetings he had scheduled. They usually went into his office and shut the door with Tim giving orders not to be disturbed.

Lori was not comfortable when Tim and Rebecca were in the office together, but Rebecca was always so sweet and helpful when she came out that Lori soon forgot her uneasiness. After all, she is just a child, Lori reminded herself.

Tim sent Lori and Rebecca after some lunch one day. It surprised Lori, but she enjoyed getting out of the office even if it did hurt her to go up and down the stairs. They bought some hamburgers and were on their way back to the office when Rebecca said, "Lori, Tim doesn't feel that you love him anymore. If you don't love him, you need to divorce him so he can find someone that will love him."

"You sound wise for a young teenager, but I'm surprised that Tim has talked about our private lives to you," Lori replied. "God doesn't like divorce, and He expects His people to do everything they can to work out their differences. I do still love Tim, but it hasn't always been easy."

"Tim, I don't think it looks right for you to shut the door when you're in the office with Rebecca," Lori whispered one day.

"I don't want to be disturbed while I'm concentrating on training Rebecca!" Tim shouted. "Try to think of someone besides yourself for a change!"

Lori turned around with her back to Tim and made another telephone call for the company.

Sam called early Thursday morning. "Sharon and I feel that Rebecca is spending too much time with you, Tim and we've decided to keep her home a few days," he explained.

Lori missed Rebecca's help, but she felt more at ease with the inner office door open. Tim had more time to help her than when Rebecca was there.

Tim and Lori had just finished supper Friday evening when the telephone rang. Tim answered it. It was Rebecca. Tim listened for a minute and said, "I'll be there to get you as soon as I can."

"Where are you going?" Lori asked.

"To help Rebecca!" Tim yelled. "I'm going to get this thing straightened out right now!" Tim ran down the steps leading from the apartment, and was soon driving out of the parking lot of the complex in his New Yorker.

Lori started cleaning up the kitchen when the telephone rang again.

"Hello, Lori, this is Sharon. I'm coming to pick you up in about ten minutes. I want you to be out in front of the complex so you can get in our car quickly. Just get out of that apartment as quickly as you can!" Sharon exclaimed.

"But Sharon, I've been sick. I don't feel well tonight. It's awfully cold outside," Lori protested. "What's going on?" she asked.

"I can't explain over the phone; just get out of the apartment quick!" Sharon repeated.

Lori did not take the time or effort to dress. She put her heavy coat on over her robe and walked slowly down the stairs. A cold wind was blowing, and there were a few skiff of snow blowing across the parking lot. Lori felt like she was going to freeze as she watched the busy night traffic along the avenue. It seemed like a long, long time before Sharon's car pulled up in front of the complex. Rebecca's older sister held the back door open for Lori while she crawled into the back seat.

"What's going on?" Lori asked as she started another terrible coughing spell.

"Tim and Rebecca have been having an affair. They have been having sex, in other words," Sharon started to explain. "I've been uneasy about them being together, and that is why I've been keeping Rebecca away from Tim. Rebecca has been like a caged lion the last few days. She has been demanding to see Tim. She has even caused her two little sisters to rebel against us. This morning, I watched her sneak a letter out to our mail box. I waited until she went back into the house, and then I went and got the letter. It was addressed to Tim. The letter confirmed out suspensions."

Lori felt like she was going to faint, then she felt her face burning again, and then she felt sick in her stomach and shaky. "I don't believe it," Lori whispered.

"Here's the letter," Rebecca's sister said. She handed Lori a small envelope. Sharon pulled the car onto a country road and stopped. She turned on the dome light for Lori to read.

> "Dearest Tim,
>
> I love you very much. I have enjoyed our sexual times together. My folks won't let me see you, but I think I can talk them into it. If they won't let me come to you, I'll run away. Nothing can keep us apart. I love you too much, and I'll do anything for us to be together, and make love. I want to be with you forever and forever, and I'm going to be, because I'm pregnant. I'm happy that I'm going to have your baby, dearest.
>
> I love you, my Dearest,
> Rebecca

"I still can't believe it!" Lori exclaimed. Her body was shaking, and her teeth were chattering.

"We have had trouble with Rebecca before. As you know, I'm Rebecca's step mother. Sam finally divorced Rebecca's mother because she had a lot of affairs with a lot of men. Rebecca's mother was wrapped up in sex, and her brother had problems when he first came to live with us. We took Rebecca out of school once because she was 'coming on' to her male teacher. We took her to a Christian counselor for help, but after the first session, he refused to work with her again. He said that Rebecca was 'coming on' to him, too," Sharon explained. "I'm sorry Lori, but if Tim is this kind of man, you might as well find it out now." She reached back into the back seat a patted Lori's hand.

"Tonight we had a fuss at home. Rebecca is influencing her little sisters and they are sassing us and not doing what Sam and I tell them to do. I finally told Rebecca tonight that I was so tired of her rebelliousness, and hearing about Tim, that she could either settle down, or she could just leave home. That's when she called Tim to come after her," Sharon explained.

"Tim came and picked up Rebecca and said that you would help him raise her. They are on their way back to your apartment right now," Connie, Rebecca's sister said.

"That's why we had to get you out of the apartment before they got back," Sharon explained. "We have called the police to arrest Tim for Child molesting, and we didn't want you there when it happens. We're going to a friend's house right now and we're taking you with us."

Lori felt too weak to argue. "Well, you don't have to worry about Rebecca being pregnant; Tim is sterile, and has never been able to have children," Lori said, trying to smile.

Sharon drove back to the city. She parked the car in front of a neat, BI-level house. The door was answered by an attractive black lady. She already knew what was going on, and she was understanding and friendly.

Jackie led Sharon, Connie, and Lori into a nice living room and motioned for them to sit down.

"May I use your telephone?" Lori asked.

"Sure, honey, it's in the kitchen right through that door," Jackie said, pointing. "Make your self at home," the pretty lady said.

Lori picked up the telephone and placed it on the kitchen table. She sat down before she dialed her own number.

"Hello," Tim said. He sounded happy.

"Tim, I'm with Sharon," Lori said. "Is Rebecca with you," she managed to asked.

"Yes she is, so tell me where you are so I can come and get you," Tim said with a giggle.

"Tim, I won't take anyone else's word for it," Lori began. "I want to ask you myself. Have you had sex with Rebecca?" she asked.

"Yes, I have," Tim answered. He almost sounded proud.

"But, How? When? Where?" Lori asked. "You're always home at night," she stammered.

"Oh, in my office, in the car, and the other night in our apartment while you were asleep," Tim answered. "Now that I have admitted it, you should be a good Christian and forgive me and let me come and get you. We can raise Rebecca together." He sounded so jolly.

"Tim did you have sex with your sister in-law when she was a girl, the way people said you did?" Lori asked

"Yes, but I was very young myself at the time, and she was consenting," Tim answered.

Lori could hear Rebecca giggling. "Tim did you ever sexually abuse your adopted daughter, Sally, the way people back home said you did?" Lori asked.

"Yes, I did, but I wasn't a Christian then," Tim answered.

"Tim, did you ever have sex with Rosita, or abuse her in any way, the way the sheriff said you did and that you went to trial for?" Lori asked.

"No, Lori, I never had sex with Rosita. Rebecca is the only other person I have ever had sex with since I married you," Tim answered. "If you're a real Christian, you'll forgive me and let me come after you. Now tell me where you are!"

"I don't believe you about Rosita. I know, now, that you were guilty and I lost everything I had trying to protect you. I even asked my mother to help. As far as I'm concerned, any feeling that I ever had for you is gone!" Lori shouted. "I'm taking off my wedding rings right now, and I'll never put them back on! I don't ever want to see you again as long as I live! I don't love you anymore so don't ever try to talk to me again!" Lori slammed the telephone down and begain to sob.

Sharon had heard Lori's side of the conversation and did not have to be told that Rebecca was with Tim. She picked up the telephone and called the Thomasville police and asked for the juvenile department. "My fifteen year old daughter has just been picked up by a fifty year old man, and taken to his apartment," Sharon explained. "Can you go to the apartment and arrest him?" she asked.

"I need to come and talk to you first and get some more information," the voice on the other line said. "Please give me your address, and I'll be there as quickly as I can."

"I'm in town at a friend's house," Sharon said. She gave the man the street address of the black lady's house.

About ten minutes later, the door bell rang. Jackie answered the door.

"Hello, I'm Sergeant Bradley. Are you the people who called to have a subject arrested on Child Molesting charges?" the man asked.

Hearing those words brought back horrible memories for Lori. She felt like she had just jumped "out of the frying pan into the fire once again".

"Yes, and here is the address where my daughter and her old, boyfriend are," Sharon replied, handing the officer a piece of paper with Lori's address on it.

"How old is the child?" the officer asked.

"She just turned fifteen, and this older man has taken my daughter to his apartment and they are there together right now," Sharon answered.

"Lady, I'm sorry, but I can't arrest this man. In this state, fifteen is considered the age of accountability. This man is breaking God's law, but not the state's law, by having sex with a fifteen-year-old. The law isn't right, but it's all I have to work with. I can't make an arrest," the police officer explained. "I can arrest your daughter for being a runaway, though," the officer said.

"Then I guess that's what you'll have to do," Sharon replied.

The officer had Sharon to fill out some papers, and walked to the door. "I'll bring her back here if I find them at this address," he said and left.

While everyone waited, Lori went back to the telephone again. She dialed her pasture's number. "Pasture Rick, I know it's awfully late, but I have to talk to you. Tim has been having an affair with a fifteen year old girl. He has admitted it. I'm leaving him. I quit coming to counseling with Tim because Tim was lying to you about our situation. Since you have such a large congregation, I felt that your time was too valuable to be wasted on us. I'm kind of angry that you talked me into coming back to Tim, but I know you tried to follow what the Bible says. Please pray for us," Lori said.

"Lori, I'm terribly sorry that things turned out like this. You're doing the right thing this time. You didn't really have Biblical grounds to leave Tim before. Now you can leave him and know that you didn't have any choice," Pastor Rick said.

"I'm going to get a divorce and change my name as quickly as I can before he gets me into more trouble. I never know what he might do next," Lori explained.

"I understand. I'll pray for you both. Please keep me posted as to what is happening, no matter what time of night it is," Pastor Rick said and hung up.

"I know he's sorry he talked me into coming back, but now I've started smoking, and I have lost my health, and I don't have a job now, and . . ." Lori told herself.

"I love him! He loves me! You can't keep us apart no matter what you do!" Rebecca was screaming from the living room. She saw Lori standing in the living room door. "It's all your fault! You didn't love him, and he needs a lot of love! He told me all about your marriage! He doesn't love you! He loves me!" Rebecca shouted at Lori.

"Lori, "I'm so sorry," Sharon apologized. "Officer, put her into my car. I'm going to take her to our home twenty miles out of town. Maybe her father and I can keep her locked up until she settles down," Sharon said.

"You can never take me far enough away from Tim! I'll run away and find him, no matter what you do to me! We love each other, and we'll do anything to be together! I'm even having his baby!" Rebecca yelled as the officer pulled the screaming girl to her parent's car. He pushed her inside, locked the door, and shut it quickly.

"You can bring the handcuffs back to the police department tomorrow," the officer said.

Sharon was soon driving down the street with the kicking child. Connie was trying to hold Rebecca and keep her from unlocking the door. It was all they could do to keep the teenager in the car, and to keep her from hurting them, and to keep her from hurting herself.

Rebecca looked liked a mature young lady, but right now, she was acting like a spoiled, sex-crazed maniac. "Oh Lord, help us," Sharon prayed loudly over and over.

"You poor woman," Jackie said. "I don't have a spare bedroom, but I'll fix you a warm bed here on the couch. I'll make you as warm and comfortable as I can." She brought Lori some blankets and a large, soft pillow.

Lori had not realized that she was shaking from the cold and from the events of the evening. She wrapped up in the blankets like a cocoon, and shook for the rest of the night. The ugly scenes of the evening kept flashing before her. The hours passed slowly. Just before dawn, Lori heard Jackie's husband get up and go into the kitchen. She heard him eating breakfast and getting ready for work. Jackie's husband left for work before daylight.

Jackie fixed Lori some toast and tea.

Lori felt more relaxed talking to this beautiful, loving lady. "I have to go back to the apartment and pick up my old car and some clothes.

I'll just wait until I know that Tim has gone to the office, and I won't have to face him," Lori said.

Lori called the office at nine-thirty to see if Tim was there. "Hello, may I help you?" Rebecca answered cheerfully.

Lori hung up the phone without answering. She knew Rebecca would recognize her voice, and she did not want to give the girl any more satisfaction than she already had. "I just can't believe that Sam and Sharon would let Rebecca be around Tim ever again," Lori told Jackie.

Jackie nodded her head to agree. She led Lori out to the garage and helped her into her nice car. Jackie spoke words of encouragement and scripture all the way to Lori's apartment. "Do you want me to come in with you?" Jackie asked.

"No, but thanks anyway," Lori answered. "I'm just going to pack a suitcase and leave as soon as I can," she explained. "Thanks for all your help. I don't know what I would have done without your help last night. May God bless you." Lori squeezed Jackie's hand and waved good-bye.

Lori slowly walked up the flight of stairs, and then rested. Her hands shook as she unlocked the apartment door. She felt like she was walking into someone else's apartment. It did not feel like home anymore. "I don't feel like I have a home, or belong anywhere," Lori said to herself with tears rolling down her cheeks. Looking around the apartment made her shiver as she thought about the love-making that had gone on there the night before and the night Rebecca stayed with them. She was thankful that the walls could not talk.

Lori picked up the telephone and called Mitch. "Son, Tim is having an affair with a fifteen year old girl. I don't know what to do," Lori said sobbing.

"I'm not surprised. All the family knew he was that kind of person. Get yourself down here to my place as quickly as you can. We'll get your furniture later," Mitch said. "Do you have enough money for that much gas for your car?" he asked.

"When did you become so wise?" Lori asked. "Yes, I have twenty-four dollars. That should be enough to get me there," she answered.

Lori said good-bye and made another telephone call. "Aunt Martha, Tim is having an affair with a fifteen year old girl, and I'm leaving him," Lori explained again.

"I'm not surprised. I always felt uncomfortable around him, Lori," Aunt Martha replied.

"How strange," Lori commented. "How much would you charge me to store my furniture in the little house on your property that you used to live in?" Lori asked.

"Nothing, you can use it as long as you need to," Aunt Martha answered. "You just get yourself out of there."

Lori thanked Aunt Martha and hung up. She looked up and saw Tim standing in the doorway staring at her with his terrible looking eyes. She had not heard him unlock the door. A cold shiver went up her spine. "I'm leaving you, so don't try to talk me out of it!" Lori screamed.

Tim did not reply. His face was extra white and expressionless.

Lori let go of her many hurts and penned-up emotions. She hit Tim in the face as hard as she could. He still did not speak or show any expression. He acted like a zombie. Lori hit Tim again. Tim had the same response. The third time Lori hit Tim in the face, his glasses fell to the floor. Tim got down on his hands and knees, completely bind, and felt around on the carpet in an attempt to find his glasses.

Lori sobbed as she watched the pitiful sight.

Tim finally found his glasses and put them back on. He stood up and looked at Lori. Lori hit him again. Tim did not even try to protect is face when he saw Lori's blow coming. He seemed to be dead of all feeling. Lori had never seen him so lifeless. She was reminded of something Mike had said once.

"Mom, Tim has no life of his own; he lives on the life that comes from you," Mike had said. Now Mike's statement seemed to make more sense, Lori was thinking.

"You and Rebecca will be good for each other because you're both sex crazy!" Lori shouted.

Tim did not answer.

"She will have to worry about you when she has her periods because you can't go very long without it!" Lori shouted.

Tim nodded his head to agree, but still there was no expression on his face.

Lori lit up a cigarette. It hurt her lungs, but she felt so mortified and confused that she did not know what else to do.

"Light up one for me," Tim said in a strange, unfamiliar voice.

"Get your own!" Lori shouted. She picked up her purse and hit Tim with it until he left the apartment. Lori cried while she packed her suitcases. She cried as she told her Tabby Cat good-bye. She cried as she left the apartment of horrible memories.

Lori took the road that left the city to the east rather than driving through "downtown" traffic. She tried to avoid all the traffic she could because it was hard to see the road through her tears. Lori cried for the first two-hundred miles. She felt like something black and slimy had it's tentacles around her and would not let her go.

Lori drove over the familiar road that led to her mother's and both of her sons'. "I must think about the future and not the past," Lori said aloud. As Lori crossed over a small bridge, she felt the slimy thing let go. Her crying stopped and she begin to breathe easier.

"Praise the Lord!" Lori shouted and begain to relax. "I wonder if I dare look toward the future?" Lori asked herself. "Lord, I know you take care of babies, and dummies. Right now I feel that I qualify in both categories. I know that you'll take care of me, Lord." Her voice echoed through the station wagon.

CHAPTER VIII

STARTING FROM GROUND ZERO

Lori drove slower and slower as she ended her journey. "It's going to be so embarrassing to go home again with another marriage crashed upon the rocks," Lori told herself. She knew her family would be nice to her. They would be sure that she didn't have to sleep in the street, like Tim had said, but she would rather die than to be a burden to any of her family.

Mike was starting all over again, financially. Mitch had two boys to raise. Staci had a good job, but it seemed to take all she could make in her medical profession, and all Mitch made swathing feed and running cattle, to meet their monthly expenses.

Mother has enough to take care of me, but she raised me thirty-five years ago, and she shouldn't have to help support a fifty year old daughter, Lori was thinking. "I should be able to support myself with the education I have," Lori said aloud.

Although Tim had been hard to live with the last five years, Lori felt lonely and unloved again, like she did when she and Hollis split. "What's wrong with me? Why do the men I marry end up wanting younger women? I must be the oldest-looking, most unattractive female in history," Lori said aloud.

"Oh Lord, I have no home, no job, no husband, and no income. Please take me home to be with you before I ever become a burden to my family," Lori prayed. "And Lord, take me home to be with you without any pain, please."

Lori's mother had not wanted her to go back to Tim a year ago, but Lori went back anyway. Now she felt too embarrassed to face her mother tonight. Lori passed Elizabeth's house and drove on to Mitch's.

Staci met Lori at the door and gave her a big hug. "We're glad to see you," Staci said as she led Lori into the living room. Staci always made Lori feel welcome. Mitch had really found a treasure when he married Staci.

"Mom, I didn't think we could ever live in the same house before, but I've changed my mind. If you need to live with us, I want you to feel welcome," Mitch said. He gave Lori a big hug. His 250 pound body squeeze took Lori's breath.

"Thanks," Lori replied. She fell into Mitch's huge arms and begain to sob. Lori was proud of this large, tender-hearted, muscle man she had raised.

"Lori, I'm so glad you're here to stay. I was always afraid of Tim," Staci said. "That's why we didn't come to see you more often. Tim made me feel uneasy and I didn't want him around my kids."

"I never knew that," Lori replied. Lori heard the same thing from all of her relatives and most of her friends in the next few months.

Mike was on a long haul, in the gas truck, and was traveling through some eastern states. He called Mitch one evening and Mitch told him what had happened to Lori. Lori had told Mitch about Tim taking all of Mike's money.

"How come you let that shyster take your money?" Mitch asked.

"I guess he did a sale's job on me, but I wanted to see mom have a better life is the main reason, I guess," Mike replied.

"Well, what's done is done," Mitch said. He handed Lori the telephone.

"I left Tim for good this time, Mike. He was having an affair with Rebecca. I have a Biblical reason to leave him this time. I know it's for the best, and I'm so sorry for the way Tim cheated you," Lori sobbed.

"Don't worry about it, mom. I can get another start and I know Tim did everything he could to make the business work. As far as Rebecca was concerned, I knew she was available, but I didn't think Tim would take advantage of the kid," Mike said. "I'll be home to help you as soon as I can, mom, and don't worry. Things will work out. I know you'll be happier now, than you were with Tim."

"Thanks Mike, but I can't help thinking that if it wasn't for me, you would have never known Tim, and you would still have your money," Lori said.

"Just try to forget the past, and don't blame yourself for everything," Mike said.

"I'll try," Lori promised and hung up the phone.

"Lori, my grandmother is blind. She has a mental degeneration disease and is not able to take care of herself anymore. My family is looking for someone to take care of her," Staci said. "Would you be interested in the job?" she asked. "It only pays four-hundred dollars a month, but it would give you a place to live and you wouldn't have any living expenses," Staci explained.

"Well, it's the wrong time of the year to find a teaching job. I'll take it, for a little while anyway," Lori answered.

Staci called her dad, who called the rest of the family. Lori was hired by phone within thirty minutes.

"We'll go after your furniture Tuesday, mom, if you have a place to store it," Mitch said. "If we don't hurry, Tim might hock it and disappear."

"Aunt Martha said I could store everything in her small house for as long as I need to," Lori explained.

Lori and Elizabeth drove to Thomasville Monday to get things ready to move. Lori was thinking how hard it was going to be to enter the apartment again. She was deep in thought, driving automatically when her mother said, "Lori, you need a car. I don't want you to turn this station wagon over to Tim or the bank. I'll pay it off so you can have it. You can pay me back when you get the money. Let's go to the bank first."

It was early afternoon when Elizabeth followed Lori into the bank that had loaned Tim money for the New Yorker and station wagon. It was this banker that had "been impressed by Tim's reputation", so Tim had said. The banker was in and the secretary motioned for the two ladies to go on into his inner office.

Lori had decided not to tell Mr. Hillcock that she had left Tim in case it might hurt his credit. She was trying to be as fair to Tim as she knew how. "Mr. Hillcock, this is my mother, Elizabeth Ardent. We have come in to pay off the station wagon," Lori explained. "How much do we owe on it?" she asked.

Mr. Hillock shook hands with both ladies. "I like to see people pay off their loans early," he said. Mr. Hillock called for his secretary to bring in some papers. After looking at the bank note, he said, "It looks like you have your loan down to only seven-hundred dollars."

Elizabeth took out her check book and had Lori to fill it out before she signed it. Mr. Hillock looked rather puzzled, but only said, "Thank you," signed the title, and handed it to Lori. The three shook hands again and the ladies left the bank.

"Lori felt tears rolling down her cheeks again. "Thanks, Mother, and I WILL pay you back," she said.

"I know you will, dear," Elizabeth answered. "Now pick out a good place to eat and I'll buy us some dinner. We're going to need all our strength for the next few hours," she said.

Lori was glad that Tim was not in the apartment when they got there. She would be so glad when she would not have to see his face again. Tim came by in the middle of the afternoon to watch Lori pack so she "wouldn't take any of his things".

"You have always worried over YOUR things," Lori said. "I sold my piano, my accordion, guitar, and some of my furniture to help pay rent. I was reminded that we haven't sold anything that belongs to you!"

"I told you before, my things are more valuable than your things," Tim repeated. "It wouldn't have made sense to sell anything I have. It's still mine and I don't want you to take one thing of mine," he shouted.

"I don't ever want to be around anything that belongs to you, anyway," Lori shouted back.

"I have started moving out of the apartment and storing some of my things. I guess you can go to the storage unit with me and see if I took any of your things by mistake," Tim said. "I'm honest."

"What would you have done to Lori if she would have had an affair with someone the way you did, Tim?" Elizabeth asked.

"I would have killed her," Tim answered, coolly.

"That's what I thought," Elizabeth replied.

Everyone was silent for awhile.

Tim helped Lori and Elizabeth pack boxes. Tim asked Lori for some advice concerning the business. Tim now seemed like he had never been anything more to Lori than a business pardoner. They worked until past midnight. Lori and Elizabeth slept in the spare bedroom. Tim went to the office the next morning.

Mitch hooked up his longest horse trailer to the four-wheel drive pickup. He asked a friend and his wife to help. Kris rode with Staci in the car, and Dan rode with Mitch in the pickup truck. They were at the apartment by nine o'clock Tuesday morning.

Lori's furniture was loaded into the large trailer and both cars were filled with the breakables and clothes. "I wish I could have my large secretary desk and electric typewriter," Lori said, thinking aloud.

"Where are they?" Mitch asked.

"At the office," Lori answered.

"We'll pick it up for you on our way out," Mitch replied.

"But Tim is using it for the business and it's not closing time yet. Tim won't let you have it anyway, and I don't want you two to get into a fight," Lori protested.

"You lost everything you had to that guy. You want that desk and you're going to get it!" Mitch said with authority. "I'd love to have a fight with that shyster, anyway."

"I'll show you where the office is located, if you promise not to fight," Lori said.

On the way out of Thomasville, the caravan which consisted of Mitch and Dan in the truck, Staci and Kris in Mitch's car, and Lori and her mother in the station wagon, stopped by the office.

Lori went in first. A woman she did not know was sitting at the desk. Tim was in the inner office. Lori walked into the familiar office. She had quick visions of what had taken place there. Where was there enough room for such activity, she wondered as a shiver went down her back. "We're taking the secretary desk and typewriter," Lori said.

The woman nodded her head "yes" and backed away from the desk. Tim stepped out of his office when he saw Mitch coming. He started to argue when he saw Mitch picking up one end of the huge desk. Mitch was wearing a "Come on and make my day" smile, and flexing his large muscles.

"I guess it's all right, if you take it, if you wait until closing time," Tim said.

"We don't have time to wait," Lori said. The woman that Lori did not know had disappeared by this time and Tim watched helplessly. Lori remembered the many times Tim had bragged about how he could easily whip Mitch. Now he had the chance to try and was backing away. As usual, it had been only talk.

Mitch and Dan quickly took the desk legs off and Dan took them and the typewriter to the trailer. Tim and Mitch just glared at each other. Lori kept looking at Mitch and shaking her head "no".

Mitch and Dan were going down the stairs of the office building with the large desk ten minutes after they had entered the building. People stopped in the hall to watch what was going on.

Lori stopped at the top of the stairs. She took a minute to look at Tim for the last time. She remembered how handsome she thought Tim had been when they were first married. Now, what she saw was a fat, old man, with thick glasses, and a helpless look on his face. He had taken her and her family for about one-hundred thousand dollars, and had nothing to show for it. Tim was wearing his three-piece, pin-striped suit that was now old and worn. He almost looked like a wino on "skid row".

"How could I ever have been so blind?" Lori asked herself. "And, how can pretty, talented, very young Rebecca be so blind?" she whispered. Lori shivered and descended the terrible stairs for the last time.

It was soon dark. Lori begain to relax a little and felt the terrible tiredness overcome her body again.

"Lori, you're broken financially, physically, and spiritually. You'll bounce back, but it will take time," Elizabeth said. "Try not to get discouraged and give up. Have faith in God and He'll help you regain what you've lost."

About midnight they turned onto a less traveled highway. Lori was so tired she started to weave from one side of the road to the other. Staci pulled her car in front of Lori's station wagon and made Lori stop. "You're too tired to drive. I'm going to take over driving your car, and Kris will drive our car," Staci said. "You crawl into the back seat and try to get some sleep."

Lori did as she was told. With all the love she felt around her, she was able to go to sleep. It had been almost a week since the nightmare had started and Lori had not had a night's sleep since.

The next morning Lori's furniture was unloaded at Aunt Martha's. She moved into grandma Grace's house that afternoon.

Grace's place was small, but clean. There were three small bedrooms and Lori was given the smallest one. The room contained a cot, small table with a lamp on it, and a small chest for Lori's clothes. Lori was glad to see an old piano in the living room.

Grandma Grace seemed happy to have Lori move in until Mitch and Staci, and the rest of the family, left. "I don't need you here. You're just here to steal my money!" grandma Grace shouted.

Lori felt angry. Then she took another look at the small, white-haired woman. She had to feel her way from room to room, around furniture, and around the yard outside. Grace tried to keep things clean and she had even planted some flowers outside by the front step. "I must remember that she isn't thinking clearly either," Lori told herself.

"You do need me here. I'll be living here with you for awhile so you won't fall and hurt yourself. I'll cook your meals and clean your house.

You might as well get used to me being here. This is my job and I have no where else to go," Lori said.

"We'll see about that!" Grace shouted and stomped into her bedroom. She slammed the door and was still in the bedroom when Lori called her to dinner.

Grace was hungry. She was at the table by the time Lori finished setting on the food. "Tell me what I'm eating!" Grace demanded.

Lori filled Grace's plate. She took Grace's hand and touched her finger on each section of food. "This is meat-loaf, this is peas, this is cottage cheese, and this is a piece of cake for desert," Lori said.

Grace asked the blessing. She felt over her food again as she pushed it into a spoon and on her fork. Lori tried to start a conversation, but Grace did not want to talk. They ate in silence.

Lori was tired and wanted to go to bed early. Grace had taken a long afternoon nap and wasn't ready to go to bed. At ten p.m., Lori ordered Grace to go to bed. Grace felt around the house and checked each door-lock before she went into her bedroom and slammed the door.

Lori snuck out of the house quickly and quietly. She stood in the cool night. It had been many hours since Lori's last cigarette. She smoked two quickly, although they still hurt her lungs. Lori looked toward the northwest. Three hundred miles away was Thomasville and Tim. "Oh Lord, take care of Tim, and help him to get right with you again," Lori prayed. She had a hard cry and smoked another cigarette before she went back into the house.

Lori had just gotten to sleep when the squeaking floor awoke her. Lori knew, by the sound of the squeaking floor, that Grace was walking toward the back door. "She'll walk into the busy street that goes in front of the house if I don't catch her," Lori moaned. She jumped up out of bed and ran outside to find Grace.

"Grace, you can't come outside alone. You could get run over by walking into the street. You must stay inside unless I'm with you!" Lori exclaimed. She grabbed Grace's hand and tried to pull her back into the house.

Grace argued, sassed Lori, and drug her feet, but Lori finally got her back into the house. Lori was asleep by the time her head hit the pillow the second time.

Lori soon learned that her new job was a twenty-four hour a day job. She tried to take naps in the day time so she could listen to the squeaking floors at night in case Grace tried to sneak out. One day the telephone rang. Lori answered it, turned around, and Grace was crossing the busy street in front. "Thank God, no cars were coming," Lori said as she dragged Grace back from the street and into the house.

Lori was so disappointed with life that she was smoking more again. She was tired of going outside in the cold every night so she opened the window and screen in her bedroom. Lori leaned out as far as she could to smoke so there would not be a smoking smell in the house. If the wind was in the wrong direction, Lori had to crawl out the window and stand beside the house to smoke.

Lori stood in the dark smoking one night. She looked at the tiny, white object between her fingers. "I wonder how anything as small as a cigarette could make a person a slave like me; sneaking outside, coughing, shaking, hurting, and knowing I'm probably going to die, and I'm shrinking in the shadows of the house for this?" Lori asked herself quietly. She remembered how much fun she thought smoking had been when she was a teenager and had just began. After quitting for thirty years, it had once again entrapped her into its deadly grip.

Lori drug herself through the routines of cleaning house and cooking breakfast. She was terribly sick again. She was wheezing and coughing. One morning she felt like she was going to die. Lori called an old friend. "Dorcas, would you please pray for my healing," Lori managed to ask. "I feel like I'm going to die, I'm so sick."

"Oh God, touch Lori's body and heal her in the name of Jesus," Dorcas prayed. "And heal her emotionally too."

Lori said thank you and hung up. She felt a little better. Staci came by that afternoon. "Lori, you have a fever. You're sick. I'm calling some of the family to take care of grandma, and I'm taking you home with me," Staci said.

Staci put Lori in the bedroom downstairs. She gave her medicine to bring down her fever and more medicine to control her cough. Lori slept a lot and started to feel better. Mike came home from his trip and rushed over to see how his mom was doing.

"I'm never going to smoke again," Lori said. "Just to prove it Mike, I want you to go get the carton of cigaretts out of the station wagon and either throw them away or use them," she said.

Lori was sick and ran a fever for three days. When she felt strong enough, she returned to work. Grace had smelled smoke in Lori's bedroom. "You can't smoke in this house! This is my house and no one has ever been allowed to smoke in my house!" Grace shouted.

"You're right and I won't ever do it again," Lori replied. When Grace took her usual nap in her large lounge chair, Lori laid down to rest. She was so discouraged with herself and life in general. Again, Lori had a dream about the tall, handsome stranger in the large motor-home, taking her to his beautiful mansion and taking care of her, and her family's, needs.

Was Jesus really trying to talk to her, or was she just day-dreaming in order to survive the circumstances she now found herself living in. Lori wondered.

Although Lori knew everyone in town, she did not have time to visit anyone. She did not really want to visit her old friends. Lori was still embarrassed about another busted marriage, and the poverty she had gotten herself into. She gave every penny she could to Elizabeth to pay for the old station wagon.

Staci's family gave Lori one day a week to go somewhere and relax. Aunt Martha was taking care of an elderly woman in another state. Lori spent her days off, alone, at Aunt Martha's. She seemed to enjoy being alone more than being with people. Many times she went to the little house and looked over her belongings and furniture, wondering if, and when she would ever get to use them again.

The telephone rang one evening. Lori answered it. "Lori, this is Tim. I want you to come back home. I have been going to a minister for counseling. I have gotten right with the Lord again. I'll work hard and take good care of you," Tim said. Please come back," he begged.

"Do you have Rebecca with you?" Lori asked.

"Yes, but I just think of her as my daughter. Her folks kicked her out and she had no where else to go," Tim answered.

"I will never come back to you," Lori said. "Please don't ever call me again," she shouted and slammed down the phone. Lori cried. "Maybe he can't take care of himself," she whispered. There was no way she could allow herself to get caught in Tim's trap again. Lori wondered how Tim had gotten her telephone number. Lori was so frightened that she ordered papers needed to get a divorce without a lawyer.

Two weeks later Tim called again. "Lori, I don't have Rebecca anymore. I have prayed and prayed about what I have done to you," Tim explained. "Please come back," he pleaded.

"I have started divorce proceedings, Tim," Lori said. "I'm trying to get the divorce without the expense of a lawyer. I can do that if you'll sign the papers I'm going to send to you," "Will you please do that for me?" she asked.

"If you're sure that what you want. Just send them to me and 'x' the places you want me to sign. I'll sign them and send them right back to you," Tim answered.

"Thanks," Lori said and hung up.

Lori mailed the divorce papers to Tim that day. When she went over to her mothers on her day off, Elizabeth was crying. "What the matter?" Lori asked.

"Tim just called. He wished me Happy Mother's Day and said I was the only real mother he ever had. He said he loved all of us and wanted you to change your mind about the divorce," Elizabeth sobbed.

Lori was angry. She called Tim. "Tim, don't you ever call me or any of my family again or I'll have you arrested for harassment. And, if you ever set foot in this area, I'll have you arrested and you know what that means!" Lori shouted, but she remembered that she needed Tim's help by signing the papers. "He might not work with me if I make him mad,"

Lori told herself. "Tim, just sign the divorce papers and send them back to me, please so we can get on with our lives," Lori begged.

"All right, if you're sure that's what you want," Tim whispered.

"I'm sure, so please do it," Lori replied.

Lori received the papers back signed, but Tim had failed to have them notarized. They had to be notarized so Lori sent them right back to Tim, begging him to have them notarized. She even put in two dollars to pay for the Notary. The papers came back to her the next week. The large envelope said that the person had moved with no forwarding address.

"Oh Lord, what am I going to do now?" Lori asked herself. She called Vance Jackson's number, which was the only friend's number in Thomasville that she still had. Vance's wife answered the telephone.

"Yes, Lori, we do know a little about Tim," Nancy said. "He was trying to hide Rebecca when the police was looking for her. He even had the nerve to ask us to keep her. We told him we would not get involved. The last we heard, he skipped town with Rebecca, and the authorities are looking for him because of Rebecca, and he didn't pay off the New Yorker, and because of other bills he neglected to pay. I don't know how you, or Vance, could get mixed up with a guy like that," Nancy said.

"I'm asking myself the same question every day Nancy," Lori replied. "I need to find Tim so I can get a divorce before he marries Rebecca and can be arrested for Bigamy," she explained. "I don't know what I'm going to do now."

"You can petition your District Judge to issue a divorce without Tim's signature. He has the authority to do that if the second party can't be found, which is where you are right now. I'm sure that Tim is in some other state, or country by now," Nancy said.

"If anyone knows how to lose his identity, it's Tim," Lori replied. "Thanks for the information and take care of yourself."

Lori drove to Dannon to talk to the District Judge. It was the same old judge that had announced Tim's Non Contendra in the hearing. Lori told the judge her story and asked for his help.

"I'm not surprised," the judge said. "I'll have to have authorities in Thomasville try to find him. If he isn't there, I'll grant your divorce. I realize why you're in such a hurry, but it will take six months. It will be October before the divorce is final. We'll just hope he doesn't get married before then," the judge said.

Lori thanked the judge and hurried back to her job at Grace's.

Lori stopped by a few weeks later to stay at Aunt Martha's house again. The place was located a mile north of a small town. Lori had grown up on a farm seven miles south, and she had gone twelve year of school in the town. She was feeling well again and had started smoking again. She had not planned to ever smoke again, but at a time she felt terribly depressed, she had found herself falling back into the same old habit.

Lori sat on the edge of the high patio in back of the house and smoked. She tried to make some plans for her future and feel more optimistic about life. The sun was setting too quickly. Lori went inside before dark and locked the doors.

Lori had watched TV, listened to some music, and read a little scripture before she felt sleepy. She was crawling into bed when she heard something. It took her a few minutes to figure out where the noise was coming from. Lori shivered with fright. Someone was outside and had turned on an outside faucet.

"I wonder if it's just someone playing a joke, or if it is Tim?" Lori asked herself. She shivered again. She had seen Tim unlock any door he ever wanted to go through. It was almost like a talent Tim had. "These locked doors won't stop him if he wants in," Lori told herself. It was early morning before Lori went to sleep. She didn't get her needed rest that day off.

Lori had finished cleaning up the kitchen from breakfast. She sat down in the living room where Grace was sitting. Lori played several hymns on the old piano. "Grace, would you like for me to start your story tapes for the blind, or would you like for me to read to you this morning?" she asked.

"I want to hear you read!" Grace snapped.

"Lori starting reading an old book she had found on one of the shelves in the hall. The pages were discolored and worn. It had been copyrighted in 1904. The story was a mystery. Lori read until her voice gave out. She went to the kitchen for a drink of water and saw a car drive up to the house. Lori watched an old friend walk up to the door and knock.

Rosy was Hispanic. She was a sweet Christian lady. Rosy had cleaned house for Lori most of the years Lori was teaching school while her sons were still at home. She was one of the cleanest ladies Lori had even known. "Come in, Rosy," Lori said as she held the door open for her friend.

"Lori, I remember the many kind things you did for me all the years we have known each other. I remember when God healed my son's mind when you prayed for his class before school started one day, when you were teaching my kids. I remember how much you paid me for cleaning up a house that was already clean. You have always been my dear friend. Now I have something for you," Rosy said.

Rosy took Lori's hand and tenderly put something in it. Lori looked down and saw a ten dollar bill. "It's not much, but I know you are going through hard times. I just wanted to give you a little something," Rosy said.

"Oh Rosy, I can't take your money," Lori replied.

"Please take it," Rosy said. She gave Lori a big hug and left before Lori had a chance to argue.

Lori looked at the money through tears. "I can't remember anything I ever did for her," Lori said. "I have had so many people thank me for things I have done for them in the past. I can't remember doing any of the things that they are talking about. It's almost like they are talking about someone else," Lori told herself.

Lori was feeling depressed one day when she received a letter from Cousin Elaine. The letter said: Dear Lori,

I know you must be terribly discouraged at this time and I know you must have a very low opinion of men. Not all men are bad. I know this guy that goes to our church. He is a fine Christian man and his wife died with cancer several years ago. He has a daughter in college. I just talked to Ben yesterday. He sounded so lonesome that I showed him your picture and gave him your address. I don't think he'll write you because he is rather bashful. If you would like to have a pen-pal, his name and number is Ben Lee, 104 10th Street, Osborne, NE.

"I guess it wouldn't hurt to write him if we never meet," Lori told herself. "I need someone to tell my troubles to that I don't know," she said. Lori wrote Ben.

Ben answered Lori's letter and told Lori about his job delivering furniture for a large furniture store and that he had worked there for eight years. Ben said he had worked for a lumber company for twenty-three years in California before he moved his family to Nebraska. "That the same time period I spent in each of my marriages," Lori mused.

Lori found Ben's letter to be interesting and encouraging.

The second month Lori worked with Grace, the family raised her wages to six-hundred dollars. Most of it went to pay off the station wagon.

Grace begin to accept Lori a little, but she was still trying to sneak out of the house at night. Ruby, Grace's only daughter, came several times a week to visit. She usually brought her three boys with her. Ruby and her boys were always cheerful and helpful.

It was during one of these visits that Ruby said, "My brother and his wife from new Mexico are coming to visit. They can take care of mom and give you a few days rest."

"I need the rest, but I also need the job," Lori said with a smile.

Grace's son, and his family, drove in late the next evening. Lori stayed long enough to meet the relatives, then she drove over to Aunt Martha's place.

When Lori returned to work the following week, Grace's entire family was at the house. "Mom has decided to go home with my brother to New Mexico," Ruby said.

"We hated to put you out of a job, so we decided that we'll give you the job of painting the outside of mom's house," Staci's father said.

"We heard that you have painted houses before. All you'll have to do is charge the paint at the hardware store here in town. My brother owns the store, you know," Ruby explained.

"Thank you for the offer. I'll take the job," Lori replied.

Lori waved good-bye to Grace and her family. She ate a sandwich for supper and went to bed early. Lori slept well in her own bed all night. It seemed nice not to have to listen for footsteps during the night. Early the next morning, Lori drove downtown to the hardware store. Grace's son helped Lori figure out how much paint she needed. They also decided that Grace would like the house to be white with green trim.

Lori put on her old clothes and found a chair to stand on. She started painting the area just below the roof. Lori felt the paint splashing on her face and clothes. She knew she looked terrible.

Lori looked up and saw Hollis's wife driving by in her new Cadillac. Lori felt embarrassed to let her first husband's young wife see her looking like this. Before the day was over, Hollis drove by, slowly, in his new pickup truck.

Lori acted like she did not see anyone driving by. She felt people watching her. Lori felt so poor, ugly, and alone. A few friends drove by and yelled at her. "Keep up the good work; you're helping beautify this part of town," many of them said. Lori tried to smile and yell back some kind of greeting.

The house had several additions. Part of it was bare cement. It took two coats of paint to make the white walls all look the same.

The summer days were long and Lori painted for ten hours the first day. She painted eleven hours the second day. The third day, Lori painted the green trim. Two weeks work was done in three and a half days. The house looked pretty.

The shower, to get off all the dirt and paint, felt refreshing. Lori put on clean clothes and typed several resumes, in hopes of getting a teaching job in the fall. In her resumes, Lori told about her college credit, teaching experiences, hobbies, interests, and how much she enjoyed working with students.

Lori also took time to write Ben and tell him about losing her job, painting the house, and asking for prayer to get a teaching job. She also gave him her mother's address.

The next day Lori bought manila envelopes and had several copies of her college transcripts made. She mailed a complete set of papers to each school in the surrounding area. Lori was praying for a good teaching job, but she did not feel very confident. I know my age is against me. Schools would rather hire younger, cheaper teachers, and not have to pay for all my extra college hours and years of teaching experience, Lori was thinking.

Lori was paid that evening. She washed her clothes and bedding, and cleaned up the little house for the last time. Lori returned to live with Elizabeth and Arther. She still owed two-hundred dollars on the old station wagon.

"Mother, I want you to have these for what I still owe you on the car," Lori said. She handed Elizabeth the wedding rings Tim had given her. The set had a ruby and five diamonds in it.

"I don't want to take your rings, dear," Elizabeth said. "Don't worry about paying for that car until you get back on your feet financially," she said.

"Please take them, mother. They don't mean anything to me now. I won't ever wear them again. They should be worth eight-hundred dollars, but I probably wouldn't get more than two-hundred dollars if I sold them. Maybe you can have a nice dinner ring made out of them to wear on your right ring finger," Lori said.

"If it will make you happy, but you can have them back any time you want them," Elizabeth said.

"Mother, do you have any work around her I can do?" Lori asked.

"The windows need washing. I haven't been able to do it for a long time," Elizabeth answered.

Lori started washing the windows on the top level of the house first. She had to lean way out to wash them on the outside. "Why are you watching me, mother?" Lori asked.

"I guess so I can see you if you fall out the window," Elizabeth answered. "I sure couldn't keep you from falling," she added and laughed, trying to cover up her anxiety.

The telephone rang. Elizabeth left to answer it. She returned and said, "It's for you, Lori."

It was Lori's sister, Bonnie. Bonnie worked part-time doing flower arrangements for funerals. "Lori, we need someone to help us here at the Funeral Home tomorrow," Bonnie said.

"I'll be glad to help, and thanks for asking me," Lori replied.

The next day Lori was still stiff and sore from painting, but she reported to the funeral home at eight o'clock.

"We can't pay teacher's wages," the owner said. "But, we sure can use some help around her today."

Lori mowed and raked the lawn, cleaned up the family reception room, and made coffee for people in sadness. She typed some funeral memory cards and was helping Bonnie make wreaths of flowers when two other workers came in. "We thought you might like to help us work on one of the bodies," one of the ladies said.

"Not me," Bonnie said with a smile.

"I'll help you, but I've never done anything like this before and it won't be easy," Lori said.

The ladies laughed. "We were just teasing because we knew Bonnie wouldn't help, but she is great with flowers, anyway," the first lady explained.

The owner's wife spoke. "It was hard for us to fix the dead bodies too, when we first begin. My son was killed in a car wreck and the man that ran this place did a terrible job with everything. My husband and I decided that we could help people, and the Lord, by buying the Mortuary and helping take care of deceased loved ones. We try to make the families feel as comfortable as possible while they are here, and make the funerals as nice as possible, too," she said.

"You're doing a wonderful job. I'm sorry you don't need any more help after today," Lori said.

Lori received a letter from Ben that evening and took time to answer it.

The next day Lori looked through the area newspapers. She noticed that the high-school at Dannon was still looking for a Special Education teacher. Dannon was the largest school in that part of the state. "Mother, I'm going back to Dannon and ask for that job again even though they turned me down the first time," Lori said over a cup of coffee.

"I'll go with you," Elizabeth said.

Lori and her mother made the hour trip back to Dannon and Lori talked to the Personnel Director. "We are still looking for someone who is qualified for that position," the lady said.

Lori said thanks and left. She helped her mother around the house the following week. When the paper came out again, the job in Dannon was still listed. "I'm going to Dannon again to see about that job," Lori said.

Lori and Elizabeth made the long trip again. Lori did not call ahead. She and her mother were in Dannon in time for Lori to ask to see the superintendent as soon as he came back from his lunch break. Lori was so nervous, but all Mr. Cappel could say was "no" again, and she had nothing to lose to ask for the job the third time.

Mr. Coppel agreed to talk to Lori. He sat behind his large desk and looked at Lori sternly. "Yes, Mrs. Jones," he said.

"Mr. Cappel, I know I'm not qualified to teach in the Special Education position yet, but you haven't been able to find anyone that is. I have fifteen hours from the University in that field, and I have fifteen years of teaching experience. I will take all the extension classes I can this winter, and go on to school full-time next summer, and become qualified as quickly as I can, if you'll just let me have the job," Lori explained. "And, I really need the job."

Mr. Cappel was quiet for a minute. "I'm sending you over to the high-school to talk to Mr. Rosa, our principal," Mr. Cappel said without a smile.

"Thank you so much," Lori replied.

Lori picked up her mother from the Teacher's Lounge and they drove across town to the high-school. Mr. Rosa was waiting in his office.

"Come in," Mr. Rosa said with a smile. Mr. Rosa was a short, handsome, Italian-looking man, who was probably in his late fifties. His face was almost hidden in a mass of thick, wavy, gray hair.

Lori had heard that Mr. Rosa was a hard person to get along with, but she felt at ease under his friendly smile. Mr. Rosa asked Lori several questions. Lori answered the questions as best she could. She told Mr. Rosa her plans to finish her Master's degree in Special Education as quickly as possible.

I'm going to give you the job," Mr. Rosa said. "Since you're not qualified, it will be with an Emergency Teaching Certificate, and it will only be for one year. We have a full time Special Ed. teacher's aid that has been here for thirteen years to help you. Right now we are just looking for someone who can love the kids that you'll be working with and I think you will. Go back to Superintendents Coppel's office and sign your contract. I'll see you early Thursday morning at our first teachers' meeting in the gym here in this building. Good Luck,"

"Oh thank you, Mr. Rosa, I'll do my best," Lori said. "Thank you Lord," Lori whispered as soon as she had left the office. Lori signed the highest paying contract that she had ever had. She would be making $23,000, plus some extra money for extra time she would spend for talking to parents after school. On their way home, Lori and Elizabeth stopped by Nada's motel for something cold to drink. Nada was Arther's younger sister.

Nada was a few years older than Lori. She was a little heavy, like Lori, and she had the same type of very curly hair that Arther had. In fact, Arther and Nada looked a lot alike.

"Lori has just gotten a teaching job here in Dannon," Elizabeth said. "Now she needs to find a place to live before next week," "Do you know of any apartments here in Dannon?" Elizabeth asked.

"I sure do! It's right here," Nada answered. "I want Lori to stay with me until she finds a place of her own. She can stay as long as she wants to. I can give her the upstairs of my apartment in the back of the office. There is a large bedroom, nice bathroom, and a work room where she can be all to herself," Nada said. She sounded happy about Lori coming to live with her.

"I can't afford to pay you much for awhile," Lori said.

"You won't pay me at all," Nada said with a smile. "Your folks are so good to me, and I'll enjoy having you here. Let me show you around."

"Thank you Lord, and thank you Nada," Lori said aloud.

Lori followed Nada through her two bedroom apartment located in the middle of the motel complex. Nada showed Lori the upstairs.

"This is really nice, that king-sized bed sure looks comfortable," Lori said. Lori was thinking that the upstairs was even nicer than the downstairs. There were several large windows overlooking large trees and the motel area. Lori would have a lot of room for privacy.

That day Lori received another letter from Ben. She answered the letter by telling him all about her new job and new place to live. She received a letter back. Ben congratulated her on her new teaching job and encouraged her for the days to come.

Although Lori had a nice place to live, she desperately wanted a place of her own. Before she moved to Dannon, she drove over to Aunt Martha's and went to the small building where her furniture was stored. "Oh Lord, please let me soon have a place of my own so I can use this furniture again," Lori prayed. She looked at the hide-a-bed that Tim had lain on when he did not feel well. A feeling of sadness and depression settled upon her. "Oh Lord, help me to get over these memories," Lori prayed.

On the way back to her mother's house, Lori decided to drive into town rather than turning into her mother's place. She drove up and down several streets. Lori was driving down Main Street when she noticed an abandoned, battered, moble home located behind a cafe. There was a fence around the property and the weeds were high all around the house. The front door of the house was slightly open.

Lori parked her car on the street just north of the mobile home. She looked around to see if anyone was watching her. There was no one in sight. Lori opened the wire gate and closed it behind her. She walked up the wobbly steps leading to the door. Although the door was partly open, it was hard to push open enough for Lori to get through because of the dirt that had blown around the door. When she stepped inside, the dust and smell of urine made her cough.

Lori soon forgot the stench as she explored the large, old trailer. It had a small entrance with book shelves. The entrance opened up to a small dining room in one direction and a nice-sized living room in the other direction. Lori walked across the living room and found a small bedroom and a nice bathroom with a pretty sink and enclosed shower.

Lori crossed the living room in the other direction. Back of the living room was a nice-sized kitchen full of hardwood cabinets. There was an eating bar on the north side next to the dining room. The dining room was joined by a small hall. There was a small bedroom, a nice-sized bathroom with two vanities, and a large bedroom leading off the hall. There was space for a washer and dryer in the hall next to the back door. All the windows were floor length.

Lori was excited as she saw the home the way it could look. "Oh Lord, I want this home and I'll work very hard to fix it up, Could I please," Lori prayed.

Lori hurried on to Elizabeth's. The next day she made several telephone calls to find out who owned the mobile home. Lori discovered it had been bought from the original owners by a family that had moved it with a tractor, without paying any money on it, and without the owner's even knowing about it.

The second family had lived in it several months and never made their payments. They had suddenly moved into another state, declared Bankruptcy, and clamed the mobile home as their residence. The family had even left a small dog locked up in the trailer when they left. It had been two weeks before someone discovered the dog and had to tear up the front door to get the dog out.

The home had been tied up in court for over two years.

Lori called the finance company that now owned the home. "Yes, it's for sale," Mrs. Dole said. "We're asking five-thousand dollars for it, as is, with no guarantees on anything," she explained.

"I would like to buy it but I don't have any money," Lori said. "I do have a teaching job there in Dannon, though," she added.

"I think we could make you a loan for the house," Mrs. Dole said.

Lori took Elizabeth and Arther downtown to see the mobile home. Arther just shook his head and said, "It doesn't look like much, Lori, but if anyone can fix it up, you can."

"Oh Lori, I hate to see you take on another mess to clean up, you have fixed up so many houses already," Elizabeth said. "I remember when we went to your farm bankruptcy sale and I saw the large, old farm house you fixed up, just going to waste, and I just wanted to cry for you," she said. "And this isn't much to work with."

"But mother, this is my only chance of getting my own home again," Lori tried to explain.

Lori took her sister, Bonnie, to see the mobile home. Bonnie almost cried when she saw the terrible mess. All she could say was, "No Lori, no!"

Bonnie had always had a nice place to live so she could not understand.

Lori borrowed eight-thousand dollars from the finance company so she would have enough money to hire a carpenter to fix the floor, and do things she could not do. She also needed enough money for new carpets for the whole trailer. Lori planned to put down Kangaback carpets that were pre-stretched. She could do this herself, but the trailer was large enough to need a thousand dollars worth of carpet.

Elizabeth insisted on signing the loan papers with Lori so the payments would not be so high. Lori had a hard time finding someone to move the trailer the fifty miles to Dannon. The people she hired took over a month to do the job.

Lori moved in with Nada. The motel was an interesting place to live. It seemed that Nada collected stray people like some people collect stray cats and dogs.

Carlos had been a high-school buddy of Nada's son. He had come home from the Viet Nam War with several problems. He was usually drinking and could not hold down a job. Nada had given him a home down in the basement of the apartment.

Nada's son, Ryan, was a handsome thirty-year-old who worked at one of the local cattle feed yards. He and his wife, Flo, lived in one of the motel rooms. They ate with Nada and Flo did nothing to help in the kitchen, or anywhere else. She had other men around while Ryan was at work.

Flo's teenage brother, Tom, was also living in the basement. He had quit school and gotten in trouble with the law. Nada had paid to get him out of jail, and Tom was to work off the debt by doing odd jobs around the motel.

There was also one permanent resident in one of the motel rooms. Steve was a six-foot, four-inch, quiet man who dressed in western clothes. He was older than Lori and spent a lot of time sitting in the lobby reading newspapers. Steve had been recovering from a terrible accident and was not working yet. He was so quiet that Lori hardly noticed that he was there.

Lori had rushed from her new living quarters into pre-school meetings and school. She was thankful for her good job and excited about getting back into teaching after four years. She enjoyed the teacher's meetings. There were fifty teachers on the large high school staff, and only five of them were women. They were some of the nicest people Lori had ever met. Lori's Aid was a tiny, cranky, older, crippled woman, who talked like she hated kids.

After two days of teacher's meetings, it was time for the kids to show up. Lori was up early Monday morning, and at school early. There was already fresh donuts and coffee in the teacher's lounge.

Lori's knees almost buckled as she caught her first feeling of the reality of her new job. She walked into her room and was greeted by twenty-five large, young men who did not want to be there. They looked at Lori like she was some kind of freak. It was a drastic change from being greeted by sixth graders anxious to be back in school. There were a few nasty remarks and giggles. Lori felt like she wanted to run.

"Shut up and sit down!" someone shouted with authority from the back of the room.

Lori turned around and saw her tiny aid, Mrs. Ming. The students scowled, but sit down. Lori proceeded to explain what class this would be, the material they would cover, what she expected them to do to pass the class, and what kind of behavior she expected from everyone. She opened up the textbook and tried to share some of her knowledge with the group.

Most of the boys were Mexicans, but it did not make any difference to Lori what nationality they happened to be. She had always worked with some Mexicans and loved them dearly. In fact, she would have adopted Rosita if things had not gone wrong.

With Mrs. Ming keeping order, the first three classes finally passed. Lori and her helper were ready for their planning period. They took a break with another donut and cup of coffee. Lori went home at noon to eat a sandwich and take a smoke break. She did not want her students to see her smoke because she wanted to be a good role model. "If only my students could realize what a slave-driving habit smoking really is," Lori told herself.

The afternoon classes were not as difficult as the morning classes. There were fewer students and Lori ended up with four girls to teach. Two of the girls were sophomores with no visible handicaps, and were "street wise". Betty was a handicapped girl that walked by swinging herself on crutches. Sue was a senior with such a nervous condition that her parents had to take her out of school for half of the previous year. One class was going to be a great challenge where several students were working on all levels of Math at the same time.

Lori knew most of the kids by the end of the first week. Mr. Rosa was right, she soon loved every one of them.

The second week Lori came home from work to find police surrounding the motel complex. When she started to get out of the station wagon, she was approached by a police officer.

"What are you doing here, lady?" the lawman asked gruffly.

"I live here," Lori answered. "What's going on?" she asked.

"One of the high-school girls has been reported missing. We think Tom has her hidden somewhere around here since they have been seeing each other," the officer explained. "I guess you can go in, but don't try going anywhere until all this is over."

Lori went up to her room to work on her next day's plans. The police left after they found Tom's girlfriend hiding under one of the beds in the basement. Tom was almost arrested again since he was on probation. He promised the officers that he would "shape up" to stay out of jail.

Before the second week was over, Lori joined some other teachers that were traveling forty miles to another town to take graduate courses in Special Education. Her days and evenings were busy, and very stressful.

"Lori, would you mind taking care of the motel for me this weekend?" Nada asked. "Ryan is working long hours and I don't think his wife could handle it. I have a chance to go to the mountains to see my daughter. Since I don't drive, I hate to pass up the opportunity."

"I'll be glad to, if you think I can do a good enough job," Lori replied.

"You'll do just fine, and if you need any help, Carlos will be here," Nada said.

Nada had already left by the time Lori came home from school Friday evening. She changed her clothes and curled up in a large chair in the motel lobby with one of her college textbooks. She could see any customer that might come in from where she was sitting.

Lori had read several chapters when Steve came in. "Lori, would you have dinner with me tonight. This is my birthday and I'm all alone," Steve said, softly.

I wonder if he really expects me to believe that, Lori was thinking. "I'm sorry, but I can't leave the motel since Nada is not here," Lori answered.

"If I go across the street and bring back some fried chicken, will you eat here with me?" Steve asked.

"I guess that would be all right," Lori answered.

Lori and Steve had just finished their meal in the lobby when Carlos came in. He was terribly upset. "We've got to find Tom right away!" Carlos exclaimed. "His girlfriend is missing again, and if the police find her with Tom, he'll go to jail and Nada will lose the thousand dollars she put up for his bail. I think they might have gone to a rodeo in Trenton, twenty miles east of here. We have to get to them before the police do."

"You stay here and watch the motel since you don't have a car, and I'll go see if I can find them," Lori ordered.

"You better take me with you in case there's trouble," Steve said.

"Well, all right," Lori replied. "I sure don't want Nada to lose her money. She deserves more than that for helping Tom."

Lori ran and crawled into the station wagon. Steve jumped into the passenger side. Lori drove as fast as she dared without breaking the speed limit. The rodeo was over by the time Lori and Steve reached Trenton. The lights were out and no cars were around the arena. Lori turned the car around and headed back toward Dannon.

"I think I know where Tom's folks live here in Trenton," Steve said. "Let's stop by and see if they are there." Steve had Lori to pull into an old, run-down complex of small buildings that had once been a motel. Steve followed Lori up to the door of the only building that had lights on.

A lady, with long stringy hair and old dress, answered the door and asked them to come in. Lori felt like she had just stepped into the back hills of Kentucky. The people were dressed like hillbillies. There were even rifles leaning against the wall close to the door. But what Lori noticed most of all were the bottles of hard liquor on the table. There was as much booze on the table as there was food. "Have you seen Tom?" she asked.

"He was here a little while ago, but he left to take his girl-friend back to Dannon," the older of the three men answered.

"Thanks," Lori said. She and Steve ran back to the station wagon and rushed back to Dannon.

On the way back, Steve told Lori a little about himself. He and his wife had been in a serious car accident. Steve was injured more than his wife. His wife had blamed him for the accident and sued for a divorce while Steve was still in the hospital. Steve had survived the accident and the divorce and was almost well. Lori told Steve a little about herself: her two divorces, and her low opinion of men.

"I have been through three divorces," Steve said. "The first one was my fault. I wanted out of the marriage even though we had nine kids. The second one left me to go back to her first husband because she said he was making more money than I was.

The third one got the divorce because she said I was trying to kill her when we had our accident. I was hurt a lot worse than she was, but she plans to get a lot of money from my insurance company. She claims she is handicapped for the rest of her life and can't work because of a back injury, although she is still able to bowl. She has a court order where I can't even drive down the street where our home is located. She only let me have three changes of clothes when she kicked me out. I didn't even know what was going on when the police came into the house to arrest me. I didn't know she had seen a lawyer while I was still in the hospital."

"And, I thought I had problems," Lori sighed.

By the time Lori and Steve reached the motel, Tom had taken his girlfriend home and was back down in the basement. There had been no customers coming into the motel that evening, and everyone was ready to call it a day and "turn in". Lori called Tom up to the main floor of the complex and gave him a lecture on how he needed to straighten up and show some appreciation for what Nada had done for him. Lori went upstairs ready for a good night's rest.

Lori felt restless from the stresses of the day. She did not feel sleepy. Lori felt too tired to study, so she decided to write Ben again before she went to bed. She always enjoyed his letters, and she always felt better after telling Ben her problems although they had never met. "Sometimes, it's easier to talk to people you don't know," Lori told herself. She told Ben about the episodes of the day and added, "I don't want to get to know Steve any better. I don't feel like I can ever trust another man. I have been hurt enough, but if I ever change my mind, and start dating someone, I'll let you know," Lori wrote. As Lori was going to sleep, she suddenly realized how much Steve reminded her of her beloved, late father. Her father had also been tall and quiet.

The weekend passed quickly with Lori visiting a lot with Steve in the lobby. He had such a quiet, gentle manner that Lori found Steve easy to talk to.

"Lori, they are on the way here with your trailer!" Nada exclaimed the minute Lori came in from school. Nada was almost as excited as Lori.

Lori drove over to the nice mobile home park to the space she had rented. The trailer was not there yet. She looked over the space she had chosen. Just back of the space was a white, old silage tower, and behind it was a small creek with trees. Her bedroom windows would face this pleasant, country scene. Lori thought about going to meet the trailer, but she did not know what route they had taken to get to Dannon. She waited impatiently at the trailer space. It seemed like her home would never get there.

Just before dark, the men arrived with the trailer. They had had a lot of trouble with their truck and wanted Lori to pay them more for their extra time. The men did not bring the old skirting for the trailer that Lori had paid them to bring. Lori had to threaten them until they promised they would send a pickup truck back with the skirting. The railroad ties that went with the trailer had been thrown into the living room, mud and all. The next day the pickup brought the skirting, and instead of putting it on the way Lori had paid them to do, they just dumped it on the property.

Lori hired a man to repair the trailer and put on the skirting. He was highly recommended by people in Dannon. Charlie did not like to work and he kept asking Lori for more money to get things done.

The trailer was finally tied down and Lori could start working on the inside. She started by painting the ceilings white again. She was busy painting in the small front bedroom when Steve came by to see how she was doing.

Steve always looked like a male model with his tall, slender body, and pressed clothes. Lori was embarrassed on how she looked because of her plump body, messy hair, and white paint on her nose.

Steve sit down in the old, black, leather, lounge chair that had come with the trailer. He watched Lori paint for awhile. "Lori, can I help you fix up this place?" Steve asked softly.

"God knows I need help, but I can't afford to pay you anything, and I don't want any strings attached, if you know what I mean," Lori answered.

"I believe that the only way from being hurt is to not get too close to anyone."

"I don't expect you to pay me. It has been several months since I have done anything, and I think helping you with this job might help me get back into the land of the living," Steve replied. "And, I don't want any strings attached either."

"I guess you can help me then," Lori said.

Steve was back in a short time wearing old, but clean and neat, clothes. He was able to paint the ceiling without standing on a chair. The ceilings were finished in a couple of evenings, and the next few nights were spent oiling the paneled walls and kitchen cabinets with Danish Oil.

Lori and Steve became good friends and had a lot of fun working together. In October it was time for Lori to stand before the judge and listen to his decree so her divorce could be final.

"I'm taking you to the court house today," Steve said when Lori came home after school.

"You don't have to," Lori answered.

"I want to," Steve said. "I know it is a good time to have a friend waiting for you when you go through something like this."

Steve drove Lori to the court house. Lori entered the same court room where she and Hollis had finished their marriage, and Tim had been given the one years probation. Lori tried not to think about the past.

"Mrs. Lori Jones, it is the decision of this court to grant you a divorce from Tim Jones without his consent, since the second party cannot be located," the judge said. "Is there anything you want for a settlement?" he asked.

"Yes, I request to drop the name of Jones and take back the name of Wallace. Wallace is the name my sons and the name on my Bachelor's degree. I want my name to officially be Wallace again," Lori answered.

"Granted," the judge said. "What about property settlement?" he asked.

"The only thing I can ask for is 10% of Mr. Jones's profits from his health products company, since we were pardoners and my family invested a lot of money into it, providing he can ever be found," Lori answered.

"Granted," the judge said.

Lori walked away from the court house in a daze. It took such a short time to end a chapter of eight and a half years of her life, yet she felt that she had just been freed from a "life sentence" in prison. She signed deeply as she crawled into Steve's car. "My name is Lori Wallace, now," Lori said. "But, I'll still have my students call me Mrs. Jones. I think it would be too confusing to have them call me something different in the middle of the year," she said, with a sob.

"Everything will be all right," Steve said and took Lori out to celebrate over a nice meal.

When Lori returned from dinner, there was a large arrangement of fresh flowers waiting for her in the lobby of the motel. The card on it said, "Congratulations, from Mitch and Staci."

Carlos came in drunk about that time. "Gee Whize, I didn't know that people celebrate over something like that," he said and stumbled on down to the basement.

Lori just had to laugh.

On Halloween Lori dressed up to show her students they could take advantage of a school day of looking weird and having fun. She wore an old sweat suit, funny hat, and painted a mustache on her upper lip. It was a fun day although Mrs. Ming thought Lori was a little ridiculous.

Steve took Lori out to dinner that night. They were acting silly and having a lot of fun. It seemed that a lot of people were staring at them. "I guess they are jealous because we are having more fun than they are," Lori said, laughing. On the way back to the motel, Lori realized that the reason people were staring was because she looked like a man and they thought that she and Steve were probably homosexuals. She felt a little embarrassed.

Elizabeth came to Dannon one day when Lori was in school. She used all kinds of cleaners, and when Lori got back to the trailer that evening, the sinks, stove, stools, tub, and showers looked like new. "Steve helped me," Elizabeth said.

Lori went back to Aunt Martha's little house to pick up her vacuum cleaner. The next week she vacuumed the trailer, and she and Steve started pulling up the old carpets and pads. When they started with the first carpet, dust flew everywhere. "I hope there isn't any urine in the dust and carpet," Steve said through the flying dirt.

"I'm afraid there is," Lori replied.

Although Steve and Lori washed their hands with soap each time they handled the old carpet, their hands became infected. Lori was impressed by Steve's good nature over the whole mess.

One Sunday Lori was working at the trailer. Steve came by. "Will you go to church with me, Lori," he asked.

"I'd like to, but I have too much work to do," Lori answered.

"Lori, you have to put God first in your life, even above this home of yours," Steve said. "Get ready and go to church with me this morning and I'll help you the rest of the day."

Lori felt ashamed. There had been a time that she had put God first in her life. There had been so many things gone wrong and the months had gone by, and she had just been giving the Lord her "left-over" time. Lori always paid the Lord's tithe off her gross income, but did she think that was all God wanted? She remembered a scripture that said something like "If God isn't Lord of all, then He isn't Lord at all."

"I'll go back to the motel and be ready in thirty minutes," Lori said.

Steve was waiting in the lobby when Lori finished cleaning up. "Where do you go to church?" Lori asked.

"I have been going to the First Christian Church here in town, but we'll go anywhere you want to go," Steve answered.

"I like Full-Gospel churches," Lori said. "I know the minister that has the Full-Gospel church south of town," she said. "Would you like to go there?" Lori asked.

"That would be fine. I know Brother David, too," Steve replied.

"Brother David was preaching the night my ex-husband, Tim, received the baptism of the Holy Ghost. Tim later started a church. It's unreal how much his Christianity went downhill in just four short years," Lori said.

"That's a lesson to only look to Jesus for leadership," Steve said.

Everyone at the church was surprised to see Lori and Steve come in together, but they were warm and friendly. From that day on, Steve and Lori went to Brother David's church on Sundays and to the First Christian Church on Wednesday night for Bible Study.

Each evening Lori watched Steve as they pulled up the old, filthy carpet. He was so neat, gentle, and strong. Steve and Lori were pulling out the carpet in the small bathroom when there hands touched for the first time. Lori felt her heart pounding. "There is no way two people can fall in love over a bathroom stool," Lori told herself.

Lori felt weak. "Oh Lord, please don't let me get hurt again," she prayed silently. Their hands were still touching. Lori looked up into Steve's soft blue eyes. His pleasant smile always made Lori feel safe. Before she knew it, Lori was in Steve's long arms. His embrace was soft and tender. Lori felt so happy for a minute.

"Leave her alone, you dirty, old man," Steve said loudly to himself. "I'm sorry Lori," he whispered.

"Me, too, but it was my fault as much as yours," Lori said.

"Maybe I need to stop working here; I'm beginning to think too much of you," Steve said.

"Maybe you should, but I don't want you to," Lori replied. "It would be so lonely if you weren't here. I need your friendship and your help. It's so nice to be with someone close to my age after spending my days with students younger than my own children."

Lori had a lot of trouble with her students the next day. That evening, nothing she and Steve tried to do on the house had gone right. Lori finally said, "Steve, let me show you what this place is going to look like someday." She dug through a box of things that she had brought from Aunt Martha's until she found the beautiful table cloth her mother had given her one year for Christmas. Lori put the table cloth on the old dining room table that Steve had fixed. The table looked so pretty that it gave them both the boost they needed to keep on working.

Steve and Lori were working and laughing when Lori found herself in Steve's arms again. This time there was no apologizing. Lori needed Steve as much as he needed her, and she was too much in love to back out now.

The kitchen had a nice, tile floor, but Lori had to order enough carpet to cover the rest of the trailer. She ordered white carpets. Steve and Lori scraped and scrubbed the floors. The urine smell was finally gone. It was so exciting to start putting in the new carpet. The white carpet looked elegant against the dark wood paneled walls.

Steve was very particular in measuring the rooms and carpet. When Lori cut the pieces, Steve would somehow make them fit. Steve worked most days while Lori was in school. One evening, when Lori came into the trailer, she was pleasantly surprised to see that Steve and Elizabeth had put up some old, but very nice, living room drapes. They were drapes that Elizabeth had replaced in her large house. The drapes were almost the same color as the carpet.

"There're beautiful, mother," Lori managed to say.

Elizabeth had brought Lori's key-board with her that day. That evening when Steve and Lori were ready to call it a day, Lori took the key-board and played some Christian choruses. She was trying to remember some of the songs she used to sing and play. Lori looked over at Steve. She saw a giant of a man holding up his huge hands in praises to God. Tears were rolling freely down his cheeks. Lori knew that the Lord was the first love of his life. Maybe that is why he could love her so deeply. In that moment, Lori felt a deeper love for this man than she had ever felt for anyone.

"I didn't know I played that poorly," Lori said with a smile.

"You play beautifully, dear. It makes me feel God's peace all over me and I can't help but cry," Steve said.

Steve and Lori went back to the motel that evening without caressing.

Lori brought the old, gold velvet drapes, and the red velvet ones that she had used at the old farmhouse from Aunt Martha's. Steve helped Lori hang the gold drapes in the front bedroom and the red ones in the large, back bedroom. "I think everything is ready for me to move in, and it looks so beautiful," Lori said. "Thank you Lord, and thank you Steve."

Steve took Lori into his arms and kissed her.

"You can use one of my stock trailers to move your furniture," Arthur said.

It was almost time for Thanksgiving. Lori was getting ready to go after her furniture. Steve was waiting for her in the parking area of the motel. She looked out of her upstairs window. There was Steve in his western clothes and hat. Lori thought he was the most handsome guy she had ever known. "How can I be so happy again?" Lori asked herself as she ran down the stairs to meet her love.

Steve was not feeling well that day, but there were enough relatives to load and unload the furniture without his help. Elizabeth and Bonnie followed the horse trailer to Dannon to help Lori move in.

Every piece of Lori's old furniture fit perfectly in Lori's new home. All the interior colors were just right. The old furniture even looked newer. Lori's old mobile home looked like a showplace. Bonnie gave Lori a beautiful silk flower arrangement to set on the large shelf in the entrance. "I could never believe that this house could look like this!" she exclaimed.

The outside of the trailer looked pretty bad. Lori thought she might could scrub the metal and make it look better. She took a small tooth brush and tried scrubbing a small area. Steve started laughing. "It's the first time I ever saw anyone scrubbing the outside of a house with a tooth brush," he chuckled.

Lori started laughing too when she realized how ridicules she must have looked.

"At least you tried, dear," Steve said still laughing. "I don't think anything will help but a new paint job, and I'll help you buy the paint."

During the mild winter days that followed, Lori and Steve painted the outside of trailer. Steve installed the lights on the front of the house. Lori was so anxious for summer to come because she and Steve could be married during her summer vacation. Steve was the last "luxury" the house needed.

Things were going better at school, except for a few problems. One of Lori's students was on drugs. He came into class a few times and passed out letting his head drop on his desk. The third time he did this, Lori called Mr. Rosa to come and get him.

The next morning, when Lori was driving to school, she thought it was extra cold and drafty in the station wagon. She checked her window, then turned around and looked into the back seat. Someone had busted out her two back windows. She talked to her students about it, but no one seemed to know anything.

The next morning, the station wagon had been pounded with rocks that were still beside the car. That night someone threw rocks at the trailer. Lori reported the problem and the police drove past her place several times each evening, but they were never able to catch anyone doing the vandalism.

On Friday, some of the Mexican boys found out that the boy on drugs was responsible for the vandalism. They came and ask Lori if they could "take some skin off of him for hurting their teacher".

"Two wrongs do not make a right, but I do appreciate you guys caring about what happens to me," Lori replied.

Mr. Rosa called the boy's parents to school for a conference. He asked Lori if she would talk to the couple since she had been around kids on drugs. "I'll do what I can," Lori told Mr. Rosa.

Mrs. Ming took over the classes so Lori could talk to the mother and step-father of the boy in trouble. "Maybe I can get them to pay me for some of my damage," Lori was thinking while she walked down to the conference room.

Lori talked to the parents. They had tried their best with their son, and did not know how to help him. "We locked him up in the back bedroom of our mobile home to keep him from getting another 'fix'," the father explained. Timmy tore up the back of our trailer just to get out and get high again."

Lori listened to the couple's problems and did not have the heart to tell them about the damage Timmy had done to her car and house. "They have problems enough," Lori told herself. She tried to encourage them and told them to seek God for help before returning to her classroom.

There was a small Italian boy in Lori's sophomore class. Chico had muscles and seemed to be confident in his abilities. He was an average student and had caused no trouble. "Chico lives with his grandmother, who rules the entire Italian population in Dannon," Mrs. Ming said.

A few students quit school again to roam the streets. Bobby came to school with one side of his face peeled off. "What on earth happened to you?" Lori asked.

"I just wanted to see what would happen to me if I jumped from the back of a pickup going sixty miles an hour," Bobby said. "It was fun!" he exclaimed, laughing.

Lori tried to tell Bobby that he should not try to destroy the only body he would ever have. Mrs. Ming shrugged her shoulders and told Lori she was just wasting her time.

Before the week was over, Mr. Rosa called Lori on the intercom. "Mrs. Jones, we are sending you a new student this morning. His name is Larry Brown," he said.

"Thank you for letting me know," Lori replied.

Lori was starting class when the new boy walked in. Chico shouted, "Larry!"

Larry shouted, "Chico!"

Before Lori could move, the two boys were at each other's throats. It was easy to see that they hated each other enough to kill. Chico banged his heavy textbook against Larry's head. Larry picked himself up off the floor and swung his fist into Chico's face. Blood was splattering everywhere.

Lori did the only thing she could think of. She pushed herself between the two young men.

Larry started to swing at Lori when one of the Mexican students shouted, "I don't think you want to do that!" He, too, had his fists in the air.

Both students stared at Lori for a minute and dropped their fists. Lori ushered them to the nurse's office to be checked and washed up.

"Now, let's get busy with our lessons," Lori said loudly.

"And, you better pay attention!" Mrs. Ming shouted, pounding her crutches.

Lori and Mrs. Ming were glad when it was time for their break. They hurried to the teacher's lounge to relax with a cup of coffee.

"I hear that you laid your life on the line for your job this morning," one of the men teachers said with an understanding smile.

"I guess I did a foolish thing," Lori replied. "It might have helped if Mr. Rosa had told me that Larry has just been released from reform school, and that he and Chico had had trouble before."

Lori knew that many of her students were having sex so she found a good movie on the consequences of young sex. The story was about two high-school kids that had sex on their only date. Gina ended up pregnant. Carl was dating another girl in school and demanded that Gina get an abortion. Gina's mother was a single mom and knew she could not take care of another mouth to feed. She also demanded that Gina get an abortion.

Gina was determined to have her baby. Gina's mother kicked her out and Gina went to live in an old garage. Carl felt guilty and got a job to help support her, and finally moved in with her. Gina was sick most of the time and the kids fought continually.

The baby boy was finally born. Gina and Carl took care of the baby the best they could, but they were still fighting. Carl moved back home. One day he was in class when Gina brought the baby in to him and left. Carl could not find Gina. His folks would not help him take care of the baby. He had to take the baby to class and even to the senior prom.

Instead of going to college on a musical scholarship, the way he had planned, Carl got a job working in an ice cream store. Gina finally came back and they were trying to work things out, but they were poor and unhappy.

Lori finished the movie and asked, "What did you think about that?"

"If my girlfriend wouldn't get an abortion when I wanted her to, I'd kill her!" one student exclaimed. He sounded serious.

"I think you really would," both sophomore girls said, shocked.

After some discussion, Lori felt like the movie had done some good, at least for the two sophomore girls. She felt like they would make better choices in the future.

Lori had one very tall freshman that loved to make faces at Sue, the girl with the nervous problem, and make her cry.

"Sue, I can't watch Gary every minute, so the next time he makes a face at you, make one back at him," Lori said one day. "It will be like passing an important test when you can do that and laugh at him," she explained. Sue was eventually able to do that.

One day Betty came into the classroom swinging herself on her crutches. "I'm going to kill myself!" Betty said in tearful anger.

"Why!" Lori asked.

"My boyfriend just left me and I don't have anything to live for!" Betty shouted.

It was the last class of the day and all the other students were somewhere else. "Betty, I'm going down to the teacher's lounge and buy some pop and candy. When I get back we're going to celebrate you getting rid of that guy. He wasn't good enough for you, anyway," Lori said. She rushed to the lounge and brought back two Pepsis and two candy bars. "Are you ready to celebrate?" Lori asked Betty.

"Sure!" Betty shouted.

Lori told Betty some jokes and anything funny she could think of. She soon had Betty laughing so hard that Betty wet her pants. Lori had to take her home early to change her clothes.

Lori and Steve went to the football games and Lori sold tickets at the gate when it was her turn. The extra money came in handy. Steve always helped Lori with her outside duties. They ate each evening meal together, either at the mobile home or Steve would take Lori out to a restaurant to eat. They shopped together, and were always together. Lori was concerned about her students, but she had never been so happy when she was with Steve. He was peaceful, a Christian, and so much fun.

Chapter IX

Another Bump

Mrs. Jones, Mrs. Jones, there's a fight in front of the school!" Betty shouted swinging on her crutches into the classroom. "Ramon is in a terrible fight with one of the football players!" she screamed.

Lori took the time for Betty to lead her to where Ramon was fighting. In front of the school building Lori saw a bloody mess. The football player looked twice as large as Lori's Ramon. Ramon was fighting his hardest and loosing. There were several men teachers on the scene before Lori got there so she let them stop the fight. Lori did not have the nerve to step between these two, anyway.

The assistant principal and PE teacher pulled the two angry students apart and the crowd of students soon separated the two young men. The two students were ordered to separate ends of the building to restrooms to wash up for afternoon classes. Ramon was sent on to the nurses room because he had several lacerations, two black eyes, and his nose was bleeding from both sides.

Lori followed Ramon into the nurse's office. The nurse had not returned from lunch. Ramon slouched down on the cot. He looked defeated in spirit as well as body.

Lori took some soft towels and begin to wipe blood from her student's face. Betty was standing in the doorway. "Betty, please go on to class and tell Mrs. Ming that I'll be there as soon as the nurse returns," Lori instructed.

Lori turned her attention to her beloved, battered student. "Ramon, I know you had to fight, no matter how unfair it was. I know your friends were watching you, and you had no choice, even though you knew you couldn't win. In your world, I know you just couldn't walk away. I think I understand," Lori said.

Ramon smiled at her and nodded his head yes. Both of his eyes were almost swollen shut and he was holding a big wad of tissues under his nose. Ramon's nose looked crooked like it might be broken. The nurse came in and checked Ramon. "His nose is broken, but I think that is the worst of his injuries," she said.

Ramon was relaxing a little, and the nurse was working on his eyes when Lori started to class. She used some paper towels and cold water in the teacher's lounge restroom to try and get some splatters of blood out of her white blouse. She caught herself crying over this "street kid" and his mixed-up world. Lori used the wet paper towels to wipe her eyes.

Lori felt like she had already had a full day at school. She would rather go home and throw herself into Steve's arms for comfort, but instead she forced a smile, entered her classroom, and took over her class from Mrs. Ming.

"He's not worth all that attention!" Mrs. Ming exclaimed, frowning at Lori.

"I feel that he is," Lori replied. Although Mrs. Ming seemed to have no feeling for the students, and Lori loved them dearly, she knew she would have trouble controlling her students without Mrs. Ming's help. "I guess together, we are doing a fairly good job," Lori told herself.

Lori begain to work on her yearly Christmas letter to send to all her friends and relatives. She had been so much in love with Steve, and the days had gone by so quickly that she had forgotten to write Ben and tell him that she was dating someone. Lori decided to send Ben one of her Christmas letters to let him know that she had a boy-friend in her life. She wrote a poem to cover the events of the year. She mentioned her divorce from Tim at the beginning, her appreciation for all the support her family had given her, and about the tall, cowboy that had helped her remodel her new home. In the poem Lori said that she expected this "cowboy" to be around a long, long time.

"This should let Ben know that I've started a new exciting life," Lori told herself. She mailed about one-hundred copies of the letter, including one to Ben.

"Steve, it's only two weeks until Christmas vacation. What would you think about having a Christmas party for my students next week? I couldn't handle it without you. I was thinking that they don't think they can have any fun without drugs, booze, and sex. I'd like to give them a good, clean, fun evening," Lori said.

"I'll do anything I can to help you, dear," Steve said as he took Lori into his arms for another embrace

"I knew you would before I even asked," Lori said, hugging Steve's large neck. Steve was so much fun, and yet had the same assuring calmness that her father always had. It made Lori feel so safe, loved, and comfortable. Steve made Lori feel like a princes. "I'll not be hurt this time," she told herself again.

Lori made a Christmas invitation that told the place, time, and rules of the party. She took it to Mr. Rosa for his approval.

"Are you sure you want to do this?" Mr. Rosa asked.

"Yes, Steve is going to help me and I think he can handle any trouble. And, I want to have the freshmen one night, the sophomores the next night, and the junior and seniors the last night. That way we won't have so many problems at once," Lori explained.

"Good luck, and you have my blessing," Mr. Rosa said with a smile. "And thanks for caring about these kids. You've been around them long enough to know what you're doing."

"Mrs. Ming, Steve and I are giving Christmas parties for the students next week," Lori said. "Would you like to help us?" she asked.

"Not on your life!" Mrs. Ming exclaimed.

"Would you like to come to the parties?" Lori asked.

"No, I wouldn't! I don't even want these kids to know where I live! We live in the country and I don't want any of them to know where!"

Mrs. Ming exclaimed. "You're not very smart letting them know where you live either."

Lori told her classes about the party and handed out the written invitations for the students' parents to sign so they would be eligible to attend.

"Will there be dames and booze?" one of the boys asked.

"No, and nothing else either, and we're going to have a good time without things like that," Lori answered.

Lori had just dismissed her sophomores when one tall student came up to her desk. "Can I talk to you for a minute?" he asked.

Lori shook her head yes.

Sam waited for the other students to leave. When the room was empty, he asked, "Mrs. Jones, can a dead person hurt you?"

"Sam, what have you gotten yourself into?" Lori asked.

"Well, last night me and some my buddies went with some older guys that we didn't know very well. They took us to a cemetery and told us to help dig up this stiff. We started digging and when we hit the casket, me and my buddies got screared and ran. Then two nights later, me and two of my buddies followed these guys to this old house. We peaked through a window and saw them doing some strange things and we saw a human skull on the table. They looked up and saw us and came running out of the house. We ran to our car and locked the doors. We started to drive away when the other guys grabbed one side of our small car and almost turned us over. They finally had to drop us and we ran for our lives. They belong to a club. Every time they get a promotion in the club, they have another earring put in further up on their ear," Sam said.

Lori tried not to look shocked.

"Do you know how guys get into the club?" Sam asked.

Lori tried to stay calm. "No, Sam, what do they have to do?" she asked.

"They hang the guy until he turns blue, then they cut him down. We know of at least two guys they didn't cut down quick enough and the dudes died," Sam answered.

"Sam, these guys are into devil worship. But God is the one to worship, and He is more powerful than the devil, and as my grandmother used to tell me, never fear the dead, it's the living that can hurt you," Lori said. "How on earth can these guys get away with murder?" she asked.

"I knew that's what you'd say about God," Sam replied with a smile. "The police said that both deaths were suicide. I gota run now, thanks."

Lori could hardly believe that Sam had confided in her. He was the one who had been sent home from school twice for wearing T-shirts with cursing and nasty pictures on them. He was the one who had told Lori that he hated school and that he also hated all teachers. Lori had told Sam, "You might hate me, but that won't make me hate you or keep me from caring about you." "Oh Lord, help him please," Lori prayed silently as the next group of students came in for class.

That evening Lori went to the police station and talked to an officer she had met while the police were watching her house.

"Yes, we know a little about the demonic activities around here, but we need some new laws to help us fight 'far out' things like these," the officer said. "I know a little about one of the deaths the kid was talking about. They found the teenager in a closet in his bedroom hanging by a rope. Even though his feet were dragging the floor, they called the death suicide."

"Thanks for the info," Lori said and went on home. She and Steve had been praying for her students every night, now they knew of more things to pray about.

"I need each of you students to bring a gift that is valued around five-dollars, and it needs to be wrapped. We'll serve pizza and home-made candy. You kids can bring something to snack on if you want to. There will be no booze, or anything else that is against school regulations. Once you come to the party you can't leave until the party is over," Lori announced to each of her classes.

"I don't think anyone is coming to your party, Mrs. Jones," Joe said.

"I don't expect everyone to be there, but some of you will come and will have a good time, I promise," Lori replied, smiling.

Steve helped Lori decorate the trailer and Christmas tree. The Christmas tree tinsel had static electricity. It seemed that the tree reached out and hugged a person as they passed by. Steve and Lori made chocolate fudge and peanut butter candy and ordered pizzas for each of the three nights. They spent the money they were going to use to buy each other Christmas gifts for the expense of the parties.

About half of the freshman class came. They were quiet when they first arrived, but Steve made them feel more comfortable and the old trailer was soon filled with laughter. The boys brought several sacks of M&Ms and wanted to eat all the brown ones. Someone told Lori that the brown ones were supposed to make them "horny", but there were no real problems. Steve and Lori had set out several table games, but the students had so much fun talking and acting silly that the games were not used.

More than half of the sophomores came. One sophomore boy did some Bill Cosby tapes. He played the tapes, talked along with Cosby, and acted them out. He was so funny, and Lori laughed so hard, that she got a cramp in her leg. Levi did the Cosby tape of the pregnant lady and baby being born. Lori would never have guess that his girl-friend was pregnant and the sixteen-year-old would soon be going through some of the same things that the tape talked about.

Again, everyone was too busy having fun to play any of the games. No one could believe that three hours had passed and it was time for everyone to go home. Steve and Lori had to almost push them out the door, and everyone was still laughing.

The night of the Junior and senior party, Lori and Steve went to pick up Betty. Lori walked up to a dimly-lit house in a poor part of Dannon and knocked on the front door. In a few minutes, Betty opened the door. Lori saw a terribly filthy house and Betty's father sleeping deeply on an old, worn-out couch. Lori remembered that she had been told that Betty's mother had died two years ago and that Betty's father had turned to drinking for comfort.

Lori motioned for Steve to come to the door. Steve picked up Betty's frail body, carried her to the car, and gently put her in the front seat. Betty giggled all the way. Lori carried her crutches and crawled into the back seat. Betty chattered happily all the way to Lori's house. Her chattering reminded Lori of Rosita's chattering.

Steve carried Betty into the trailer. The other students came right after Lori came in. Lori had never seen Betty, and the other students, laugh so much and have so much fun.

"Heah, you're sure a big dude," George told Steve. George was one of the big linemen on the football team. "Heah, how would ya like to arm wrestle me?" George asked.

"I don't think so," Steve said, embarrassed. "I have never fought or wrestled anyone. I almost got into a fight once when I was young, but my size finally scared them away," Steve explained.

"Oh, come on; it won't be like fighten," George begged.

Steve looked at Lori. "What ever you want to do," Lori said.

Steve and George started arm wrestling. All the students watched quietly. Although Steve was larger, it looked like the two were well matched in strength at first. After a few minutes, Steve had no trouble in pushing George's hand back onto the table.

George looked disappointed, then embarrassed. Then he started to grin. George grabbed Steve's hand and shook it proudly. "Congratulations!" he said. The rest of the students cheered.

Steve smiled with relief and said thank you.

The party was soon over and the students were on their way home, Lori hoped. Steve picked up Betty and carried her to the car like she was a prized treasure. Betty held on to Steve's neck and giggled. Steve carried Betty back to her house. Betty opened the unlocked door. It looked like her father had not moved at all the three plus hours they had been gone.

"Thank you for such a wonderful time," Betty said.

Steve and Lori said good-night. "That poor girl," Lori said with a sigh as she and Steve crawled back into the car. They took time to pray about Betty's situation before they went on. Steve drove Lori back to the trailer and helped her clean up the mess.

As usual, Steve waited in the living room until Lori was in bed, then he came in and kissed her good-night. He was always sure that both doors were locked before he left the house to go back to the motel.

"Oh Lord, I'll be go glad when we're married, so we can be together all the time," Lori said. "Make it soon, Lord," she prayed.

The next day when Lori walked down the hall at school, she heard several students telling their friends that they had a lot of fun at "Mrs. Jones's party, even though there wasn't any booze or dames". She heard George talking to some of his friends. "Mrs. Jones has this great big boy-friend dude. He even beat me in arm wrestling," George was saying.

"George sure is a good sport; it's too bad that everyone can't be that way," Lori said to herself.

That evening Steve was waiting at Lori's when she came home from work. "Hello, Dear. How was your day?" Steve asked as he kissed her.

"Better, but I'm anxious for Christmas vacation to start," Lori answered. She noticed that Steve had several pictures in his lap.

"Lori, I want to show you some pictures," Steve said. "This is a wooden plaque that my youngest daughter made for me. All nine of my children's pictures a mounted on it," he explained.

Lori held up the plaque and studied the pictures. Each picture had the name and birth date neatly printed under it. "Six boys and three girls is a nice family," Lori said. "According to these pictures, you and your wife had eight of these kids in ten years!" she exclaimed.

"That's partly because our first babies were twins," Steve explained. "Here are some cowboy pictures of me when I was younger, and one of my old pilot's license, that I want you to keep," Steve said as he held Lori close.

Lori looked at the pictures and license. Steve had been an extra handsome young man. "Thank you, Steve," Lori said. She wiggled out of Steve's arms and sit up where she could look eye to eye. "Steve, I feel that it's very important for you to go see your children as soon as you can," Lori said. "After all, it has been over two years since you've seen eight of them."

"Lori, dear, I love my kids, but it's so hard to go back there. I feel that I've caused them a lot of pain because of the divorce between their mother and me, and I feel that I've made such a mess of my life, that it's just embarrassing to go back," Steve replied.

"Will you go see them if I go with you?" Lori asked.

"Yes, but how can you go?" Steve asked.

"We can go during Christmas vacation. We could wait until summer, but I'll be in college then, and I feel that it's important that you see them soon. Maybe some of them just need to talk to you or something," Lori tried to explain.

"I'll go if you go with me," Steve replied.

Steve and Lori went to Arthur and Elizabeth's for Christmas day. Mitch and his family, Mike, and all of Bonnie's family were there. The family was not happy about Lori having another man in her life; but Steve's big smile and quiet manner was so different from Tim's personality, that the family soon felt at ease with Lori's new friend. Lori did not try to cover up how much she loved this tall, older cowboy.

Arthur and Elizabeth traveled the fifty miles to Dannon to have breakfast with Steve and Lori the day after Christmas. After the kitchen was clean, Arthur and Elizabeth went back home and Steve and Lori started their trip to South Dakota.

Steve had bought a newer Oldsmobile that had a sun roof in it. It was much nicer than Lori's old station wagon. "I can't believe this beautiful, sunny weather for this time of year," Lori said. She took Steve's large hand and squeezed it as Steve drove across part of Kansas. Lori had never felt so happy and free. The warmth of Steve's hand sent tingles through her body.

It was late by the time they crossed Nebraska and entered South Dakota. Their destination was only one hour away. "Steve, tell me the names of your kids, their spouses, and your grandkids so I'll know who they are when I meet them," Lori said.

"Okay dear. Tonight we'll stay with my youngest daughter, Carrie, her husband, Bob, her daughter, Fran, and young son, Bret. Tomorrow we will see my son just younger than the twins, Benny and Kate, and their two daughters, Sparkle and Trina. Then we'll meet the twins, Gene and Dean and their families," Steve said. He was silent. Steve's eyes were intently watching the road in the darkness.

"And . . ." Lori said.

"Don't rush me!" Steve shouted.

Steve had never yelled at Lori before. Lori did not know what to say. The car had suddenly become very quiet.

"I'm sorry, dear," Steve whispered. "I was having trouble remembering all of my new grandchildren's names, and it made me so angry at myself."

Lori just squeezed Steve's hand again. "It's all right, Honey," she said.

It had been dark for several hours by the time Steve and Lori reached Carrie's home in the country. "Oh dad, it's so good to see you again," Carrie said as she hugged her father. "It has been too long since we saw you last."

Steve introduced Lori to the first part of his family. Carrie and Bob made Lori feel "right at home" with their gracious hospitality. Fran was six and Bret was four. They, both, were soon on Lori's lap. Lori had brought her key-board and gave Fran a piano lesson. It was past midnight by the time everyone went to bed. Steve and Lori were given bedrooms at each end of the basement. Lori was sleeping in Bret's bed while he slept on the couch upstairs.

Bob had to leave early the next morning to feed cattle and take care of some farm business. Lori was awakened by Bret and Fran bouncing on her bed. She loved these children. "And they will soon be my grandchildren," Lori told herself.

After a large country breakfast, Steve and Lori said good-bye and drove north to town. Steve showed Lori around the small town where he had attended school and grew up. The Missouri River went through the western side of town. Steve and Lori crossed the long bridge and traveled north again.

"This land on both sides of the river once belonged to my family. The Indians used to live along the river, but when the government put in all the dams, they had to build homes for the Indians on higher ground," Steve said as he pointed in several directions.

Steve drove past a group of run-down houses. "The Indians don't know how to take care of their homes and they don't understand our culture. Most of the electricity was pulled out of the houses the first few weeks the Indians lived in them. Most of the men don't know how to find jobs, and drinking is a terrible problem here," Steve said.

Steve drove to Benny's place in time for dinner. Benny looked a lot like Steve except he had dark hair and was two inches shorter. Kate was short, pretty, quiet, and nice. Lori gave Sparkle, who was ten, a piano lesson on her old piano. She found Kate and Benny's girls easy to love, too. Sparkle thought her granddad was the most important guy in the world. She spent a lot of time on his lap, or just hugging his neck any time he sit down and she could reach it.

Kate was taking care of two mall children. "I'm the only daughter-in-law that doesn't work. That's why I babysit. We don't have as much as the other kids, but I didn't have my two daughters for someone else to raise," Kate explained to Lori.

"You're very wise to feel that way," Lori replied.

The next day Steve and Lori went to Dean's place. On the way Steve slowed down as they passed a farm with a lot of trees. "My first wife lives there with a farmer. They have never gotten married. They just live together. I'd like to stop and ask her forgiveness for leaving her and the kids, but I just don't have the grit to do it," Steve said.

"Maybe this isn't the right time," Lori replied. "Let's pray about it and maybe you'll feel like talking to her before we go home."

Dean's place was just two miles on down the road. "Dean works for his mother's boy-friend," Steve said. "They have just finished building a new, two story house on this farm. Dean did most of the work, but I imagine his boss helped him with the expenses," he said.

No one was home. Steve and Lori toured the nice home. Dean's wife soon came home from the dress shop where she worked in town. "We're all invited to Uncle John's tomorrow for dinner. Most of the family should be there and you can meet the rest of the clan, Lori," Mitzy said.

Dean came in from the field. He was handsome, but he did not look much like Steve. He did have Steve's blonde coloring. Dean was almost a foot shorter than Steve. He was quiet, but glad to see his father.

Again Lori and Steve were given the children's bedrooms while the kids slept on couches. Dean and Mitzy left early the next morning so Mitzy could help Dean's aunt with the large meal.

"I'll try to help you learn names, dear," Steve said. "But, you'll have a lot of people to meet today. You will meet my brother John and his wife Ruby, my other brother Spade and his wife Karen, and eight of my kids and their families. Oh yes, there is also my step-mother and her three adopted Indian kids. My mother died several years ago. When my dad was seventy-five, he married a twenty-five year old lady. She is real nice and we all love her. After dad died, she adopted the Indian children. She helps other people too," Steve said.

"I'll try to remember everyone," Lori replied.

"John is living on the place that I once owned. It's the place where my kids grew up. When the kids got older and in school, we built a house in town just like the one in the country so we could live in town during the school year," Steve explained. "It used to be a pretty place, but I'm afraid it's run-down by now. I dread seeing it."

"You sound like you used to be pretty wealthy, Lori said.

"We were. We had several thousand head of cattle and several thousand acres of land at one time," Steve replied.

"What happened?" Lori asked.

"The cattle market fell. I was the oldest in my family and the leader in the business. When I left my family and moved to another state, I sold out to my brothers. Things haven't gone too well for them," Steve answered. "Things would have been so different if I would have stayed. But, I would have never met you, dear."

Steve drove through what looked like a flat pasture. "We are coming in the back way," he explained.

Steve drove into a ravine and below was a beautiful farm topped off with a large brick house. Steve smiled. "John has done a great job of taking care of the ranch," he said with a sigh.

Lori was overwhelmed with Steve's family. She was introduced to his other daughter, and family, other sons, and families, seven brothers and sisters and their families, besides the step-mother and her family. "Don't try to learn everyone's name at once; it will take some time," Trina, Steve' pretty middle daughter said.

Lori visited with everyone while walking around the large living room, dining room, and kitchen. Steve's family was the most friendly people she had ever met. "Why are you guys so nice to me?" Lori asked Trena.

"Well, you're pretty nice, yourself, but this is the first time we've seen dad really happy. We know you love him and he certainly loves you. You're not anything like the other women he has been married to that seemed to just love what he could buy them," Trena answered.

"Then you all approve of us getting married?" Lori asked.

"We sure do," the group of ladies said. "Dad has gotten his wits and laughter back, and his health too," Steve's sister said.

"Thanks," Lori said, but she was concerned about how pale Steve had been that day. "I guess it's just the stress of seeing everyone again, and visiting so many places of memories," Lori told herself.

Lori was visiting with Steve's youngest brother. "Steve looks so much better than he did the last time I saw him," Ropper said. "I heard that Steve had been in an accident and I called him while he was in the hospital. He said he was doing fine, but he didn't sound good. I drove to Dannon to visit him. Here's a picture of what he looked like then," he said. Ropper handed Lori a snap-shot.

Lori almost fainted when she looked at the picture. Steve's head and face had been so covered with bruses and lacerations that Lori could not believe the picture was Steve. "I see what you mean," Lori said. "It's a miracle that his face isn't covered with scars!" she exclaimed.

"I wasn't very happy about meeting you, but I've changed my mind, and John and I want you guys to stay with us tonight," Ruby said.

"It's okay with me if Steve wants to," Lori replied.

"Lori, I just can't seem to get rid of this headache," Steve said after the rest of the family had gone home.

Lori brought Steve some asprin. "You just sit down in that large chair and relax," Lori ordered. "I'll get our clothes and other things from the car," she said.

Steve did not argue. John saw Lori bringing in the suitcases. "I wish my wife would wait on me like that," he said with a laugh. "When are you going to make Steve do things for himself?" John asked.

"When his color gets better," Lori answered.

Lori slept in the basement that night across from the large family room and play rooms. "This house is well-designed for raising nine kids," Lori told herself. The room was cold, but Lori did not want to complain. She missed Steve's good-night kiss, but the family probably would not understand.

The next day some of the family returned. Lori was playing cards with Steve and two other family members. She could have won the game with the hand she had, but all she could think of was how much she loved Steve. Lori let Steve beat her without realizing what was happening.

The last day they were in South Dakota, Lori and Steve stopped by to visit with some old friends of Steve's. The house was a new, elegant, brick home overlooking the Missouri River. Steve's friend was as tall as Steve. Lori had been amazed by the number of tall men she had seen in the area. "This area must have been settled by tall Swedes," she told Steve.

"My kids wanted me to come and see you," Steve told Tony. They told me that you were in such bad health that you were confined to a wheel-chair, but now you are as active as you've ever been," Steve said.

"The doctors had given up on me ever getting well," Tony explained. "Then my wife got me to go to this herbal health specialist and he got me to taking all kinds of vitamins and minerals, and I have slowly gotten well," he said.

"Do you have some literature or addresses you can let me have?" Steve asked.

"Sure," Tony replied. His wife found several brochures and gave them to Lori.

Steve and Lori left to meet more family for dinner. They met at the large tourist complex where Dean's wife worked. Gene and his family were not able to join Steve at Uncle John's house so they made a date to join Steve at Lori at the complex. They were about the only family members that Lori had not met yet.

Dean and Gene were identical twins. When Lori walked into the restaurant and saw the two men sitting next to each other, she did not know which one they had spent a night with. Steve introduced Lori to Gene and his family. Gene and Sally had two girls, and they had just adopted a boy. They were just as nice as the rest of the family and Gene was as quiet as Dean.

Steve and Lori, and some of Steve's children, ate a large meal together. The time went by too fast. Everyone said good-bye and Steve and Lori started home. They were crossing part of South Dakota when Lori took out her key board and played some choruses. She and Steve were singing praises to the Lord.

Lori suddenly noticed that Steve had quit singing. She looked at Steve. His head was hanging down and he was acting drunk. He was not paying any attention to where he was driving on the busy Interstate highway.

"Steve! Steve!" Lori shouted. The car was going eight-five miles an hour, and Steve was giggling and hanging onto the steering wheel loosely. The Oldsmobile was heading into the middle of the concrete median between the four-lane highway. It took all of Lori's strength to push Steve out from under the steering wheel so she could take over. She took her foot and pushed Steve's foot off of the foot feed. Lori took her left foot and pushed down on the brakes.

The car came to a jolting halt. Lori looked up and saw what looked like a huge, black monster in the middle of the median, ready to swallow them up, but hey were safe. Lori eyes filled with tears as she said, "Thank you Lord". She did not know what she was really looking at, but she did know that she had to get Steve to a doctor quickly.

Steve opened the car door and fell out. "Whatcha doin?" he stammered as he got up and stumbled into the back of the car.

"I stopped the car because you almost wrecked us!" Lori screamed.

"So what?" Steve said with a slurry laugh. He started to get back under the wheel.

"Oh no you don't!" Lori shouted. "I'm driving now!" she exclaimed. "Now I know what happened when you had your accident and why your ex thought you were trying to kill her," Lori said.

Steve shrugged his shoulders and fell back out of the car. Lori helped him up and into the passenger's side, fastened the seat belt, and locked the door. Lori crawled under the steering wheel and pulled the car back upon the highway. She started speeding down the highway in hopes to be stopped by a patrol car, in order to get help.

Lori saw a patrol car going down the other side of the highway. She turned her head-lights off and on several times when she passed the State Trooper. "Praise the Lord!" Lori said when she saw the Patrol car turn around and follow them to a stopping place by the side of the road.

"Something is wrong with my boy-friend!" Lori exclaimed. "He's acting drunk and he doesn't drink!" she tried to explain.

The officer looked at Steve through the window for a minute. "There's a hospital in a little town five miles up the road. You just follow me, and I'll take you there," the law officer said.

Lori had a hard time keeping up with the patrol car. He pulled up in front of a combination doctor's office and hospital. A nurse came out and examined Steve. "We need to get him to the hospital in Pierre quickly," she said. "I'll send the ambulance around to pick him up," the nurse said.

"Stay right behind us and you won't have to worry about getting a speeding ticket because I'll have the emergency lights on," the ambulance driver told Lori.

Lori had been used to driving fast, but following the ambulance to Pierre would be one fast trip she would never forget. She prayed for Steve to be well all the way to the large hospital.

The nurses soon had Steve in a hospital gown and in bed. Lori waited in the waiting room. "What if Steve needs surgery? I can't even sign for him," Lori told herself.

A nurse came in and walked toward Lori. She sat down and asked Lori some questions. Lori told the nurse every detail about what had just happened. "I'm so worried about him, and I can't even sign for him if he needs surgery," Lori sobbed.

"Steve is going to be all right, and I'm glad to meet you; I'm Steve's sister, Peggy," the nurse said. She put her arms around Lori and gave her a hug.

"What!" Lori exclaimed. "I can't hardly believe it; Praise the Lord," she said. "I guess you're one sister I hadn't met yet," Lori added.

The doctor came out of Steve's room. "I can't find anything wrong with him, but by his behavior, I'd say that oxygen wasn't getting to his brain. As soon as you people get back home, I want his personal doctor to send him to the heart specialists in either Phoenix or Kansas City. I'm sure it's his heart, and they are the only clinics advanced enough in the field of heart problems that can help him," the doctor said.

"Do you think we should call his kids?" Lori asked.

"It wouldn't be a bad idea," Peggy answered.

By the time Steve's brother Bart, Benny, Dean, Carrie, and Trena got to Pierre, Steve had been released from the hospital and they were at Peggy's house.

There was an unscheduled family gathering at Peggy's. Lori watched Steve as he talked and joked with his family. It seemed like nothing had really happened. "I'm sorry to have bothered you, but I was so frightened," Lori apologized.

"We're glad you called us," Carrie said. Everyone else agreed.

Suddenly, the events of the evening hit Lori like a ton of bricks. She had almost lost the most important person in her life. Lori snuck off to the bathroom where she broke down in deep sobs. It was the first time she had cried for quite awhile. Lori could not control her deep sobbing.

"Lori, my I come in?" Steve's soft voice came through the closed, locked door. Lori did not like for anyone to see her cry, but this man was different. She slowly opened the door and fell into Steve's loving arms. She clung to him with all her might.

"Don't worry, Lori, we'll be together a long, long time. My grandfather, and father, had nine kids and lived to be ninety. And, I will too, and I'm only sixty now," Steve said softly, kissing Lori on the top of the head.

Lori nodded her head yes. She did not want to ever let go of Steve's body, but they had to return to the living room where the rest of the family was waiting. Lori felt embarrassed over her red, swollen eyes when she and Steve joined the family.

"We understand, and we're glad you love him so much," Trina said.

As each family member left for home, they gave Lori a hug and thanked her for calling them.

CHAPTER X

AN UNSCHEDULED JOURNEY

Steve and Lori traveled into Nebraska. They spent the night with cousin Elaine, her husband, Walter, and Aunt Martha, who was visiting. Elaine was the one who had given Lori Ben's address in hopes that they would someday meet, but she liked Steve right away. Elaine took pictures of Steve, Lori, and Aunt Martha.

After dinner, Elaine played the piano and Lori played the keyboard. They enjoyed music until after midnight. The rest of the family listened, visited, and joined in singing hymns from time to time.

"What kind of wedding would like, dear?" Steve asked on their way home.

"I don't care, except I want to be married in church, and I want as many of our families there as possible," Lori answered. "I feel funny to ask everyone to come to another one of my weddings, but this will be the last one," she said with a smile. She squeezed Steve's large hand. "The only thing I feel bad about is that I'll have to be gone most of the summer to work on my graduate degree, but we can be together weekends, and when summer classes are over."

They were soon parking beside Lori's trailer.

One of the last things Steve had added to the trailer was a stool on the front step for Lori to stand on when he kissed her.

Steve visited for a short time. "I need to go home so you can get ready to go to work in the morning." Steve said.

Lori followed Steve to the front door. Steve lifted her upon the stool to his level. Lori clung to Steve again as they kissed good-night. She never wanted to let go of this precious, giant of a man.

Lori waved good-bye and went into the house and started washing clothes.

Lori felt tired, but happy, when she went to school the next morning. Her day was as challenging as the other ninety days had been. Steve was waiting for her at the trailer when Lori came in from work.

"Lori, I want you to talk to my doctor," Steve said. "I told him what the doctor in Pierre said about my heart. He said he was sure there was something wrong with my brain and not my heart. He has me scheduled for a 'cat scan' tomorrow; I have had so many of those I don't want another one," Steve said. "Could you please call him right now and tell him what happened in South Dakota," he asked.

"Sure, Babe," Lori answered. "What's his number?" she asked.

"I'll dial him for you," Steve replied. He dialed the number and handed the phone to Lori.

"Is Dr. Monty in?" Lori asked the receptionist. This is Lori Jones, and I need to talk to the doctor right now," she explained.

Dr. Monty answered the phone.

"Dr. Monty, this Lori Jones; I'm Steve's friend. Steve wanted me to talk to you about what in South Dakota, and about his heart," she said.

"Mr. Jones, from what Steve told me about his condition, while you were in South Dakota, I'm sure it's a brain problem and not his heart," Dr. Monty said. "Will you describe his condition during that time just as you saw it?" the doctor asked.

Lori described the terrifying episode she and Steve had experienced on the Interstate highway. She tried to remember every detail. "The doctor that examined him said he was sure it was his heart; he said his heart was not working right and not getting enough oxygen to his brain. That's why he acted drunk. The doctor told us to have you send Steve to a heart specialist in Kansas City, or Phoenix, because those were the only two places that could help him," Lori said.

"Ms. Jones, I'm sure we need to this 'cat scan' first. If we don't find anything there, when the tests get back, Ill send him on to a heart specialist," Dr. Monty said.

"Please hurry," Lori replied. "He needs to see a heart specialist as quickly as possible and he needs to be sent by a doctor like you."

Steve was tried after the 'cat scan' on Tuesday. He felt even more tired on Wednesday. Steve was so tired Wednesday night that he kissed Lori good-night right after supper, and went back to the motel to rest.

Lori was in a deep sleep when the telephone rang. Her first thought was that her mother might be sick. "Hello," Lori said.

"Lori, this is Nada at the Motel. "I thought you ought to know that the police found Steve two blocks from here. He didn't have any clothes on except his shorts. He was knocking on a Lady's door. The police thought he was drunk and took him to jail. I sent some clothes down to him, but I thought you might like to go down to the police station and check on him."

Lori could hardly believe what Nada had just told her, and she felt a lump coming up in her throat. "Thanks, I'll get down there as soon as I get dressed," she said.

Lori quickly put on the clothes she had worn that day. She walked carefully through the four inches of new snow to get to the car. Lori drove slowly the ten blocks to the police station. She opened the back door into the building and walked down a hall to the only room with lights on.

Steve saw her coming and met her at the door. "I'm sorry, dear, to get you out this time of night. I'm glad you're here, though," Steve said, trying to smile.

A police officer was sitting behind a desk. He stood up when Lori entered the room. "Sit down, Mrs. Jones," the officer said, pointing to an empty, leather chair. There were two other police officers in the room.

Lori sat down in a chair beside Steve. She held his large hand tightly. The officer sat back down behind the desk. "I guess you can take him," the officer said. "We found him two blocks away from where he lives. A lady called us because he was trying to get into her house. He didn't have many clothes on, and it scared her. We thought he was drunk. By the time we got him down here to the police station, he was perfectly normal. He knew who he was, but couldn't remember what had happened, or how he got to the police station."

"We checked his feet for frostbite, but his feet weren't even red. He asked us to call the motel to get him some clothes. We couldn't understand how anyone could sober up so fast, and then he told us that he doesn't even drink. Our test proved that there was no alcohol in his blood. You can take him from here if you'll have someone watch him the rest of the night to be sure he doesn't do the same thing again," the officer said.

"I can watch him for the rest of the night," Lord replied.

"Thanks for all your help," Steve told the three police officers.

"You're the nicest guy we ever picked up," one of the officers said. The other officers agreed and shook hands with Steve.

"Thanks for taking care of my guy for me," Lori said as they left the station.

Steve followed Lori out to the car. He was extra quiet.

"Steve, when you told me that you didn't remember running your car into that cement wall when you had your terrible accident, I couldn't understand how that could happen, but now I understand," Lori said.

Steve did not answer.

"Steve, don't be embarrassed about what happened," Lori said, softly. "You couldn't help it, and the police officers knew it." Lori took Steve's hand again and held it while she drove back to the trailer.

Steve finally spoke. "My ex-wife didn't ever understand; she just thought I was trying to kill her and had me arrested for abuse. She has sued my insurance company for one-hundred thousand dollars."

Lori parked the station wagon and started to get out.

Steve grabbed Lori's arm. "Lori, my ex came to see me the other night. She said she had a lot of money now, and we can have a lot of fun together, if I came back to her. She was driving a new expensive van. I told her it was too late. I told her that our divorce is final now, and that I love you," he said.

A chill went down Lori's spine at the very thought of loosing Steve to his ex-wife. "I'm so glad you told her that," she said, squeezing Steve's giant hand again. "I guess I can't take you home tonight. I hope people will understand you spending the night here," Lori climbed out of the car and Steve followed her into the house.

"Lori, I have to wash up," Steve said. "May I use your bathroom?" he whispered.

"Of course, use anything you need," Lori answered. "Everything I have will soon be yours too, anyway," she added.

"This is so embarrassing. My body didn't work right at the same time my mind wasn't working right," Steve tried to explain.

"It's all right now, so don't worry about it." Lori replied. She lay down on the bed for a short rest. The alarm would be ringing in less than two hours. Steve came in a laid down beside Lori. Lori held Steve's hand tightly again. "I'll never let him go," she said to herself.

The alarm sounded. Lori got up and got ready for school. Steve was still asleep. "I'll take you home on my way to work," Lori said when she woke up her 'sleeping treasure'.

Lori waited until Steve was safely inside his apartment before she drove on to school and a full day's work.

Lori called Pastor David to come and pray for Steve's healing after school that evening. Pastor David and his wife came an hour after Lori called them. The four prayed for Steve's healing and complete recovery. Pastor David had counseled Steve and his ex-wife in an effort of saving the marriage when they were having trouble.

"Thank you for being such a fine pastor and friend," Steve told Pastor David. Everyone shook hands before the pastors left. Steve and Lori spent a quiet evening together.

Steve was waiting for Lori at the trailer when she came in from work. "Lori, I have felt better today than I've felt for a long time," he said, smiling.

"Praise the Lord!" Lori exclaimed. She hugged her tall cowboy and they sit down together on the couch.

"Lori, I've been thinking. I want to go back into the cattle business. Spending time at my old ranch in South Dakota gave me the courage to believe I can be successful again," he said.

"That's wonderful," Lori replied. "How are you planning to get back into the cattle business?" she asked.

"I'm going to all the cattle sales within driving distance. I want to learn all I can about the present cattle market; and then I'll know what I'm talking about when I go to the bank and ask for a business loan," Steve explained.

"I know more about cattle than anything else, and I probably know as much about cattle as most people that are in the business," Steve said. "I believe that the Lord is leading me to use what I know to earn a good living for you, and to leave something to my kids after I'm gone."

"I don't want you to go back to work just for me, until you feel well enough," Lori whispered.

"Lori, I feel great, and the one-thousand dollars I receive each month from the insurance company from the accident will soon run out. I don't want you to support me after we are married," Steve said. "I want to give you as many nice things in life as I have my other wives." Steve put his long arms Lori and held her tight. "I've made plans to go to two cattle sales this week and two next week before I go talk to my banker," he said.

"Just being with you is all the luxury I need," Lori replied. "You do sound happy at the very thought of going back into the cattle business, though," she said.

"I was also thinking about renting some cattle pasture in the mountain valley where you will be going to college this summer. We can be married as soon as school is out, and have a weeks honeymoon before you have to start classes, and be together in the evenings," Steve explained.

"That sounds great!" Lori exclaimed. She snuggled up to Steve's chest and begain to relax from the events of the day. "I'm sure my 'cat scan' won't show anything," Steve whispered. "Lori, I have something to show you, that is if we can use your VCR," he said.

"Anything that is mine is yours," Lori repeated with a smile.

Steve went to his car and brought in a package. "My family started taking family movies in 1941, when I was only twelve. My brother, Bart, has put the movies together on video. He has added descriptions and music, and has made copies for all the family. I haven't even seen it yet," Steve explained.

The video lasted for three hours. It showed movies of Steve's aunts that had been dead for forty-five years. There were great movies of Steve's parents, brother, sisters, and Steve's first wedding. One of the cutest movies was of Steve' youngest sister, the nurse at the Pierre hospital, when she was learning to walk. Bart had added the song, "I Need Someone to Lean On" while the baby toddled around, falling, and getting up again.

There were several movies of Steve's nine kids when they were growing up. One impressive movie was the huge family ranch at branding time. There were thousands of head of cattle being driven into the ranch pens to be vaccinated, castrated, and branded. The heard was so large that there was cattle as far as the eye could see.

"That should encourage you to go back into the cattle business again," Lori said, laughing.

Lori fixed some sandwiches for them to eat while they finished watching the video. It was time for Steve to go home when the video was over. He waited until Lori was in bed before going in to kiss her good-night. "Sleep tight, Dear, and I'll see you tomorrow," he said. Steve had a spring in his step as he checked both doors and left.

"Steve seems happy, and so much younger," Lori told herself just before she went to sleep.

Steve attended the two cattle sales that week. He felt so young and energetic. Steve had a surprise waiting for Lori when she came home from school Friday evening.

"Who's Lincoln Town Car is that parked in front of the house?" Lori asked when she came into the living room where Steve was sitting.

"That's ours," Steve answered. "I know how much you liked that Town Car the company let you drive when your old Ford was in the shop. I wanted one to drive you around in," he said, hugging Lori.

"Steve, you shouldn't have, but it might help you keep the determination to work the cattle business just to pay for it," Lori said.

"Lori, the way I feel, I know we're going to prosper together. The car will be impressive when I talk to other people about deals," He added. "People might not know how honest I am just by looking at me."

I guess that's honest," Lori replied.

"Lori, I thought it would be fun to go to your mother's and watch the Super Bowl with the rest of your family, Sunday," Steve said. "You don't spend enough time with your family anyway."

Lori sat down on the floor and laid her head on Steve's knees. "I don't remember being this happy. I love you and it will be fun being your wife," Lori said.

Steve came back from Thursday cattle sale excited. "I felt like I was home again watching the sale of the cattle, Dear," he said with a smile. "I wrote down the prices, and I checked prices on pasture and cattle feed today. I think I'll have some solid figures to present to my banker next week," Steve explained.

Steve and Lori had fun grocery shopping on Saturday. Steve scooped a couple of inches of snow off the driveway next to the mobile home. It made him too tired and Lori scolded him for doing the extra work.

On super Bowl Sunday, Steve and Lori drove to Elizabeth and Arthur's in time to go to church with them. They took Nada along. After church, the rest of the family joined them for dinner at Elizabeth's big house. Steve had another one of his headaches and sat down in the living room. Lori gave him two aspirin. They did not seem to help. "I have something a little stronger," Elizabeth said. She opened a kitchen cabinet, and brought back two tablets and a glass of water for Steve.

"Thanks," Steve said. Thirty minutes later, he felt better, and played basketball with Mike, Mitch, and Lori's two grandsons.

"It sounds great to hear Steve' laughter with the laughter of my kids and grandkids," Lori said.

It was time to gather in the large family room and watch the Super Bowl football game. Arther put on his bright orange hat for the home team, and Staci served the family orange Crush pop. It was a fun day except the home team lost by a large margin.

After the game was over the rest of the family went home. Elizabeth sat down in the large chair in the living room to visit with Nada, Steve, and Lori. "Arthur, would you please bring me the blood pressure machine and check my blood pressure. I feel like its too high this evening," she said.

Arthur went upstairs and brought back the machine. He wrapped one end tightly around Elizabeth's arm and pumped it full of air. Arthur read the digits on the other end. "Yes, your blood pressure is too high," he said. "You need to rest the next day or two, and see if you can get it down."

"While you have the machine handy, maybe the rest of us should check our blood pressure," Nada suggested. Her blood pressure check out a little high.

Lori's blood pressure checked out low as usual.

Arthur put the machine on 'Steve's arm. "I don't think the machine is working right. Maybe we need to get a new one," he said. "I can't get the same reading twice." He tried several times before he took the machine back upstairs and put it away.

Steve, Lori, and Nada said good-night and started home. Lori sit snuggled close to Steve all the way back. The new car was so much nicer than Lori's old station wagon. "It seems like the world is finally right for us," Lori said with a sigh.

Steve squeezed Lori's hand and smiled while he drove them back to the motel. They let Nada out and Steve took Lori on to the mobile home.

"I've never been this happy before, either," Steve said. "It's late so I won't come in tonight. I'll let you get a good night's rest before you go back to work," he said. "It's not fair to keep you up too late. You have to get up early every morning and I don't have to get up until I want to. But, that's getting ready to change."

Steve led Lori to the front door and helped her step up on the stool, and then he took her in his long arms and kissed her. Lori had never felt so loved and relaxed. She felt so happy and satisfied. Lori knew she could face anything with Steve by her side.

"Good-night, Dear," Steve said. He unlocked the door and held it open for Lori. "I love you and I'll be glad when we're married so I won't have to leave you every night," Steve said. He waited until he heard the door lock before he walked back to the Town Car.

When Lori came home from work the next evening, Steve was sitting in his favorite living room chair. He had his lap full of more pictures. Steve showed Lori a picture of the airplane he once owned. "I had a private landing strip close to the farmhouse. One time I took off when the wind was blowing. I gained a little speed and just let the wind carry me for a few minutes. I looked down where my mother had been waving good-bye. This time she was waving her hands in a panic at me. I landed the plane and ran to her. I thought something terrible had happened. She said that she was afraid for me because the wind wouldn't let me down," Steve said, laughing.

"That is pretty funny," Lori had to agree. "Thanks for the pictures," she said. Lori put some of the pictures on the bulletin board next to the kitchen door. "The picture on your flying license is twenty years old, but you don't look any older now than you did then," she said.

"Love is blind," Steve said with a chuckle.

"May I never get my normal sight back," Lori laughed. She put the license in her wallet in order to see Steve's picture often. "I'm going to make you a supper of spaghetti, and mean balls," Lori said.

"That's one of my favorites," Steve replied.

They ate supper sitting close together on the two high stools at the kitchen bar. Steve helped Lori do the dishes. After the dishes were done,

Steve took Lori in his arms and they danced around the kitchen to a favorite song coming over the radio.

"I remember going to dances with my folks all the time when I was a child. It almost seems like I was raised on a dance floor. Since I'm a Christian now, I feel that going to dances is wrong, but I have always liked to dance," Lori said. "You're one of the smoothest dancers I ever danced with," "Oh thank you, Lord, for such happiness!" Lori shouted.

"I don't think it's the dancing that is wrong, it's the other things that go with it," Steve said.

"Maybe, but I would never want another woman to be as close to you as I am now," Lori replied.

"I guess I wouldn't want anyone this close to you either," Steve said with a smile.

"I'm so happy, let's sing praises to the Lord," Lori suggested. She ran into the living room and uncovered her key board. Lori started playing some scripture songs that they both knew. Steve stopped singing. Once again, Lori saw Steve raise his huge hands toward heaven. Large tears were running down his face as he praised his Lord. "You have found peace with God and with yourself, haven't you?" Lori asked.

"Yes, I'm so glad that God has forgiven me for my crazy, mixed-up past, and helped me to forget most of it," Steve whispered. He helped Lori sing a few more songs. "Lori, I hate to say this, but it's time for me to go home. I want you to get enough rest again tonight," Steve said.

Lori kissed Steve and bounced into the back of the house to get ready for bed. "I'm in bed now," Lori yelled.

Steve came into the bedroom and kissed Lori good-night. He was ready to leave when he stopped and said, "You know, Lori, the cattle deal might not work out. Sometimes I think I should encourage you to find a younger guy that has a lot of money," Steve said. "I'm seven years older than you are, and you need someone like your principal, who is divorced and has a good income, to take good care of you. He is younger than I am, too."

"Steve, you're the most precious person I've ever known. You can give me things that money can't buy. You have given me the happiest days of my life. You're the only one for me, and don't you forget it!" Lori shouted.

"All right, if you say so, Dear," Steve answered. He kissed Lori good-night again.

Lori squeezed Steve's hand until he slipped away.

Steve checked both door locks and shut off the light before leaving.

Lori rushed to school the next morning. She and Mrs. Ming took time for a donut and coffee in the teacher's room. Mrs. Ming was still reading the morning paper when Lori went on to her room to get ready for her first class. Lori had already started lecturing in her first History class when Mrs. Ming came in.

""Mrs. Jones, you're wanted on the telephone in the teachers lounge," Mrs. Ming said. "I think it's urgent, so I'll take over the class while you check on it," she said in her usual bossy way.

Somehow, Lori knew. All feeling left her body as she walked down to the teacher's room and picked up the telephone on the wall.

"Lori, this is Nada. We have just found Steve in his room. He is dead. His ex-wife is here causing a scene. She came banging on my door early this morning and said she couldn't get Steve to answer his door. She was screaming and said she knew that there was something wrong. She says that he isn't dead because his body is still warm, and she won't let the funeral home take his body. Don't come here. I have called your mother and she is on her way to Dannon and to your house. You go on home and she will be there soon." "Lori, are you all right?" she asked.

"I don't know, but thanks for letting me know," Lori answered. She hung up the telephone. "Oh God, No!" Lori whispered. "Steve was my completeness and my everything. I had finally found a place where I fit in this life, and now it's gone!" she sobbed "Why?" she asked.

"Mrs. Jones, may I see you in my office right away," Mr. Rosa was saying.

Lori followed Mr. Rosa into his office. She felt like a zombie.

Mr. Rosa closed the door and turned to face Lori. He motioned for her to sit down. "You already know, don't you, Lori?" Mr. Rosa asked.

Lori nodded her head yes. Her body started to shake.

I wanted to get you in here and sit you down and tell you gently," Mr. Rosa was saying. "I'm so Sorry, Lori. We all thought a lot of Steve. You may stay in here as long as you feel that you need to."

"Thank you. I'll try to teach my best today. That is what Steve would want me to do," she whispered. Lori gritted her teeth and marched back to her room.

Mrs. Ming had given the students an assignment by the time Lori got back to the room. She motioned for Lori to follow her into the small storage room in the back of the room. "What was the call?" Mrs. Ming asked.

"They have just found Steve. He is dead," Lori said. She burst out in tears and fell across Mrs. Ming's shoulders.

"I though it might be that," Mrs. Ming said.

"We were planning on getting married when school was out this spring," Lori said with a sob.

I thought that too," Mrs. Ming replied. "You need to go on home. I can cover for you here. Maybe you'll feel better tomorrow," she said.

"I can't afford to take any time off," Lori protested. She wiped her face and started back into the classroom. Mr. Rosa was walking through the classroom toward them.

"I think it's best for you to go home now," Mr. Rosa said.

"I can't afford to miss any days off from school," Lori said again, sobbing.

"Don't worry about it. You have sick leave coming anyway. I'll take care of it," he said, patting Lori's hand.

Lori left the room with her face turned away from her students. She heard several students ask, "What's wrong with Mrs. Jones?"

"Sit down and be quiet, and I'll tell you," Mrs. Ming was saying.

Lori felt like she was walking in an aquarium as she tried to see her way down the hall and out to the station wagon. She lit up a cigarette before she pulled out of the parking lot. Lori drove the long way home.

She did not want to drive by the place where Steve had died. She did not want see Steve's body because he was not in it.

Lori stumbled into the living room and into the laundry room where she had done Steve's last laundry. Lori grabbed one of Steve's large, western shirts that was hanging above the washer. It had been his favorite old shirt. Lori stumbled into the living room and fell into one of the large chars. She squeezed Steve's shirt and cried until the shirt was wet.

"I had two husbands to leave me for younger women, but you really got away from me, Steve!" Lori screamed. "You promised me you would live to be ninety like your father and grandfather, because they each had nine kids too! You only lived to be sixty!"

Lori could almost hear Steve whisper, "It's all right, Dear. Everything will turn out all right."

"Without you Steve Hanson, I have nothing to live for," Lori shouted through sobs.

"I'm so sorry, Dear," Lori heard someone say. She looked up and saw her mother coming in. Elizabeth patted Lori's shoulder. "Can I do anything to help?" she asked. "I know what it's like to lose someone after forty-nine years," Elizabeth said, softly.

"But, you and Daddy had those forty-nine years to enjoy each other, and Steve and I didn't even have time to get married!" Lori exclaimed.

"May I come in?" someone asked through the door.

Elizabeth went to the front door and invited Pastor David in. The Pastor came over to Lori. He saw Lori rocking back and forth with Steve's shirt. "She really loved him," Pastor David said.

The pastor sat down next to Lori and took her hand. "Lori, I can't say that I know a person is in heaven, but I can say that Steve was as ready to go there as anyone I have ever known. He really loved the Lord. He gave more than his tithe of money to the Lord's work. He was a good man. And Lori, you made him more happy than he had ever been in all the years I knew him," Pastor David said.

Lori nodded her head yes.

"Lori, I thought Steve was healed when we prayed for him the other night, but I guess he is really healed now," Pastor David said. He patted Lori's hand. "I also feel that if he couldn't believe for his healing, he chose to go and be with the Lord rather than take a chance of having another wreck and both of your being killed."

Lori nodded her head yes again.

"I want to pray with you, Lori, before I leave," Pastor David said. He squeezed Lori's hand. "Oh Lord, we don't understand this situation. We don't understand why Steve was not healed and given more time on this earth, but we do know that you are the only One that can get us through a time like this. We are asking that You heal Lori's broken heart, and comfort Steve's family members too. We ask in Jesus name. Amen,"

"Let me know if there is anything else I can do here," Pastor David said. "I'll try to telephone all of his children and let them know. I'll be honored to do a memorial service for Steve, if that's what you want," the Pastor said. "I'll see you later this evening."

"Lay down on your stomach and I'll rub your back," Elizabeth said. "It might help you relax."

Lori remembered the time Elizabeth had rubbed her back to relax her the day Tim had been arrested for child molesting. "Yesterday the hours just flew by, and now I've never seen time go so slow," Lori said with another sob.

"Lori, I remember when you stopped by my house once, when you and Hollis were getting your divorce. You were crying and talked like you thought it was the end of the world. You thought that there was not place for you in life, but your life gradually got better. You had some happy years with Tim, and you have had some happy months with Steve. I know you'll be happy again, and time will start going fast again," Elizabeth said.

"I'll never love anyone else after loving Steve. I'll never be happy again, or feel like I really belong anywhere again without Steve," Lori said sobbing. "With a divorce, there's always a hidden chance for things to get back together again. With a death, it so final that I can't see any life for me beyond it," she said.

Pastor David came back to check on Lori later that evening. "All of the children have been notified. Two of the boys are coming for the body tomorrow. They want to take him back to South Dakota for burial," the Pastor said. "One of the daughters asked me if I would have a memorial service here in Dannon for him, and I said I would."

"Steve told me he didn't want to be buried in South Dakota," Lori replied. "But, if that's where the kids want him, I think that is where he would want to be buried. I'll never tell them any different."

"Lori, I was thinking, you and Steve went to the First Church for Bible study and came to my church for Sunday services. What do you think about Pastor Williams and I having the memorial service together?" Pastor David asked.

"I think that's what Steve would want," Lori answered. "Steve told me how much Pastor Williams helped him through his last divorce, and how much he thought of both of you. I think it's a good idea."

"I'll be back later. You write down anything you think Steve might like said, and what scriptures he might like read. You can also write down his favorite songs and give them to me. I'll plan the service around them," Pastor David said.

"Steve would want people to have a chance to accept the Lord and commit their lives to Him, and he liked the new scripture songs we sang together," Lori replied. "That's all I can think of right now."

"That's a great start," Pastor David said. "Please call me if there is anything else I can do," he said. He patted Lori on the shoulder one more time and left.

Lori went to bed wrapped up in Steve's shirt. She did not sleep. She cried until she thought she could cry no more, and then the memories of Steve's voice, laughter, smile, or the touch of his hand, would send Lori into deep sobs again. She felt so helpless.

"Mother, it seems like my life has been a mess every since I was twenty-one. Just the time I was beginning to feel like I really fit into the world, and with someone, it all comes to a terrifying end," Lori said.

"Lori, you have always been such a good girl, I don't know why things happen to you," Elizabeth said. "I do know that the Lord has a plan for your life and that you'll be happy again someday. No matter how you feel now, or how hopeless things look right now, you will be happy again."

Lori put a cold, wet washcloth over her eyes to get rid of some of the swelling before she went to school the next morning. She did not go by Steve's motel on the way to work. Lori dreaded facing the teaching staff, and her students, with a swollen face. She did not know if she could keep from crying or not.

The teachers' room was full of the forty men and four women when Lori came in to check her school mail. She tried to sneak in and out of the room without talking to anyone. Mr. McClean, the vice principal, walked up to Lori and threw his arms around her. "Lori, I'm so sorry. We all liked Steve." He said and sobbed so deeply that it shook Lori's whole body.

Lori could no longer hold back her own tears. She sobbed helplessly in her boss's arms. "Thank you for caring," Lori finally managed to say.

"Mrs. Jones, may I talk to you in my office," Mr. Rosa said.

Lori followed Mr. Rosa into his office. He did not close the door this time, but motioned for Lori to sit down again.

"Lori, I think you should take some days off and go to Steve's funeral in South Dakota. Don't worry, because we won't dock you any pay," Mr. Rosa said.

"I appreciate your concern, but the tires on my old car are worn out. I don't have money to get new ones, and I don't see how I can go to South Dakota," Lori replied.

"Maybe you can go by Amtrak, or maybe a tire company will sell you some new tires on credit," Mr. Rosa said. "You need to go to that funeral."

"Thank you,' Lori replied. She left Mr. Rosa's office and felt several teachers squeeze her hand on the way out. Lori heard several teachers offer condolences before she reached the front door.

Lori lit up another cigarette and inhaled deeply. Nothing numbed the pain she felt inside. She slowly drove back to her mobile home, avoiding the street that went past Steve's motel. Every store on Main Street brought back memories of the fun she and Steve had shopping together.

Elizabeth was waiting for Lori at the house. "The school let me have the rest of the week off and told me to go to South Dakota for the funeral," Lori explained.

"Then, that's what you better do," Elizabeth replied. "Do you want me to take you?" she asked.

"No, Mother. Arthur needs you at home, and it would be a hard trip for you," Lori answered, "I'll find some way to get there."

Lori's numbness from shock was gone the next day and she seemed to hurt from reality more deeply than she had hurt the day before. "I don't know why I can't be like some other people and just let sadness bounce off me," Lori told Elizabeth.

"You are more soft-hearted than a lot of people, Lori," Elizabeth replied. "Maybe that's why you've had so many men in your life."

Steve's two sons came to the house early that afternoon. "We have been to the mortuary. Dad died of a massive heart attack. We're having his body flown back to South Dakota," Gene said. He handed Lori Steve's Bible.

Lori could almost see Steve's large hands holding the Bible. She took the book and hugged it. "Thanks, this book meant a lot to him," Lori said.

"Do you have any idea where Dad's saddle is?" Dean asked. "His ex-wife won't let us look for any of his stuff at her place. She says she has no idea where the saddle is. She said he probably sold it, but we know that Dad would never sell that saddle. He has had it since he was a teenager, and he had it repaired several times. We think it's at her place, but we would have to get a search warrant to find out," he explained.

"I don't know where any of his things are," Lori answered. "I know that she only let him have just a few things when she kicked him out.

She had a restraining order put on him so he couldn't go get any more of his things."

"She never cared about him," Dean replied. "All of us kids want you to come to the funeral, and give us any ideas you might have with the arrangements,"

"Thank you. I'll try to be there," Lori replied. She hugged Steve's two, young, handsome sons.

"We have to get started back to South Dakota to be there in the morning when the plane brings in Dad's body," Tom said. "We're having the funeral in a Protestant Church. Our priest did not want the funeral in our Catholic Church because Dad had left the church. We don't know anyone in the protestant church, but they were glad to open up their church to us. They are planning to fix a dinner for our large family, to feed everyone after the funeral."

"What about the Town Car?" Lori asked. "Steve took out insurance to pay for the car if anything happened to him," she said.

"The auto company said that since no payment had been made on the insurance yet, it was not really in effect," Dean answered. "By the time we hired a lawyer to handle the case, we probably wouldn't clear much, even if we won."

"Well, so much for that idea; I was hoping it would belong to you kids and at least pay for the funeral," Lori said with a sigh. She and Elizabeth followed Dean and Tom out to the van and saw the few items that had belonged to Steve. "What a few things to show for such a great man's life," Lori said with another sob. "But, he did leave a wonderful family."

The others agreed. Lori hugged the young men again. She and Elizabeth waved good-bye as the van drove away from the trailer.

"What nice, young men. Steve must have been very proud of them," Elizabeth said.

"They are, and the others are just as nice, including their families, Steve's step mother, and all his brothers and sisters. They treated us like royalty when we were in South Dakota," Lori replied.

Lori and Elizabeth walked back into the house and had just sat down when the door bell rang. Lori answered the door and saw Steve's ex-wife.

"I want Steve's Bible! I gave it to him and I want it!" the woman screamed. "You are the whore that took him away from me and you have no right to any of his property!"

Lori stepped back from the door, speechless. Elizabeth came to the door and shouted, "You have no right to talk to my daughter like that! Go away and leave her alone!"

Lori had never had a good look at Steve's ex-wife. The woman was slender, and very pretty, except for the cruel look on her face. "You had your chance! You pushed away the most wonderful man in the world and treated him like dirt!" Lori screamed. She slammed the door in the woman's face.

Steve's ex rang the doorbell again. Lori and Elizabeth went back into the living room and waited for the woman to leave. She rang two more times before she gave up and left.

Lori had another sleepless night. The next morning she spent an hour on the telephone, trying to make Amtrak connections between Dannon and Templeton, South Dakota. Amtrak went through both cities, but the trip would take her all the way to the west coast and back. It would take a week for her to get there, and it would be expensive.

"I don't know what to do now," Lori said.

"God will make a way for you to get there," Elizabeth said. "If nothing else works out, I'll take you,"

"Arthur needs you at home and I don't want to be a burden to you," Lori said again. "I think I'll call this Christian man that Steve knew. He owns a used car lot and tire company. He might sell me some tires on credit," Lori looked up the number and dialed it.

"I'm sorry to hear about Steve. He was a good, Christian man, and you two always looked happy together. I imagine this is pretty hard on you," he said "You have a good teaching job, and I trust you, so I don't see any reason I can't sell you some tires on credit. We can put them on for you today, right after lunch, and you can pay for them later. I know you will need what money you have now for the trip."

"Thanks, I'll have my car at your place at one o'clock," Lori replied. She hung up the phone and dialed her cousin in Nebraska. "Elaine, Steve just died, and his funeral is going to be in South Dakota," Lori explained. "Would you be able to go with me, if I pick you up on the way?" she asked.

"Oh. Lori. I'm so sorry to hear that," Elaine answered. "I'll be glad to go with you and I'm glad you asked me to go."

Lori hung up the phone and called Steve' youngest daughter in South Dakota. "I have finally made arrangements so I can come to the funeral," Lori explained, trying not to cry. "When and where is it?" she asked.

"I'm so glad you are coming. We want you to be a part of our family because you made dad so happy," the young lady said. "There will be a Catholic memorial service tomorrow evening, and the funeral will be the next morning. You don't have to worry about Dad's Ex. My brothers have called the police there in Dannon to keep her from leaving town and coming to the funeral. She was always such a problem that we don't want her here."

"Thanks, that will make it easier for me, but it's sad that you have to go to so much trouble to keep her from being there," Lori replied.

Lori hung up the phone and joined her mother for a light lunch. She had the tires mounted and signed a bill for one-hundred and forty-five dollars. The owner offered condolences and wished God's blessing for her trip.

Lori had another sleepless night with Steve's shirt. After breakfast, Elizabeth went home, and Lori started her long trip to South Dakota. She could not help thinking about how happy she had been when she and Steve had traveled the same road together, holding hands all the way. Now Lori felt so alone. It seemed that everything she had to do was causing more pain. She cried across Kansas. Nothing seemed to ease the pain in her chest. She could not seem to pray, or praise the Lord, and she felt so lost and not a part of the world anymore.

Lori was in Nebraska by early afternoon. She did not go to Elaine's first, but found a flower shop instead. "I need a funeral wreath made a certain way," she told the woman at the shop. "I want it to have a barbed wire on it, a horse in the middle, and please hurry. The memorial service is in South Dakota tonight."

Lori sat down to wait. Although the arrangement took only thirty minutes, it seemed more like two hours. Lori cried when she saw the arrangement. It was just what she wanted. Inside a circle of barbed wire was an arrangement of large dried flowers, surrounding a beautiful black horse. The horse had a bridle in its mouth and one end of the rein was left loose. "He's free from being tied to sickness, hurt, and other things, now," Lori commented.

"I understand," the lady said with a professional quiet manner.

Lori paid for the wreath and went to pick up Elaine. Her cousin had her bags packed and was waiting by the front door. The two women were soon on their way north. Lori was able to praise the Lord for weather that was still warm and shiny.

"I want to show you what I just had made," Lori said. She reached into the back seat and carefully handed Elaine the wreath.

"This is different, but pretty, and it looks like a wreath for a man," Elaine said. "I think it's appropriate although I didn't know Steve very well. We just met him that one time, but he seemed to be really nice."

"We were planning to be married when school was out this spring. I was so determined to never be hurt over another man, and here I am, crying again," she said.

"Lori, I wish you wouldn't smoke so much," Elaine said. "I remember when you almost died of pneumonia not so long ago."

"I was about ready to quit, then this happened, and now I'm trying to smoke enough to make me numb, and it isn't working," Lori replied.

"You'll get over this. You have always had God's help to get you through the terrible heartbreaks, and you'll be happy again, but it will take time," Elaine said.

"Do you remember sending me one of your friend's addresses last summer when I was taking care of Grace?" Lori asked.

"Yes," Elaine answered. "He's a nice guy that goes to my church. His wife died about five years ago from lung cancer. I just thought you two might become pen-pals, and I wanted you to know that not all the men in the world are as bad as the two you had been married to."

"Ben and I wrote for a few months," Lori said. "And then I met Steve. We fell in love so fast that I forgot about everyone else. Ben and I had promised each other that if either of us started dating, we would let the other one know so we wouldn't write anymore. Ben wrote me several times then quit. I decided to let him know by sending him one of my copied Christmas letters. As you know, it was filled with my love for Steve. I knew when Ben read the letter, he would know why I quit writing," Lori said. "That was a terrible way to let him know, although we were only pen-pals. I thought when we come back from the funeral, I would like meet him and apologize," she said. "I don't have his address anymore, and I know there will never be anyone else for me. I'll spend the rest of my life alone because no one can ever measure up to Steve."

"Just give your self time to heal," Elaine said.

"Elaine, we don't have much time to get to the memorial service tonight," Lori said. "I'm going to have to drive faster than I want to."
"This is a new, straight highway with no traffic, and maybe we can make up some lost time on this stretch of road,"

Lori had driven about ten miles and not met one vehicle when she saw two red lights flashing behind her. "Oh! No!" Lori exclaimed. She pulled off the highway and stopped.

The state trooper pulled in behind Lori's old station wagon. The officer got out of his car and walked up to Lori's window. "Lady, you were driving a way too fast. I'm going to have to fine you forty dollars and take some points off your license," the young man said.

"I'm sorry officer, but I'm late for my boyfriend's funeral," Lori tried to explain. "Please do what you have to do and hurry."

"I need for you to come back to my car with me," the officer demanded.

Lori followed the stern-looking man back to his patrol car and crawled in on the passenger side.

The officer waited a few minutes before he started the fining procedure. He made two calls on his mobile phone, and finally started filling out several pages of paperwork. "Here's your bill; you can mail it to us," the officer finally said. "If we don't get your money within two weeks, you will have to show up here in court."

Twenty minutes had passed before Lori was back in the car and ready to travel again.

"I'm letting my partner up ahead know that you are coming in case you break the speed limit again, and we'll have to haul you into court," the officer said.

Lori and Elaine watched the police car pull onto the highway and on down the road before Lori signaled and pulled back onto the highway. "It's too late now; I don't know even if we should try to make it to the service or not," Lori said. "He took all the time he could just for the fun of it."

The service had started thirty minutes before Lori and Elaine arrived at Templeton. "We're late, but I want to go anyway," Lori said. They found the funeral home and had to park some distance away.

The room was filled with Steve's family and many friends. Steve's casket was at the front of the room, unopened. The priest spoke a few words and led in some kind of Catholic service. Lori remembered the special prayer that Steve, and his family, always prayed together at each meal. The prayer was so beautiful that Lori had Steve to write it down so she could memorize it and pray it with the others.

Steve's family saw Lori and Elaine standing by the door and made a place for them to sit. After the service, the family invited Lori and Elaine to join them at John's Steve's fourth son, place. They were ushered from the car to the house by Connie, Steve's middle daughter. "There is someone I want you to meet, Lori," Connie said. She led them into a small living room and introduced Lori to Fran, Steve's first wife.

"Lori, this is Fran, our mother, and mother, this is Lori, dad's girlfriend," Connie said.

"I'm glad to meet you, Fran said. "My kids have told me a lot about you," she added.

"You really have a wonderful family," Lori replied. "May I talk to you alone?" she asked.

"Sure," Fran answered. She led Lori through the living room and into a small bedroom. It looked like a hundred coats were piled up on the bed.

Fran pushed the coats back and motioned for Lori to sit down beside her. She took out a cigarette and lit up. "Well?" she asked.

It's strange that seven of her children don't smoke, Lori was thinking. She looked at the woman that Steve had married many years ago. Fran looked like she had lived a pretty rough life. She was probably pretty at one time, but having eight kids in ten years, and raising them had left its toll. Fran did not seem the type that Steve would have married, but even more amazing, was that this rough-talking woman was the mother of Steve's soft-spoken children and Lori had already grown to love.

"Now what did you want to talk to me about?" Fran was asking in her hoarse voice through a ring of smoke.

Lori took her time and thought about what she wanted to say. "You probably know that Steve and I were planning to be married in May," she said.

"Yes, I know. You would have been wife number four," Fran answered. "My kids have told me about you, and they really like you. They said that their dad seemed happier when he was with you than they had ever seen him before."

"I was happier than I had ever been before," Lori replied. "Well, when we were in South Dakota three weeks ago, Steve showed me all through this area. We drove by the place where you live now. When we drove by your place Steve said that your marriage could have been worked out if he had been willing. He said he knew that the divorce had been mostly his fault. Steve said he knew that he messed up your life and the lives of your kids. He said that he wanted to stop and ask you to forgive him, but he didn't have the courage to talk to you yet. I'm telling you how he felt, and I'm asking you to forgive him."

Lori watched Fran's hardened face soften. She heard thirty years of bitterness coming out of Fran's heart. Lori and Fran put their arms around each other and sobbed deeply.

"Thank you for telling me that," Fran managed to say. "We need to join the rest of the family," she said. Fran opened the bedroom door and Lori followed her back into the crowded living room.

"Lori, you and Elaine are staying with me tonight," Connie said.

Lori and Elaine told everyone good-night and followed Connie out to where all the cars were parked. They followed Connie's car to another part of the city. "This is the nicest family I ever met!" Elaine exclaimed.

"Yes, I know," Lori replied.

Connie's place was small but neat. "I'm getting ready to move to another part of the state so that I can go to college. Connie said. "I married my high school sweetheart. He was from a nice family, but I found out he was on drugs after our son and daughter were born. We got a divorce and his parents are helping me financially. They are even helping me to go to college."

"That's great!" Lori exclaimed. "What do you kids think about your mother going back to school?" Lori asked Connie's two children.

"Ooh, I guess its okay," the daughter answered. "I'm in middle school and I hate to change schools." Her younger brother was agreeing with her by nodding his head.

Being around Steve's large family took Lori's mind off of her grief. She was crying less often. Connie showed them to their bedroom. Lori slept a little better than she had been sleeping. Connie fixed a light breakfast and all the family met at the Protestant Church.

When Elaine and Lori came through the front door, Steve tallest son, Tom, was standing next to the casket. He spent several minutes looking down at his father. He showed no emotion. "I wish he could cry," Tom's wife whispered. "He's too much like his dad used to be to show any emotion, in fact, he's more like his dad than any of the other kids."

Tom stepped away from the casket and joined his waiting family.

Lori walked toward the casket. She had not seen Steve since the night he had left her house. He was feeling so well and happy then. "I must tell him good-bye for the last time," Lori told herself. She gritted her teeth and walked up to the brown casket. Steve looked so natural, and so handsome. His large body completely filled the casket. Lori gently put her hands on Steve's huge hands once more. The large, warm, tender hands now felt like cold rocks. The reality of her loss hit her and she started to weep again.

Lori felt someone's hands around her and looked up. It was Steve's oldest daughter, Carolyn. Carolyn was the largest woman Lori had ever seen. She was at least six feet, two inches tall, and probably weighed around three hundred pounds. Carolyn led Lori into a pew at the back of the sanctuary away from the rest of the family. "You can sit here with me," she said.

Lori fell into the pew and cried on Carolyn's shoulder. Carolyn showed no emotion.

The Protestant minister gave a good message. A man sang three Protestant songs, and the service was over. The family walked toward the large line of cars. There was a black limousine behind the hearse to carry the pall bearers, and several cars to hold the members of Steve's large family.

Lori and Elaine rode to the cemetery with Carolyn. Carolyn's car was much older than Lori's old station wagon. This was the child that Steve worried over more than the others. "I'm afraid that a Mexican married her just to become a US citizen," Steve had told Lori. "After they were married, he wasn't good to her, and I feel that he has another family in Mexico."

The weather was still nice for late January in South Dakota, but it was cool enough to wear a coat. Carolyn was wearing white jeans and a light Coca Cola jacket. She looked different from the rest of the family dressed in dress-up, dark clothes. Lori wondered how Carolyn found clothes large enough to fit her.

Lori cried on Carolyn's shoulder as the pretty casket was lowered into the brown earth. "There is nothing as final as death," Lori said.

Carolyn drove Lori and Elaine back to the church where the family was served a large meal.

"We want to thank these church people for the nice service, and wonderful dinner they have prepared for us," Dean announced. He led the family's Catholic prayer. Lori felt blessed saying the beautiful prayer with Steve's family.

When Elaine and Lori were through eating, Lori stood up and announced that she and her cousin had to hurry back home so she could go to work the next morning. "Thank you for inviting us and taking such good care of us," Lori said. She tried to tell everyone good-bye individually.

"Please come and see us again, and bring your cousin too," several of Steve's family said.

Lori promised that she would return. The family followed Lori and Elaine out to the station wagon and waved good-bye. Lori was soon driving and smoking.

It was late on Sunday afternoon when Lori drove up to Elaine's house. She helped Elaine carry her two bags into the house, and said good-bye.

"Lori, why don't you stay here tonight and go home tomorrow," Elaine said. "You'll only miss one more day of school and the rest will do you good," she said. "I'll call Ben and see if he can come over and you can apologize."

"You talked me into it," Lori replied with a sigh. "I think I'll go upstairs and lay down for awhile, if you don't mind."

"Go head; I'll visit with my family, and call Ben. I'll let you know if he's coming by."

Lori stretched out on the bed in the guest bedroom. She was soon asleep. She dreamed about Steve, but the dream was not as sad as reality. She suddenly realized that Elaine was calling her. Lori got up and combed her hair before she started down the stairs. At the bottom of the stairs was a small, white-haired man, in a blue suit, with a pleasant smile.

"Lori, this is Ben, and Ben, this is Lori," Elaine said. "I guess you kind of know each other, so I'll leave you two to talk. We're all in the back in the family room so you can be alone to talk in the living room."

"I'm glad to meet you," Ben said and shook hands with Lori. Ben followed Lori into the living room a sat down across the room from her.

"I just wanted to apologize for not letting you know about Steve, the way we promised each other we would," Lori said. "That was very rude of me to let you know through my Christmas letter the way I did."

"Have you started dating anyone?" Lori asked.

"I have a close friend that I date once in awhile. She goes out with other guys, too, and we aren't serious," Ben answered.

"Well, I just wanted to let you know that there will never be anyone else for me, even though Steve is dead," Lori said.

"That's fine with me, but we can start writing again, if you want to," Ben replied. "The next few months are going to be pretty difficult for you, and it might help to have a pen-pal."

"I think it will help to write someone who has lost a dear one. You probably know more about what I'm feeling than most of my friends,' Lori replied.

"You look pretty nice considering all you've been through," Ben said, kindly.

"Thanks. I'll need a lot of prayer to get through this sad time, if I ever do get through it," Lori said. She shook hands with Ben before he left.

"Is Ben already gone?" Elaine asked when she came into the living room. "I was going to ask him to stay for supper."

Lori felt a little stronger from her short nap. Visiting with Elaine and her family helped to get her mind off her loneliness. She slept about six hours that night which was the most she had slept since Steve's passing.

The next morning Lori began the rest of her trip home, alone. It would be six hours before she reached her destination. The road seemed long and lonely without Elaine.

Lori was taken back to the happy memories of her and Steve returned home on the same highway only three weeks earlier. They were so happy. Who would have ever imagined so much could have taken place in such a short time?

Lori felt extremely tired when she parked her car in front of the trailer house. She slowly walked up the sidewalk to her front door. She looked at the stool that Steve had set up for her so she could be tall enough to kiss him. Lori let a mournful wale. She shook herself, unlocked the door, and stepped inside.

Lori turned on the lights. She could see Steve helping her paint the acoustic ceilings. Lori could see Steve helping her tear out the old carpet and put in the new. They had fallen in love changing the carpet. The first time Steve had kissed her was over the bathroom stool in the front bathroom. Lori could see Steve hanging the drapes and cleaning the old stove. Everywhere Lori looked was vivid memories of Steve.

Lori shook herself again and took her suitcase of dirty clothes to the laundry area. There hanging above the washer, was still the last washing she had done for Steve. Lori saw his three western shirts and three pair of western-styled pants. Lori dropped her suitcase and ran to the bedroom. She grabbed Steve's old favorite shirt off the bed and put it on again.

Lori tried to go to sleep. Nothing seemed to relieve the pain she felt. She watched the clock as the hours slowly passed. She remembered the thousands of nights she had watched the clock when she was waiting for Hollis, her first husband to come home. "But I don't have to guess now, because Steve will never come back," Lori whispered. "Oh, God, please help me," Lori prayed. The last time Lori remembered looking at the clock, it was three thirty in the morning.

CHAPTER XI

MORE SURPRISES

The alarm sounded loud, but Lori was not sure she was asleep when it went off. She crawled out of bed and tried to decide what to do to make her face look better. Lori put on some extra makeup and curled her hair with the curling iron. "Lori, old girl, you've had enough time off. Steve is not a part of your life anymore, and your students deserve the best you can give them today," Lori said to the reflection in the mirror. "Steve would not want you to keep crying, so straighten up," she shouted.

Lori almost disobeyed her own orders at the beginning of the day when one of her students came into the classroom. Jenny was Hispanic and the youngest of seventeen kids. She had quit school in December.

"Jenny, what are you doing here? Did you start back to school?" Lori asked, hoping.

"No, Mrs. Jones. I just heard about Steve and I came to school to tell you how sorry I feel about him dying," the beautiful young lady said. Jenny put her arms around Lori and gave her a hug. "Didn't you tell me once that you have had two divorces?" Jenny asked.

"Yes," Lori answered.

"Well, I think if I were you, I would just give up on men," Jenny said with a smile.

"I think you're right, but I've always had a problem with loneliness, Jenny," Lori replied. "But, Steve was such a great guy. This is probably it, if you know what I mean."

"Yes, we all liked Steve," Jenny replied. "I need to go now, but I just wanted you to know that I was thinking about you."

"Please consider coming back to school next year, Jenny," Lori said.

Almost every student told Lori how sorry they were that Steve had died. "These hardened, wild, teenagers still care about people," Lori told herself. Mrs. Ming even seemed a little sympathetic.

Lori was able to go to the motel, where Steve had died, and visit with Nada a little after school. Nada was sweet and understanding. "I lost my husband years ago, and I thought I had fallen in love with another man, but I realized that I just liked him because he was tall, and reminded me of my late husband," Nada said. "How do you like your new home?" she asked.

"I loved it until Steve died. Now it's just memories of him because he helped to remodel it," Lori replied.

"I sure hope you learn to enjoy it again. You guys put so much work and expense into it and it's so pretty," Nada said.

"Well, I have to go home sometime, and it might as well be now," Lori said. She drove on to the trailer. As she parked she could almost see Steve helping her paint the outside. In fact, he had finished the job while Lori had been at work.

Lori forced herself into the house. One of the first things she saw was Steve's pictures on the bulletin board next to the kitchen. "I can't stand to look at them and I don't want to take them down," Lori said to herself. She looked at the old pilot's license and Steve's picture and started to cry again. She decided to call an old friend who had lost her husband in an automobile accident before their children were grown.

"Vera Lee, how did you get over your husband's death?" Lori asked. "I need some suggestions since I lost Steve."

"Lori, one thing I had to do was to put all my husband's pictures away for awhile," Very Lee said. "And I keep as busy as I can, and I even get out into the country and run when things get tough."

"Thanks," Lori said and hung up. Lori carefully took Steve's pictures down and put them in a drawer. She did not feel like eating alone and didn't eat much. Lori was smoking instead of eating. She tried to watch TV until it was time to go to bed.

Lori decided to go down town and buy some sleeping medicine from the drug store. She took two tablets before bedtime. Lori crawled into Steve's shirt and into bed. There was no bedtime kiss. Lori started to cry again. She could not go to sleep. "I've got to get out of here!" Lori exclaimed. She jumped out of bed and dressed. Lori drove back to Nada's. It was about midnight when she knocked on the door.

It took Nada a few minutes to answer the door.

"Nada, can I stay here for the rest of the night? I just can't take it in the house anymore," Lori said, crying.

"Sure Lori, come on in," Nada answered.

"I miss Steve too, and I sure didn't want him to die in my motel," she said. "I think he did come to this old motel to die, but you gave him a reason for living."

"I guess it wasn't a good enough reason," Lori said, trying to laugh.

"Do you want to sleep upstairs in your old room, Lori?" Nada asked.

"I think I just want to sleep here with you," Lori answered. "Please forgive me for being such a baby."

Lori got a few hours sleep before she went back home to get ready for school again. The phone was ringing. It was one of the Elementary teachers that Lori had gone to class with when she met Steve. Steve had taken Lori to class after they became such good friends.

"Lori, this is Judy. Sorry to hear about Steve. The reason I'm calling is that we are starting another graduate class and wondered if you would like to take the class and share in our car pool," Judy said.

"I'd love to, and thanks for letting me know," Lori answered. "This will help me stay more busy with going to class three hours once a week and studying every night."

"We'll see you in two weeks," Judy said and hung up.

The next night Lori did not want to bother Nada so she took and hour drive east to see some friends. Violet was now running a beauty shop in a border town.

"We didn't get to meet this guy of yours, Lori, but you seem pretty broken up," Violet said.

"I'm so lonesome without Steve around when I come home from school in the evenings," Lori said.

"Maybe what you need is a pet," Violet said. "I know these people that run a dog kennels here, and they were trying to give away a registered Laso Apso dog," she explained. "Let's go see if they have her."

Lori climbed into the same Oldsmobile she had ridden in the first time she left Tim. Violet drove a few blocks and parked in front of a large white building with pens in the back. It was feeding time.

"Do you still have that little dog you wanted to give away?" Violet asked.

"Yes we do. Come on in and I'll show her to you," the lady replied.

Lori followed the two other ladies into the building. About fifty dogs ran up to greet them. Half of the dogs were while, short-haired dogs, and the other dogs had long hair and were black or brown.

"We'll have to look for her,' the caretaker said. "She is the only dog that runs and hides when we come into the building. She was abused as a puppy and she is the only dog we have that hasn't gotten over it. We paid one-hundred, and seventy-five dollars for her. We wanted her for breeding, but she lost her first puppies, and she just couldn't seem to get pregnant after that."

The caretaker found a little, black, long haired dog hiding under some boxes. "Her registered name is Lady Diana, but we just call her Lady," the caretaker said. She handed the shivering dog to Lori.

"It sound like your life has been as mixed up as mine," Lori told the dog. She petted the frightened animal. "I'll take her if there isn't any charge,' she said. "She won't take the place of the tall cowboy I just lost, but she will give me someone to talk to in the evenings."

"Thanks, Violet," Lori said when she drove home with her new pet. As soon as Lori turned Lady loose in the house, she ran under the bed. Lori pulled her out and talked to her, but as soon as she turned the dog loose, Lady ran under the bed again. Lori picked up the dog and put an old leash on her and tried to walk her outside. Lady was too frightened to wet or dirty outside.

Lori finally gave up and went to bed in Steve's shirt and her arms around a small, shaking dog. The next evening she cut Lady's hair and gave her a bath. Lady still hid under the bed or furniture. It was nice to have someone to talk to in the evenings, and Lady soon learned to lie on Lori's lap.

The days were getting easier away from memories of Steve, but the evenings were still like "Hell on earth." Lori enjoyed traveling with the four other teachers forty miles to class. She sometimes did her studying at Nada's just to get out of the house and its memories.

One evening Lori had lady in her lap and was studying for a test when someone rang the door bell. Lady ran and hid. Lori answered the door and saw an old friend. She had taught Terry her first year of teaching. Terry was the son of some of Lori's friends from the church she attended before she met Tim. "Come in, Terry," Lori said. "How are you?" she asked.

"I'm fine, but I've been worried about you since you lost Steve," Terry answered. "I drive by your house pretty often and would like to stop by and visit, but my girlfriend is too jealous to let me."

"What about tonight?" Lori asked.

"We had a fight tonight and I don't care if I make her mad or not," Terry answered, smiling.

"I appreciate your concern, but I don't want to cause you any trouble, Terry," Lori said. "Terry, are you sure that you want to marry someone that is that jealous over you?" Lori asked.

"Well, tonight, I don't think I do," Terry answered with a laugh. "I must be going, and I just wanted to be sure that you're all right."

"Thanks for coming by, and I hope your social life gets better," Lori said. "I do have a little company now, a dog, but she is so afraid of people that she spends most of her time under the bed."

Lori was studying one evening when the doorbell rang. This time is was Carolyn, Steve's oldest daughter. "I didn't have a job when I got back to Texas after dad's funeral," Carolyn said. "Worse than that, my husband had written a check for cash and took all our money out of the bank and went back to Mexico."

"Oh you poor girl, come in," Lori said. She fixed two cups of hot coffee and sit down at the dining room table with Carolyn. The two ladies lit up cigarettes. "What are you going to do?" Lori asked.

"I don't know yet," Carolyn answered. "You told me I could come and visit you and I thought this might be the right time to do it."

"Well, it's taking all my money to meet expenses and go to school, to work on my master's degree, but you can stay for awhile," Lori replied.

"It will be nice to have someone else around to help me forget my loneliness," Lori said. "You can sleep in the small spare bedroom. I have my sewing machine, desk, and typewriter in the larger front bedroom."

"No thank you. I'll just sleep here on the hide-a-bed," Carolyn replied.

It didn't sound like it would do Lori any good to argue so she found some extra blankets to put on the hide-a-bed.

Lori pulled Lady out from under the bed to walk her outside.

"Oh, what a cute dog," Carolyn said. She tried to pet lady but Lady was frightened. She growled and snuggled up against Lori. Carolyn took Lady anyway and the dog started to shake.

Lori took lady to the vet's the next evening. "I need to have her spade. I work and I don't have room for a bunch of puppies," she explained.

"You can pick her up tomorrow evening and bring her back in a week to have her stitches taken out," the vet said.

The thirty-five dollars it cost Lori to have lady spade was a strain on Lori's budget, but it was worth it not to have to worry about a dog in heat.

Carolyn talked about going out and looking for a job every evening, but she never did. Lori's grocery bill doubled, and the utilities were higher since the furnace wasn't turned down during the day. Lori could not figure out how Carolyn had money enough for cigarettes but nothing else. Lady was still frightened of Carolyn, but Carolyn insisted on picking her up all the time and making her lay on her lap. Lady was continually shaking.

Lori had forgotten how it was to come home to a dirty house after working all day. Carolyn fixed a meal once in awhile, but most of the time she expected Lori to do all the work. When Lori insisted that Carolyn get a job, Carolyn talked about how bad she was feeling. Lori did not have money enough to go to the doctor herself, little only take Carolyn. "But, Carolyn belonged to Steve, so she is precious," Lori told herself many times.

The only characteristic Carolyn had that reminded Lori of Steve was her height. Carolyn was dark, with dark hair like her mother. She was loud and pushy, but Lori felt like she had to take care of her for Steve.

"Your father was such a wonderful man that I can't imagine the number of women that let him get away," Lori said one evening.

"Ooh, he wasn't as wonderful as you thought he was. His second wife was a great person and I think their divorce was more his fault then hers," Carolyn replied.

"Your dad told me that Geri's father had planned for her to get a divorce from her first husband and marry him. He said that they got him into a cattle setup that he knew wouldn't work. After he lost a lot of money, Geri went back to her first husband who was having some success in the cattle business," Lori said.

"That's what he wanted you to believe, but frankly, I'm still friends with Geri"! Carolyn said.

Lori felt the strain of school and her student's problems, the strain of adjusting to being without Steve, the strain of the house training a little dog, and keeping a house guest she could not afford. When she thought she could go no further, she always received a cheery, inspirational card or letter from Ben. One day Lori received newspaper clipping from Ben about a snow storm they had in Nebraska. The pictures showed cars buried in the snow and escaped cattle walking down the streets of their city. Lori put the pictures on the bulletin board to cover up the empty spaces. Lori always found time to answer Ben's letters.

Ben called Lori one Saturday just to see how she was doing. They had a good friendly visit. Lori caught herself calling Ben when she needed him to pray about something, or just a friend to listen to her problems. Although Ben had some sadness in his life, he did not let them get him down. He had a deep faith in God that nothing could shake.

Lori felt that she just had to get away from Carolyn and the house. During spring vacation, she and Lady went back to Nebraska to visit with Elaine. Lori and Elaine went to church together and Ben joined them after he finished driving the Sunday School bus. The family had been invited to Elaine's daughter's church that afternoon for her grandson' dedication service. Ben was invited too, so Lori rode with Ben the forty miles to the service.

"Have you started dating again," Lori asked.

"No, my old girlfriend is going steady with a truck driver now," Ben replied.

"Are you interested in dating again?" Lori asked.

"Maybe, but I would never be interested in dating you. You still think Steve was perfect, and I'm not. I could never measure up to a guy like that even though you didn't know him that long," Ben said.

"You're probably right, but I do appreciate your cards, letters, and phone calls. They have helped me get through some awfully hard times," Lori replied. "Working my job, getting my master's degree, and meeting all my expenses since Carolyn's been living with me are enough to keep me busy for life."

It had been a relief to be away from Carolyn's negative attitude for a few days, but Lori had to go back. She could not tell if Carolyn was glad to see her or not. It was harder for Lori to study since Carolyn always had the TV on or wanted to talk. Carolyn could not understand why Lori had to study so much since she had never gone to college.

After three months of studying, Lori passed her college class and added three more college hours to her degree. She should be able to almost finish her master's degree by taking a full load of classes at the college the coming summer.

"Mrs. Jones, I need to see you in my office," Mr. Rosa said during Lori's planning period.

"What now?" Lori asked herself as she followed her principal into this office.

Mr. Rosa closed the door and sat down behind his nice desk. "Mrs. Jones, I have more bad news for you," Mr. Rosa said kindly. "You know that you are not qualified, by college hours, for your teaching position here, and that you were hired on a one year's contract. We have several people applying for your job that are qualified, and we have to hire one of them. I'm sorry; I think you have done a fine job here."

Lori was stunned. "I thought if I finished my degree as quickly as I can, that I could keep my job," she said.

"There's no way you can have your master's degree completed by the time school starts next fall, so we have no choice in not renewing your contract," Mr. Rosa explained. "I know that credentials do not always prove that a person is a better teacher, but we have to comply with the law, and we have to have certified teachers when at all possible. I hope you can find a good teaching job in the area you are certified to teach, Mrs. Jones." He stood up and held the door open for Lori to leave.

"Maybe it will be easier to go somewhere else and get away from the memories of Steve," Lori told herself while walking back to her classroom.

When Lori came in from school that evening Carolyn had a little male dog on her lap while watching TV. "Where did that dog come from?" Lori asked.

"I'm taking care of it for a friend while they are on vacation," Carolyn answered.

"I think you should have asked me first," Lori replied.

"They'll only be gone for a week, and I didn't see what it would hurt," Carolyn replied.

Lori did not know what she could do about the circumstance. She was terribly angry when she saw the dog trying to ride Lady. "I'm glad Lady is spade, but you keep that dog away from her, understand!" Lori shouted.

"Oh, all right," Carolyn said. She picked up the dog and made him stay on her lap.

The next evening Lori caught the dog lifting its leg and wetting on one of the lounge chairs.

"Carolyn, I will not put up with that!" Lori exclaimed. "My furniture isn't new, but it's the best I have; if I find anymore messes, the dog is out of here!"

The owners did not come and pick up the dog after a week. Carolyn called the owners and found they had been home several days and had no plans to pick up the dog. "Tell them to come and pick up the dog, or we'll call the dog catcher!" Lori shouted.

Carolyn told her friend what Lori had said. The next day when Lori came home, the male dog was gone. "Praise the Lord!" Lori exclaimed.

Lori obtained permission to use one of the school's white vans to take her junior class for a field trip to the highest suspension bridge in the world. It was a fun day as well as educational. A week later, she used the same van to take her senior class to visit the Museum of Natural History in the state capital. It was a long day, but fun.

While they were at the museum, Betty was given a wheelchair to use during the tour. She enjoyed the large theater presentation on the seven-story screen. The movie they saw was one that had been taken from a camera attached to the leg of a sea gull. It made Lori a little sick at her stomach to be floating over the coastline. She decided that the equilibrium of a bird was much different than a human's.

It was great to see a crippled student enjoy "flying" once in her life. Betty squealed through the whole presentation.

Betty needed to go to a rest-room after the movie. Lori pushed the wheelchair to a door that said "Women" on it. She pushed the wheelchair through the door and gasp. There was a flight of steps leading up to the restroom. It was about the only restroom Lori had seen for a long time that was not built to accommodate handicapped persons. There was no way to get Betty up the stairs, so Lori had to hurry and find another restroom since Betty was not always able to wait.

By May, Lori was satisfied with the progress of the students who had not quit school. Even the Hispanic student that had been on probation had attended well and did well on his tests. Lori had gotten used to signing a progress report for his probation officer every week. It was a part of the new world that she was teaching in.

Special Education was a hard field, but Lori loved working with these troubled kids. Most of them were smart, but didn't fit into the environment of a regular classroom, and most of them failed to see the importance of school all together.

Once again, at the end of the year, it was hard to tell the students, other teachers, and even Mrs. Ming, good-bye for the last time. "I should be used to it by now," Lori told herself. "Carolyn was still sitting, eating, and watching TV when school was out for the summer. Lori felt guilty when she was angry over the way the carpet and chairs were beginning to show wear. "Carolyn is more important than my carpet and furniture," Lori told herself.

Lori scraped together enough money for her books for the summer college semester, but she had to borrow money from her mother again for the tuition. She planned to take sixteen hours if the college would let her.

It was a hot day in late May when Lori made her first trip to the college in the valley. The old station wagon did not have air conditioning, and it was hot even with the windows rolled down.

"Someday, I'm going to have a car with air conditioning," Lori promised herself.

Lori entered the large three story office building and waited in line to talk to a registrar. It seemed like a long time before she was ushered into the office. "I'm working on my Master's Degree in Special Education, and I want to take all the classes I can this summer to finish as quickly as I can," Lori explained. She handed the lady the transcripts of all her college hours, including the fifteen hours she completed at Thomasville University.

The lady called Dr. Coolie. Dr. Coolie had been the professor that Lori had just taken the two extension courses under. Dr. Coolie would also be head of the committee to help Lori obtain her Masters degree.

"Dr. Coolie says that you must take Current Events in Education over under him," the lady said.

"Oh! No!" Lori exclaimed, helplessly. There went her three hours under Dr. Snead. Lori had worked so hard for that A, although she had enjoyed the class and learned a lot.

"Here are the classes that Dr. Collie has lined up for you," the lady said, handing Lori a schedule sheet. "We only allow a student to take sixteen hours in one summer. You may go to one of the desks down the hall and pay your tuition now, and classes start tomorrow." She held open the door for Lori to leave and the next person in line to come in.

Lori used the blank check Elizabeth had given her and filled out the tuition and dorm bill. "Who do I talk to in order to find a place to live? I've never stayed in a dorm before:" Lori asked.

Lori was assigned a three bedroom apartment. "Sometimes you have the apartment to yourself, but this summer, I imagine that all bedrooms will be filled," the manager said.

"It would be nice to have an apartment to myself in order to study more," Lori replied. She drove across the campus and found the right number on one of the apartment buildings. The apartment was on the second floor of the complex. Lori felt tired by the time she had carried all her clothes, toiletries, and kitchen supplies up the flight of stairs.

Lori put her bedding on the bed in the first bedroom. She put up her groceries and hung up her clothes. After resting, Lori drove around the campus, and town, to find out where the class building, library, and town businesses were located. She went to the library and bought all the books she needed for her five classes. The books were expensive and heavy. It looked like she would be doing a lot of reading. "I might as well go to the apartment and get started," Lori said to herself.

Lori unlocked the apartment and thought she was alone when a person walked out of the bathroom. The person was tiny, but Lori could not tell if the person was a man or a woman. The person looked more like a man. "What are you doing here?" Lori asked, shocked.

"I'm your new room-mate," the lady answered. "Didn't aim to startle you; my name is Charley," she said.

"I thought at first they had assigned me a man room-mate," Lori said, embarrassed.

"Oh, that all right; it happens to me all the time," Charley replied. "It would be ^&*()%^& fun to have a man room-mate for the summer though, wouldn't it?" she said with a laugh.

"I don't think so," Lori answered.

"%^$*&^@$, you must be a poor married soul," Charley said.

"No. I'm not married," Lori answered.

"I'm not either, so let's have some fun this summer; that's what we are here for," Charley said.

"I'm here to work on my Master's Degree and I don't think I'm going to have any time to have any fun," Lori explained. "Besides, my finance died last January, and I'm not over it yet," she said.

"I'm sorry about that, but #@%$^* life goes on," Charley replied. "Loosen up and have a good time," she added. "I got my Master's Degree in Physical Education a few years ago, and it's not all that %$#^@%@ hard," Charley explained.

"It will probably be hard for me because I don't have a Bachelor's Degree in Special Education; and I might as well start studying now," Lori said. She walked into her bedroom and closed the door.

Lori sat down at the small desk next to her bed. She lit up a cigarette and took a mouthful of M & Ms. Lori looked through the Table of Contents of each book. "Lord, I would have liked to have had a

Christian room-mate: why did you send me one like Charlie?" Lori asked in prayer. "I guess the apartment won't be too crowded with just the two of us, and I'll try to get along with her," Lori said to herself.

Two hours later, Lori heard a knock on the front door. She listened while Charley answered the door. Lori could hear two lady's conversation. Pam was the other room-mate and she sounded as worldly as Charley. "Oh Lord, please help me," Lori prayed. She lit up another cigarette and tried to relax when she heard Charley say, "Pam I want you to meet our other room-mate," as she knocked on Lori's door.

Lori answered the door. "Lori Jones, this our other room-ate, Pam Andrews; Pam, this is Lori Jones," Charley said. "Lori is kind of in morning for a guy that died last winter," she explained.

"It takes a little while to get over a death," Pam said. "Glad to meet you," she added. "Aren't you here to have a good time?" she asked.

"No, I'm here to study," Lori answered.

"Too bad; I'm married, but I come to summer school to have a good time, and my husband doesn't care," Pam said.

"Glad to meet you," Lori forced herself to say. She excused herself to become more acquainted with her books before the next day.

Pam and Charley did not try to cover up their ways of the world. Lori wondered how much of the teacher population had the same values on life as her two room-mates. These were the younger people that were teaching in the schools now days.

Lori picked up another one-credit hour the next week to bring her schedule up to sixteen hours. She spent all her time going to classes, studying, and doing research in the library. Pam and Charley were not taking many hours and Lori never saw Charley study. Pam would study once in awhile. She was glad when the weekend came and she could go home, even though she still had to study while she was at home. Carolyn was always so cranky that Lori was glad to get away to go college. It seemed that she had very little space to relax.

Lori's room-mates ate out most of the time. Lori did not feel that she could afford to eat out, even at the school cafeteria. Lori took a little time to visit with her room-mates and get to know them better. She learned that Charley had never been married. She had fought with her father because of their different views of the Vietnam War and she had never forgiven her father for being in favor of the war. Charlie's father was now deceased, but Charley still seemed bitter.

Pam had married a widower that was old enough to be her father. "I used to be fat and didn't date much," Pam told the others. "Then I fell for this older guy and married him; and I've lost about eighty pounds since we have been married. His kids don't seem to be crazy over me, but I feel that Bud and I have a good marriage," Pam said. "Let me show you a picture of Bud and me," she said, handing Lori an eight by ten inch picture.

Lori was shocked when she looked at the picture. Bud was a very dark Negro.

Pam started to laugh. "But he is predigest against minorities, especially blacks," Pam said. "One of our friends took the picture she had of us and sent it off and had Bud painted like a Negro. He about had a heart attack when he saw it," she said, still laughing.

The third evening, Pam brought a friend to the apartment. Larry was a handsome, music teacher that Pam had know for years. He spent part of the evening at the apartment visiting. Larry talked about his job and his children, who were in Elementary School. He sounded like he was happily married.

A few days later, Lori realized that Pam and Larry were having a "summer affair". Charley went to the movies one evening with the. She came home before Pam did. "Lori, we found out tonight that Larry has never been weaned," Charley said, laughing.

Lori mumbled a reply and excused herself to go to her room to study. "Oh Lord, these people are the people that are teaching our kids," Lori said. "They may be good teachers, but what kind of examples are they?" Lori asked the Lord.

Lori had a hard time keeping her mind on her class-work. She had several term papers and spent a lot of time in the library with books a microfish. Lori often wondered how other students got by without working.

The class of Current Events was only lectures from Dr. Coolie. Most of the material Lori had covered in Dr. Snead's class. Lori had to read a lot to pass Dr. Coolie's tests. It seemed that his lectures did not help the students on the kinds of tests he was giving.

Lori took a class on counseling Parents with Handicapped Children under Dr. Coolie. The class was interesting and the students interviewed several parents with handicapped children. Lori learned that the number one fear the parents talked about was dying before their handicapped child and there would no one that would take care of their child.

The students had to do research on certain handicaps and learn all they could about it in order to ask the right questions. Toward the end of the Semester, "Turner Disease" was the subject. Dr. Coolie said that the students probably would not find much information on this handicap. Lori was determined. She found a small medical library and a lot of information which she shared with the rest of the class. Dr. Coolie seemed impressed with Lori's research.

One class that Lori enjoyed was Dr. Carson's class. He was not a regular teacher, but came to the campus during the summers to teach. His lectures seem to make sense and Lori felt that Dr. Carson had high moral values. He talked about his family in many of his lectures. "Today is my birthday, and I want all you students to join me in celebrating at Johnny and Susan's, the pub downtown, tonight," Dr. Carson said.

Lori debated about going. Charley and Pam thought she should go. "It'll do you good to do something besides study," they both said.

Lori decided to go. She soon felt out of place. There was a lot of drinking and couples getting together. One lady teacher did a nasty illustration with a napkin on the table. One guy about Lori's age, that she did not know, asked her to dance. The music was fast, but the man let her know that she was a lot of fun and he would not mind spending some time with her. Lori felt so filthy after the dance that she quietly left the noisy party. She felt disappointed in Dr. Carson, too.

Lori drove back to the apartment. "Oh Lord, take me home. I don't belong here," Lori prayed before she got out of the car. She said hello to

Pam, Charley, and Larry, and went on to her room. Lori indulged by eating a lot of M & Ms and smoking.

Lori was expecting the utilities at the trailer to go down during her absence at summer school. Carolyn was running the swamp cooler night and day. The utilities were going "sky high".

"Carolyn, you are going to have to get a job to help pay these utilities, or find another place to live; I can't afford this electric bell," Lori said. "You've lived here four months and not helped with anything, and I can't afford to take care of you any longer," she tried to explain.

"I've been baby sitting Lady for you; doesn't that count for anything?" Carolyn snapped. She did not look at, or talk to Lori the rest of the weekend. Lori was glad when it was time to leave to go back to college.

The next weekend when Lori came back to the trailer, the house was empty. She called Nada. "Nada, do you know where Carolyn and Lady are?" she asked.

"Lady is here waiting for you; she is such a cute little dog," Nada said. "Carolyn left Lady here when she moved in with an old friend that is on Welfare," she explained.

"I'll be right over and get Lady and Carolyn's new address," Lori replied. Lori picked up Lady, said thank you, and drove over to an old trailer that had the same address that was on the paper Nada had written down for her.

Carolyn saw Lori coming and came out of the old trailer. "Did you find Lady?" she asked.

"Yes," Lori answered. "How are you doing?" she asked.

"Fine, I guess," Carolyn answered.

"Carolyn, I hated to kick you out, but I didn't have enough money to pay all my bills last month, and I just didn't have a choice. I'm sorry," Lori said.

"That's all right. I'm staying with a friend here and I'm getting ready to go to a vocational college and study secretary skills in another week. The government is going to pay for it and it'll help me get a job and support myself," Carolyn said.

"Well, take care of yourself," Lori ordered. She gave Steve's daughter a hug and left. Lori was a little lonesome without Carolyn there, but lady seem not to be afraid anymore and did not spend all her time under the bed. On Saturday, Lori took lady to Elizabeth's because she could not take her back to college with her.

"Mother, I hate to ask you to take care of Lady, but I don't know what else to do; I have to get that degree so I can find another job," Lori tried to explain.

"I think we will enjoy Lady, and don't worry," Elizabeth said. Lori hurried back home to study and get ready to go back to school.

The last week of the summer semester the campus was filled with lunchroom personnel, taking classes in nutrition. They, too, seemed to be have a good time. Lori had studied for about two hours. Charley and Pam were in their bedrooms too. Lori walked out of her room to get a drink of water from the kitchen. She screamed. She could not get into the kitchen. Someone had filled the apartment living room, eating space, and kitchen with large braches from trees.

"How could this happen with all three of us here?" Lori asked herself. Then she heard the loud music coming from the other two bedrooms. Lori, too, had been playing music while she studied. It had not been difficult for some people to drag in all the tree limbs.

Charley and Pam heard Lori scream. They ran out of their bedrooms to see what was the matter. Charley begin laughing. "I bet it was those silly #$@%$^^ cooks saw the place where they were trimming trees and decided to fill our apartment," she said.

The rest of the evening was used in cleaning up the apartment. Lori had to work late that night to finish up a paper that was due the next day.

Lori finished her last test and told her two roommates good-bye. She did not feel that she had been a very good Christian witness to them. Charley was anxious to get back to her PE classes and coaching, and Pam was anxious to get back to her teaching job and husband. It was almost like the summer had never happened.

Lori took another route back to Dannon. She drove to a mountain town and looked for her retarded aunt. She finally found a large, green-colored house that was a group home. "Does Mary Stoner live here?" she asked the lady that opened the door.

"Yes me to!" Lori heard her Aunt Mary shout as she ran to the door and hugged Lori. Lori visited with her aunt for awhile and then it was time for her to leave. "Come back again, kiddo," Aunt Mary said when Lori left.

Lori drove to the next town to stay with another aunt. She enjoyed visiting with Aunt Francis. Aunt Francis had lived a "dog's life" with her first husband, and the father of her two sons, and had not had a stable relationship since then. She understood some of Lori's heartache.

Lori left early the next morning to drive thirty-five miles to a larger town where they were having a Job Fair. She just had to find a job, and school would be starting in just three weeks.

The people at the Job Fair were nice, but no one was looking for another teacher. Lori visited with a dark man that was a principal from a large school in the state capital. He asked Lori a lot of questions about her ideas on teaching. "If I needed a teacher, I would hire you," the man said.

Lori thanked the man, but his comments would not help to pay her bills. She drove on back to Dannon, disappointed and praying for some job to open up in the last part of the summer.

Lori picked up her week's mail. In it were two invitations for interviews from two different schools. Both schools were looking for Elementary Special Education teachers. Lori called one school and sit up an appointment for the following week. She then called the second school. The superintendent sounded friendly. "I'll be able to interview you one hour after you finish your first interview. It will take you about forty-five minutes to get from there to here," the man said. "Our administration building is at the end of Main Street on the right," he explained.'

The next week, Lori received her grades in the mail. She had made an A in all her classes but Dr. Coolie's. Dr. Collie had given her all B grades. Lori cried when she saw the B replacing her A from Dr. Sneads class form Thomasville University. "I think I know why some kids get so discouraged with college," Lori told herself.

Lady and Lori traveled to the first school for the first interview. The school was small, but the people were friendly. "I think the job is yours if you want it," the superintendent said.

"I probably will take it, but I have another interview before I decide" Lori replied. "I'll let you know tomorrow," she said.

"I understand" the superintendent said.

Lori had finished her first interview early. She drove around the small town. It seemed rather lonely for a woman living alone. Lori drove on to the next interview. Wasco was located on an Interstate highway. It was a much larger town and many businesses. There was a High School, Middle School, and Elementary School in separate buildings. Lori still had time to walk Lady and eat dinner before her next appointment. She chose a restaurant with an upper eating area overlooking the main part of town.

Lori walked lady again. She found the superintendents office without any trouble. "May I use your restroom?" she asked the secretary.

"Sure, it's right over there," the lady said.

Lori combed her hair that had been messed by the blowing wind. She put on a little rouge and lipstick and tried to look her best. "I wish I could make you look younger," she told the reflection in the mirror.

Lori was ushered into a nice office with black, leather furniture. The superintendent stood up and said, "I'm Dr. Bloomingdale, the superintendent you talked to; this is Mr. Walker, the Elementary principal, and this is Mr. Wilson, the Middle school principal. Mr. Little, our Special Education Coordinator could not be here this afternoon," Dr. Bloomingdale said. "Gentlemen, this is Ms. Lori Wallace,' he said.

Lori shook hands with everyone and sat down. Although the men were friendly, Lori felt like she was under a microscope. Mr. Bloomingdale asked several questions while he looked over Lori's transcript. Lori answered with feeling.

"Tell me, Ms. Wallace, why you only taught at Dannon one year and let go?" Mr. Bloomingdale asked.

'Because I wasn't qualified and was only hired for one year," Lori answered. "I have taken sixteen hours of graduate credit this summer and only lack four more hours to complete my Master's Degree in Special Education," Lori answered.

"That's very commendable," Mr. Walker said. He asked several questions pertaining to the Elementary level. Mr. Walker seemed satisfied with Lori's answers.

"I'm just listening and learning today," Mr. Little said. "This will be my first year with the administration; I'm a farmer and on the school board," he explained.

Lori was asked to wait outside while the three men discussed her answers. She tried to get interested in a magazine she found in the secretary's room, but her mind was still in the inner office.

"We have decided to hire you, even though we have to hire you on a Temporary Emergency Certificate until you complete your degree," Mr. Bloomingdale said.

"I understand and thank you," Lori replied.

"Ms. Steel, please get the contract papers ready for Ms. Wallace to sign," Mr. Bloomingdale told the secretary.

Lori had just signed the papers when Mr. Walker asked her to ride over to the elementary school with him. I want to show you our building and supplies and your room," the principal said.

Lori was impressed with the friendliness of Mr. Walker. He was proud of his domain. "I'm afraid this is all we have to offer you at this time," Mr. Walker said when he showed Lori where she would be teaching. Lori's classroom was a large, single wide trailer. "Our school has grown faster than our buildings," Mr. Walker explained. "At least you don't have to worry about bothering any other teachers out here," he said. "Our other Special Education teacher's room is in that part of the building. Her door is close to yours, and she will help you in any way she can," Mr. Walker said.

Lori said thank you when she was returned to her car. "I need to find a place to park my trailer home," she explained. Lori drove all over town. She only found two small trailer parks. She went to talk to the owner. "I think I found a space I like in the smaller west park," Lori said.

"There are some older trailers in that area and the people have lots of kids," the owner said. "Let me who you a space I have in the east park. The people there are older, the homes are newer, and there aren't as many kids around," he said.

Lori liked the east space better. "My home is seventy-five feet long," Lori said. "Will it fit in there?" she asked.

The owner helped Lori measure. She would be ten feet from the alley. It would fit. "Now I have to go home and find someone to move it for me," Lori said.

Lori and Lady rushed back to Dannon. "Thank you Lord for new job," Lori prayed. She called the smaller school and told them her decision. The next day Lori made several calls to find someone to move her home. It would cost one-thousand dollars to move the home the two hour trip. That would take most of Lori's last check from Dannon. Lori gave her freezer to the next neighbor for taking down the skirting, getting the house ready to move, and putting the skirting back up.

The day before the move, Ben called. "Lori, I'm coming through your area this evening. My mother just died and I'm bringing back her old car to Nebraska. Since I'll be coming through Dannon, I wondered if I could stop by and see you," he said.

"I guess so, Ben, but they are moving my house tomorrow and I'm in a terrible mess," Lori answered.

"That's all right. I won't stay very long," Ben replied. "See you in ten hours," he said.

"Oh well," Lori said after she hung up. After all, Ben had written and called to encourage her all during summer school. It seemed that when Lori was the most discouraged and lonely, she would receive a call or letter from Ben. His letters had been positive, inspirational, and uplifting. It would not hurt to visit with him one evening. Lori was beginning to tell herself that there weren't many men left on the planet that was as caring as Ben, but she would not let herself ever be hurt again.

Lori took all of her breakable dishes out of the cabinets and put them into boxes with papers wrapped around them. She tied down door knobs and tried to make everything secure. It was ten o'clock that night, and the house was in a mess, when Ben showed up. He had driven straight through from Arizona and looked tired.

"How are you doing?" Ben asked.

"Come on in; I'm doing better since I have a new job and a way to pay my bills," Lori answered. She told Ben about her classes at summer school, her two strange room mates, and her new job in Wasco.

Ben told Lori about his mother's stroke and not regaining consciousness before she died. He talked about his mother's wishes to be cremated and that he had buried her ashes next to his real father's grave. "I'm an only child, and I was glad that my cousin could be there to help me make all the decisions. She is almost like a sister to me." "I need to go on now and find a place to stay tonight so I can drive on home in the morning," Ben said.

"That would be silly at this time of night," Lori replied. "I have a hide-a-bed that would be more comfortable than a motel bed; It's a little worn since Carolyn slept on it for four months, but it should be plenty comfortable. You can use the bathroom in the front part of the house, and I'll see you in the morning," she said. "Good night," Lori said as she shut the door to her bedroom and master bath.

The men came to the trailer early to hook up the trailer and get things ready for the two hour trip. "While the men are working outside, I want you to go with me downtown," Lori told Ben. "I need your opinion on something."

Ben climbed into the station wagon. Lori drove to the place where she had bought the tires to go to Steve's funeral. "I'm going to trade cars today, too. My old station wagon has too many miles on it," Lori explained. "I sort of wanted this older Town Car, but my youngest son tried to convince me to buy this newer Buick Century. It's a front wheel drive and should be safer in snow and ice." "What do you think?" Lori asked.

"I know one thing; the tires for the Century Buick will cost a lot less than they will for the Town Car," Ben answered.

"Then that's what I shall buy," Lori replied. She went into the office and filled out the necessary papers. The loan company that had loaned her money for the trailer had loaned her more money to get a better car.

Ben helped Lori move everything from her old car to her newer car. The men were almost ready to move the mobile home out of the trailer park when Lori and Ben came back.

Lori and Ben were in front of the trailer when a nice car pulled up in front. It was Margaret. Margaret was the PE teacher at the high school and one of Lori's friends. Her husband was president of one of the local banks.

"I just had to come by, Lori, and wish you good luck," Margaret said.

"Thank you, Margaret, it's hard to leave Dannon," Lori replied.

"You had a lot of heartache here, but with your attitude, I'm sure you're going to be successful; the best of luck to you," Margaret said.

Lori waved good-bye to another dear friend that she would probably never see again.

The men pulled Lori's trailer out into the street and stopped. "What's the matter?" Lori asked.

"The trailer has a broken axel. We can't move until you get it fixed," one man explained.

"I don't know what to do," Lori moaned. She and Ben were looking under the trailer at the broken axel when Lori realized someone was standing behind her. She looked up and saw Harley, Terry's dad, and a long time friend. Harley and his family went to the same church Lori had attended for twenty-five years before she met Tim. "What are you doing here?" Lori asked with a smile.

"Ah, I just come by here every once in awhile to see if everything looks all right around your place," Harley answered.

"I never knew that," Lori replied. "The last time I saw you was when I was painting Grace's house."

"Well, it looks like you have some trouble here," Harley said.

"Yes, do you have any suggestions?" Lori asked.

"Well, I know a good welder here in town," Harley replied. He quickly took the wheel off the trailer and put it in the back of his farm pickup. "Ill be back as quick as I can," Harley said. He was back in less than an hour. The axel was neatly welded and Harley put it back on the trailer's rim. "I think you're ready to travel," Harley said.

"Thank you very much, and what do I owe you?" Lori asked.

"Ah, nothing. What are friends for?" Harley answered.

"Thanks again, and you are an answer to prayer," Lori said.

"That's what I'd like to be, but I'm just an old farmer," Harley said with a chuckle. "You two be careful," he said as he drove away.

The caravan, consisting of the long trailer house, Lori in her "new" Buick, followed by Ben in his mother's old Pinto station wagon, was finally staring on their two hour journey.

Lori watched the back of the trailer traveling over the small highway. It seemed like she could still see Steve painting it.

There was only one small town between Dannon and Wasco. Lori and Ben stopped for some pop, and then caught up with the trailer again. By the time the caravan arrived in Wasco, Lori's neighbor showed up to help hook up the utilities. By dark, Lori had lights and water. Ben lit her hot water heater. Lori was ready to start a new life in a new town and new job.

"I have to get back to Nebraska so I can go to work tomorrow," Ben said. "God bless you, Lori." Ben kissed Lori on the lips and was soon gone.

Lori was till standing in the living room surprised over what had just happened.

CHAPTER XII

A NEW LIFE IN WASCO

When Lori got up the next morning, she did not know her directions. The trailer was facing east now instead of west. It almost looked like the sun was coming up in the west. Lori put her dishes back into the cabinets and straightened up the house. Her neighbor finished the skirting around the trailer and thanked her for the freezer.

"I have time to take a short vacation before school starts," Lori told herself. "I feel that I need to go back to South Dakota." Lori called Connie to see if some of Steve's kids would be home if she came to visit.

"I'm moving into a new place today that will be close to where I'm going to college this fall," Connie said. "It's only an hour away from the rest of the family, and I want you to come and spend a night with me, and I'll show you around my new town."

Lori packed her suitcases and started the long trip back to South Dakota. It would be the last trip in that direction for a long, long time. Lori stopped and spent the first night at Elaine's She knew she didn't have enough money for a motel and she enjoyed her cousin's company. There was more music and fun. Lori felt strong enough to complete the journey alone this time. "I just have to close the pages on another chapter of my life," Lori tried to explain to Elaine.

Lori entered Steve's home town one more time. She did not have any trouble finding the cemetery. Lori walked through a late, summer breeze to the place she had seen "her treasure" put into the brown earth. It seemed like it had been years since Steve had left her.

"Oh, that's beautiful!" Lori exclaimed as she looked at Steve's grave stone. Steve's kids had gone together and had a small engraved stone put at the head of the gravesite. On it was Steve's name, the year he was born, and the year he died. The stone was decorated with cattle, a horse, and a windmill.

Lori dropped to her knees and touched the cool earth on the grave. "I had to come these many miles to tell you good-bye one more time, my love," Lori said aloud. "I still love you more than I could ever tell you. Thank you for all the happiness you gave me. I hope I can find the purpose that I'm still here in this life and you are gone. I feel that you chose to go and be with your Lord. I pray that I will love the Lord as much as I know you did. I know you are in a perfect place now, waiting for me. I know you don't want me to be lonely, but to go on with my life. I'll never forget you, my love. And, I'm going to try to live close to God so I can see you again, someday." "Good-bye, sweetheart," Lori said again.

Lori patted the cold dirt one more time and walked back to the car. She waited until she stopped crying before she went to visit each of Steve's children and tell them good-bye. All seven of the families Lori visited thanked her again for making their dad happy, and told her to get on with her life. Lori finished her good-byes to one of the nicest families in South Dakota.

Starting back to Elaine's, Lori cried some, ate M & Ms, and smoked heavily. Instead of stopping at Elaine's first, Lori drove down Main Street looking for Ben's house. Elaine had told Lori where Ben lived. Lori was surprised when she found the house. What she saw was a quaint, turn of the century, two-story home.

Lori drove down the alley in back of the house. She saw Ben through the back screen door. He was sitting at the kitchen table with his shirt off.

Lori walked up past a small building and a pen where a beautiful, large Labrador dog was waiting for attention. She walked up three worn cement steps to the back door and knocked. She saw Ben running out of the room and returning with a shirt.

Ben looked surprised, but asked Lori to come in.

"I have just gotten back from South Dakota; I just closed another chapter on my life," she explained. "I know you're not perfect, but you're a true Christian and caring." "I wonder if you might change your mind and want to date me?" Lori asked.

"The only way people can love each other is to really get to know each other, and I don't know whether that is possible for us or not since we live so far apart," Ben answered.

"It takes three hours to get here from Wasco and we could see each other on weekends," Lori said.

"That's impossible for me because I have to work six days a week. I work on Saturdays," he said.

"I don't, and I can stay with Elaine when I come to see you," Lori replied. "I'm impressed with your faith in God, and I need someone to help me be steady in my faith again. I'm willing to put forth an effort to get more acquainted, if you are."

Ben did not answer.

Lori felt so embarrassed. "What on earth am I doing here, taking a chance on being hurt again," Lori asked her self as well as Ben. "I'm sorry I came," Lori said walking back to the door.

"Wait," Ben said. He caught Lori by the arm. Ben put his arms around Lori and kissed her. This time he did not miss her mouth. Ben's warmth and gentleness made Lori tremble. "Oh Lord, here I go again. Please protect me," Lori prayed.

"Lori, I'm embarrassed for you to come to my house," Ben said. "I haven't done much house keeping since my wife died, and things are really in a mess. I'm not used to having company."

"Yes, I see what you mean," Lori said, laughing. "Can I see the rest of the house now," she said, teasingly.

"Well, it's not any worse than these rooms," Ben answered.

Lori followed Ben as he showed her his quaint home. The house had a full basement where Ben had a washer and dryer. The main level had a nice-sized porch, a large kitchen with eating space, a full bath, a huge dining room, living room, an entrance room, and a front porch. In the entrance was an open stairway leading to the second floor. Lori followed Ben up the stairs and through three bedrooms and another full bath.

The house had been beautiful about eighty years ago. The plush, dark-green carpets were thread bare. The antic wall paper was coming off the walls. Some of the walls were completely bare. The twelve foot ceilings needed papered or painted. There was so much litter in every room that there was only a path leading from one room to another. Newspapers were stacked six foot high in the living room. There was a huge rolled up carpet taking up most of the space in the large dining room.

"Oh Ben, this is a beautiful house," Lori said, seeing it the way it had once looked.

Ben was surprised with Lori's comments. "My kids and step kids have left a lot of things here," Ben tried to explain, "Most of this stuff isn't even mine."

"I can help you clean it up on the weekends I'm here. It will give us something to do," Lori said.

"Maybe your help is what I need," Ben replied.

"I need to get on to Elaine's. We're going to church in the morning. Hope to see you there," Lori said.

Ben kissed Lori good-night, and this time he hit her lips perfectly. Lori wanted to cling to Ben's solidness, but instead she slipped away and said good-night. Lori drove over to Elaine's.

Elaine was glad to see Lori, but she was not glad to see Lady. "Lori, would you mind if Lady stayed in the car?" Elaine asked.

"I don't think that's a good idea, but I'll see if Ben will keep her for me," Lori replied. She called Ben.

"I guess she can't hurt anything over here. I can put her on the back porch. It's warm out there she can't hurt anything out there," Ben answered, thinking aloud.

Lori took Lady back to Ben's. "I hate to ask you to do this, but I don't know what else to do," Lori said.

"She'll be okay," Ben said again. "I'm still taking care of my kids' old dog, Bo."

"Yes I saw her outside," Lori answered. Lori received another good-bye kiss before she went back to Elaine's.

Lori told Elaine that she and Ben had decided to start dating. "He's a good Christian," Elaine said. "I wouldn't have given you his address if I hadn't thought that he was all right."

"Elaine, the only way we can date is for me to drive here on weekends and stay with you," Lori said. "Would you mind if I did that?" she asked.

"I'd love to have you here, and I wouldn't let you stay at Ben's anyway," Elaine said, laughing.

"Thanks Elaine. You've always been like a sister to me," Lori said. She said good night and went to the guest bedroom for some sweet sleep.

Elaine and Lori went to church the next morning. Ben came in after he had taken the Sunday school children home.

Lori watched Ben walking down the church isle. This was the man she had decided to trust some of her time to. Ben was taller than Lori had remembered. He was about five foot, nine inches tall. His hair was silver gray and he wore silver rimmed glasses. Ben probably didn't weigh over a hundred, sixty pounds, and looked neat in his double knit, blue suit. Ben was wearing a light blue shirt with no tie. There was chest hair decorating the top of his shirt.

Lori realized that there was a man and woman walking in with Ben. They looked different. Lori knew from her training that they were mentally handicapped people. Ben helped the lady sit down beside the Pastor's wife. The tall man followed Ben to where she and Elaine were sitting.

Ben sat down beside Lori. The handicapped man sat next to Ben. Ben was soon so interested in the minister's message that Lori knew he was unaware of the people around him.

Lori enjoyed the happy singing and Pastor's message. When church was over, Ben said, "Lori, I have to take these people back to the group home. I'll come by Elaine's and pick you up for dinner."

Lori nodded her head that she understood.

"Lori, I want you to meet a friend of mine," Elaine said. She introduced Lori to a very pretty, slender, brunette, who was nicely dressed.

"So you're Elaine's cousin!" the lady snapped. "I don't think I'm glad to meet you," she said and walked away.

"I don't understand her attitude!" Elaine exclaimed.

"Who is she?" Lori asked.

"She is Ben's old girlfriend. She told me that she was not a bit interested in Ben before I sent you his address, and now she acts like that!" Elaine said, disgusted. "She wants me to pray for her to find a Christian man, and then she dates men that are not Christians."

Lori wished that she had not seen Ben's pretty, ex girl friend. It made her feel old, fat, and ugly.

"Let's get out of here," Elaine said.

Lori followed Elaine out of the large church.

Ben came by to take Lori out to dinner, but Elaine talked them into eating with her and her family. It was a fun day. Elaine and Lori played music for awhile, then everyone joined in a game of scrabble.

"Oh dear, I need to start home," Lori said. "I have to get ready for a brand new job."

Ben followed Lori over to his house and Lori picked up Lady. She felt relaxed and visited with Ben longer than she intended. "I just have to get home" Lori said again. Ben and Lori kissed good-bye and the zing was there. Lori started her three hour journey to Wasco. "If I would have taken the other job, it would have been too far to drive here to see you," Lori said while she was putting lady into the Buick, "I don't know if I will see you next weekend or not."

As Lori started home she had a let-down feeling. She was soon smoking and eating M & Ms again. Ben's first wife had died from smoking, and she thought too much of Ben to smoke in his presence. "I need to stop," Lori told herself again.

Lori attended her first teacher's meeting the next morning. Teachers from all three schools met together in the high school gym. Lori was thinking as she drove to the gym that it didn't seem like she had had any summer vacation.

Mr. Bloomingdale welcomed the teachers. He was a friendly man, almost ready for retirement, and about sixty pound overweight. The high school principal gave a short speech and introduced the teachers that would be in his building. Mr. Walker, the Elementary principal gave a short talk. He was a nice looking man who looked to be in his forties. Mr. Wilson, the new Middle school principal ended the administration part of the meeting. He was on of the shortest, nicest people Lori had ever met.

Information papers were passed to all the teachers and papers that needed to be filled out and handed in at the main office. The teachers were dismissed for lunch, and to be in their different schools at one o'clock. Lori rushed home for a smoke and a light lunch.

In the afternoon meeting, Lori was introduced to the fourteen teachers, and four aids that made up the Elementary staff. She was the only new teacher. The other Special Education teacher, Bobbi, was friendly and helpful. Bobbi was a short, pretty blonde that looked to be in her thirties. She had already finished her Master's degree and had taught several years in that field.

Lori found the teachers to be as friendly and helpful as the teachers in Dannon. The meeting took the rest of the day. Lori was glad when the meetings were over and she could go home to relax and smoke. The trailer did not bring back so many memories parked in a different city and environment.

The next day there was a short Elementary meeting in the library that afternoon. Lori spent the rest of the day putting up bulletin boards and fixing the old mobile unit as cute as possible. Mr. Walker showed her the file cabinet where all the records were kept. "You might want to look over your students records before tomorrow," he said.

"I would rather look at them later, Lori replied. "I like to get my first impression of each student without knowing anything about them."

"That sounds like a good idea," Mr. Walker said with a smile.

Lori met all of her students on Wednesday. Kris had an older and younger sister. Her sisters were A students and very talented. Kris had a hard time in school. It was easy for her to become angry with herself, and others.

Timmy was the same age as Kris. He was a small, beautiful child, with a sweet, quiet personality. Timmy had such an allergy to milk that one drop of milk could destroy more of his brain cells. His mother was raising her children alone. She was the Home EC teacher at the high school.

The other students were younger, but a lot of fun. Lori taught the students most of the basic subjects. She soon had them working in a Language Experience program like she had used with her student in Thomasville.

Ben called almost every night. It was fun to visit with him and hour before Lori went to bed.

Lori did not plan to go to Elaine's the first weekend, but she caught herself loading her clothes before she went to school Friday morning. She left for Nebraska as soon as school was out. It was seven o'clock before she reached Concord. She went to Ben's first to leave Lady.

Ben and Lori visited about the past week, went out for pizza, and read some scriptures. Ben belonged to three bowling teams, a church softball team, volleyball team, drove the church bus to pick up kids for Sunday school and take them home, gave transportation to two handicapped people, went to three Bible study groups, and worked sixty hours a week.

Lori enjoyed listening to Ben's life. "No wonder he didn't have time to clean house," Lori was thinking.

Ben had five step-children that lived in California, and three sons that he didn't know where they were, and his youngest, a daughter, Joyce, was a junior at the University of Nebraska. "Joyce was only fifteen when her mother died and I have probably spoiled her," Ben said.

It was later when Lori got to Elaine's than Lori had planned. Lori was thankful that Elaine always left the door unlocked for her. She slipped in through the front door in the dark.

"Hi," Elaine's son, Levi said.

"Oh you startled me!" Lori exclaimed. "I didn't see you in here watching TV," she said. "How are you and how is your senior year of school going?" Lori asked the quiet teenager.

"Fine," Levi answered.

"That's good," Lori replied. "I'm going on upstairs and I'll see you in the morning,"

Levi's bedroom was downstairs next to the small living room where the family watched TV.

Lori slept late. She and Elaine enjoyed visiting over hot tea after breakfast. "Elaine, I'm going over to Ben's and see if I can help him clean up his house. Would you like to go with me?" she asked. "Ben will be at work and I thought maybe I can find something to do over there for awhile," Lori explained.

"No, thank you. I have all I can do around here," Elaine replied, laughing.

Lori drove across town and entered Ben's unlocked house. She fed Lady and started carrying old newspapers out to the trash barrel to be burned. Ben had told her she could do anything she wanted to do, but it was hard to decide what to do with all the junk she found in the living room. By noon, the living room looked a little more empty.

Lori was getting excited about fixing up another place. It was full as the old farm house had been when Tim and Lori moved Tim's mother into her new mobile home and they moved into the large house. Lori could vision how the house must have looked in 1900. She could almost see ladies in beautiful, long dresses descending the stairs.

Ben came in for a short lunch break and they ate hamburgers together.

Lori worked in the dining room and kitchen in the afternoon. "I don't know how anyone could live like this," she told herself, but she wanted to help Ben live better and she loved fixing up old houses.

That evening Ben took Lori bowling. They went to church Sunday, ate out, and Ben helped with some of the things in suitcases and boxes that were things that had belonged to Ben's mother who had just died. Other suitcases and boxes were filled with things that had belonged to Sue, Ben's wife that had been dead for five years. Sue had sold Tupperware and jewelry.

Lori dreaded the three hour trip back home, but she found Ben to be a lot of fun, and also funny. She left about four o'clock to get home by sundown. "It will be nice when I'm retired and not have to worry about a job every Monday morning, but I do enjoy my work," Lori told Ben. There was another kiss that left Lori feeling tingly.

Lori returned to Concord the following weekend. This time she started working upstairs. She was surprised to find the closet in the guest bedroom full of Sue's clothes. The last clothes she wore were still hanging in the closet so Ben had told her. Sue had been a tiny woman so Lori took the clothes to a second hand place to be sold. The proceeds from the used clothing went to support the mentally handicapped.

Most of the things Lori found did not mean a lot to Ben so he let Lori decide what to do with them. One room Lori never bothered was Joyce's room.

One weekend, one of Ben's teams bowled in a tournament in Lincoln. Lori went to Concord and worked on the house anyway. She and Elaine always had a lot of fun together, and Lori found that cleaning up Ben's house was a pleasant break from working with students all week.

The next week, Lori and Ben were visiting over the phone when Ben said, "You don't have to come to Concord next weekend."

"Why not?" Lori asked.

"Because I'm delivering some furniture for my company in a little down close to Wasco, and I thought it would be a chance for me visit you for a change," Ben explained.

"That sounds great!" Lori replied.

That week, after school, Lori worked to make the house look perfect, and then on Saturday, she baked pies, and planned to fix Ben a good home cooked meal.

Lori was busy baking on Saturday morning when she heard the door bell. She wiped the flour off her hands and answered the door. There was an attractive, small, man with dark hair standing on the step. Lori recognized him as the brother of the contractor that was building the large, new church building for the church that Lori attended.

"I thought you might like to go play some golf with me today," the man said.

"I haven't played golf for years, Lori replied, surprised.

"That doesn't matter," the man replied. "I have a nice golf cart, and I can teach you how to play again," he said.

"I'm sorry, but I'm expecting company," Lori replied.

"That's all right. We can go golfing after your company leaves," the man said.

"I'm expecting very special company," Lori tried to explain. "It's a dear friend from Nebraska."

"Well, maybe we can play golf next weekend if the weather is nice, or whatever you like to do," the man said.

"I don't think so, but thanks anyway," Lori said as she shut the door.

Ben reached Lori's house early. Lori was not quite ready for him and still had flour on her face when Ben rang the door bell. It bothered Lori that everything wasn't perfect, but she knew that Ben would never notice. The old hide-a-bed was used once more, and it was nice not to drive for six hours on the weekend. Ben went to church with Lori and met her pastor. Lori also showed him through the new church building that wasn't quiet finished.

The next weekend Lori went to visit her mother and sons. She was on her way home when she saw a sign that pointed to the town where Violet lived. "I need another permanent," Lori said to herself and Lady. She turned and was at Violets in thirty minutes.

Lori always enjoyed Violet's company. Violet gave Lori a perm and then the two women went out to eat. "I need to get started on home, it looks like a storm is coming in," Lori said.

"Maybe you better," Violet agreed.

Lori had not gone very far when the wind started blowing harder, and it started to snow. Lori drove slower and slower to keep from sliding on the snowy roads. It was after midnight when she reached the trailer. The phone was ring when she stepped through the door.

"Lori, are you all right?" Elizabeth asked.

"Yes, mother I'm fine," Lori answered. "Why?" she asked.

"It's storming here and I knew you should be home by now, and I was afraid you were stranded in the storm somewhere:" Elizabeth exclaimed. "I called Ben to see if he had heard from you. I guess I better call the sheriff and tell him you are safe at home."

"Sheriff!" Lori exclaimed. "I just went to Violets for a permanent Mother. "I guess you have finally met Ben; How do you like him?" she asked.

"I've been so worried about you that I don't know, but he sounds nice, I guess," Elizabeth replied.

Lori had to take two days off from school and travel seven hours to her college in the valley. It was time for the "comps" that she had to take to get her graduate degree. Lori had studied on her summer materials every evening for a month, trying to remember all the things that had been in summer school at Thomasville and the Valley Universities.

It took all day to get to the college because of the cold and snow. Lori stopped to fill the car with gas at a mountain town. It was so cold that the gas pumps were almost frozen. It took Lori thirty minutes to fill up the gas tank. Lori had never remembered being so cold.

Lori carefully drove over the pass to get to her school. She found a cheap motel and rented a room. It was dark, cloudy, and snowy. Lori felt so lonesome, and nervous, and she called Ben. She always felt better after talking to him.

"Just relax and do your best on your tests," Ben said. "I'll be praying for you during that time."

"Thanks," Lori said and hung up. She tried to get warm under the blankets and go to sleep. She was thinking that Steve didn't have to fight the cold anymore.

Lori was up early and studied all her notes again. She drove onto the campus and reported to the business office. "There will be several people taking their 'comps' in that room," the secretary said. "The professor that was supposed to administer the test had to go somewhere else. He asked me if I would watch you while you are taking your test." "No one is allowed to talk while you are in the room," she said, handing Lori several pages of test.

There were twelve ladies already seated in the room; four in one group and eight in another group. Lori took out her #2 pencils and sat down in an area alone. No one was friendly, but Lori thought it was probably because everyone felt as nervous as she did. Lori read the questions. She knew about one-fourth of the answers for sure. The other questions were on materials that had not been covered in any of her classes.

The secretary was busy on the telephone at her desk in the next room. Lori was trying to concentrate when she heard one group of women discussing the answers to the test. One of the ladies walked over to the other group and asked their opinion on a few answers.

Lori was shocked about what was going on. She looked at the test again and felt like a trapped animal. Lori saw all her hard work and money going down the drain. Lori was in a state of panic, and she did not know what to do. She took out one piece of paper she had put in her purse and checked a few of her answers. She had answered them correctly. "What are you doing?" Lori asked herself. She felt so ashamed. "How can I expect God to help me if I'm cheating?" she asked, inside. She sat in a trance for the rest of the two hours.

Lori handed in her papers and started home. "I know I'm a good teacher with these kids," Lori told herself. "I'm meant to work with handicapped kids, so I will pass my test," she said over and over. The weather was a little warmer and Lori was home by early morning. She had about five hours of sleep before she had to go back to work.

The next weekend was fun to go back to Concord. It seemed like it had been a long time since she had enjoyed the peace of being in Ben's arms. The house was looking better. Joyce called from college.

"I think it's time to tell her about you," Ben said. "Joyce, I'm going steady with a lady I want you to meet; and we might get married," Ben said.

"You can do what you want to do; it's your life!" Joyce exclaimed and hung up.

Ben looked shocked. "Joyce was just a kid when her mother died. They were real close. I guess I have spoiled her since then," he said again.

"I'm sure we will get along, especially since she's a redhead too," Lori said, smiling.

The next week Dr. Coolie called. "Lori, we need for you to come back down here this Thursday for more testing. We have decided to give you some oral comps. You will meet with us, your committee, at eight a.m.," Dr. Coolie said.

"Oh! No!" Lori exclaimed. "I hate to miss more school, but I guess I have no choice."

"That's right," Dr. Coolie replied.

Lori called Ben for more prayer. She fought another mountain storm back to the college in the valley. She rented the same cheap motel room that she had rented two weeks before. The expenses seemed to never end. Lori called Ben again.

"I'll be praying for you, Lori, and praying that you will prove to your committee that you are good teacher," Ben said.

Lori felt cold sweat on her hands when she was ushered into Dr. Coolie's office. Dr. Brown and Dr. Shelly were the other two people on the committee. Lori had taken summer classes under both teachers and made an A in their classes.

Dr. Collie told Lori to sit down and begin asking her questions. Dr. Brown asked more questions, and then Dr. Shelly asked more questions. Lori was asked to define a Special Education student. "I don't like labeling a student because I think it can ruin their lives, but I think of a Special education student as being anyone that can't function in a regular classroom for one reason or another. It can be physical, mental, or emotional handicaps," Lori answered.

"Mrs. Jones, How much research have you done on Special Education since you finished your last college hours?" Dr. Collie asked.

"None, I have just started a new teaching job and I have only been out of class three months," Lori answered.

"Mrs. Jones, how many magazines on Special Education have you subscribed to since you took your last college hours?" Dr, Coolie asked.

"None, I have just moved to a new town and school," Lori answered.

"Mrs. Jones, will you please leave the room while we discuss your situation," Dr. Collie said.

Lori went back to the outer office and waited beside the secretary's desk. Twenty minutes later Dr. Coolie buzzed the secretary to send Lori back in.

Lori felt like she was going to faint as she faced her committee. "Mrs. Jones, we have decided that you will never get a degree in our school. The kindest thing we can do for you is to not ever let you attend out college again," Dr. Coolie said.

"You are in the wrong field."

"But, why didn't someone tell me that before I took all the hours for my degree, and what about my job? How am I going to support myself without my job?" Lori sighed.

"That should not be a problem; I hear that you are planning on getting married," Dr. Coolie said.

"But, I have borrowed money, and worked hard for my college credit, my grades are good and I only lack four more hours, and I feel that I'm doing a good job with my Special Ed. Kids, and I can't keep that job without my degree," Lori tried to explain.

"You are not going to get a degree in this university and you will not be allowed to come back," Dr. Coolie said as he ushered Lori out the door. "Thank you for being so easy to talk to," he said with a smile.

Lori looked at the other two professors. The two women had tears in their eyes. Lori felt the pain of being knocked down again. She saw everything she had worked for, so hard, crashing to her feet. Lori stumbled to her car and drove to a gas station. She called Ben although she was crying.

Ben tried to make Lori feel better but it was hopeless.

Lori called Elizabeth. It seemed that her mother was always helping her through tragic experiences. Elizabeth gave words of encouragement.

Lori had to hurry back to Wasco. She cried, smoked and ate M & Ms all the way. She returned to school with no sleep and to report to Mr. Walker.

"I didn't pass my comps," Lori had to tell her boss. She felt so ashamed. "Is there any possibility that you can hire me another year on an emergency Certificate?" Lori asked.

"We are satisfied with your work with our students," Mr. Walker answered. "I'll talk to the superintendent and see what we can get done,"

"Thanks," Lori said and rushed to her classroom.

Lori taped her students while they read. She let them play the tape back and talk about how they could improve their reading skills. She let them grade their own tests with tapes she had recorded with answers. She heard Timmy say, "I should have known that one because we went over and over it."

"Working with these students is so much fun, and one of the joys of my life, and it might soon be taken away from me," Lori told herself. She tried to forget her failures during the Holidays.

Lori finally met Joyce when she came home from college for Christmas. Joyce was as tall as Ben and only weighed a hundred pounds. She made Lori feel short and fat. The only daughter Lori had ever had was the year she had Rosita. Joyce had not had a mother for many years, so it took her and Lori some adjusting to get along. Before long, when Ben and Lori disagreed over something, Joyce usually took Lori's side.

After New Years there were no graduate classes offered anywhere around Wasco. Lori had to wait for the school board's decision.

Lori joined three other ladies on a bowling league. The alley was only four blocks from the trailer. Some of the teams quit so the alley dropped one of the leagues. Lori's team was dropped after a couple of months.

Lori and Ben felt like God had brought them together. They had many dates on weekends and knew each other quite well. They decided to get married during the Easter Holidays. Joyce could be home and it would give Ben and Lori a few days for a honeymoon.

They planned a simple wedding in Ben's church in Concord. More and more people asked if they could come. They finally decided to open up the church to anyone that wanted to be there.

"I ordered real flowers," Ben told Lori over the phone one evening.

"Why did you do that," Lori asked. "They are more expensive and they don't last very long," she said.

"Because a person only gets married three times in their life and they need to do a good job," Ben said, laughing.

Mike, Elizabeth, Arthur, and Lori's sister Bonnie, and brother in law, Gary, came from back home. Mitch and Staci could not come because Staci was expecting Lori's third grandchild about the same time. The crowd consisted of church friends and mostly Ben's deceased wife's family.

Elizabeth brought a beautiful wedding cake the six hour drive. Elaine, Bonnie, Elizabeth, and Joyce stood on Lori's side. Elaine's husband and Gary stood with Ben. Elaine played the piano and Arther sang two love songs. Mike walked Lori down the isle to give her away to Ben. Lori wore a silk pink dress and Ben wore his blue double knit suit.

Lori walked up to the altar with Mike and took Ben's hand. Ben looked down at her and smiled. Lori thought he was going to say, "I love you," but instead he said, "I forgot the rings." Ben kept telling the pastor not to do the rings part during the ceremony. Ben, jokingly, told his best man that it was his job to take care of the rings and that he would never use him again as a best man.

After the vows were over, Joyce rushed home to get the rings. They exchanged them during the reception. Lori placed the pretty diamond ring that Ben had worn during his marriage to Sue on Ben's finger. Ben placed the diamond rings that Sue had worn on Lori's finger. They had decided to wear these rings until they could afford other nice ones to give each other.

One of the highlights of the wedding was when Sue's mother hugged Lori from her wheelchair and welcomed her into the family. The family thought a lot of Ben and was happy to see him marry again.

Elaine's daughter, Bev, was in charge of the nice wedding reception. There were many gifts to open, but the one gift Lori remembered was a card with $13.42 in it. It was from some of Sue's family. They were poor people and Ben and Lori knew they had sacrificed to give them the money.

Lori was so happy. She had married a guy that loved the Lord just because he wanted to and not because he was trying to please her like Tim had done. Ben was a year and a half younger than Lori and was in good health. "Thank you Lord," Lori said over and over. There was a chance that Lori would lose her job, but Ben's company had just given him a raise and he was making more than Lori made teaching. It seemed like she could not be happier.

After the reception they drove a few miles away and stayed at a Holiday Inn that had all kinds of things to do. It wasn't much of a honeymoon, but the first one Lori had ever had out of three weddings. Joyce took care of Lady and came by the second day on her way back to college to leave Lady. She spent most of the day with them.

The time passed quickly and Lori had to leave to go back to Wasco and work. It was hard to leave Ben's arms and bed, and go back to the cold world. The only thing warm in Lori's world were her students. They always made her feel needed and appreciated.

Lori noticed something white in the headlights. It was drifts of snow on each side of the interstate highway. There was a large snow drift in front of her house. She called a friend to find out that school had been cancelled for the next day. Lori could have spent another day with Ben, if she would have known. It had only rained where they were in Nebraska. "If we had just known," Lori told Ben on the phone that night.

"Lori, I have had news," Ben said a few evenings later.

"Oh no, I'm afraid to ask what it is," Lori replied.

"My company is closing next month. They told us workers that we could quit any time we want to so we can look for other jobs. They have been so good to me that I'm going to stay with them until they close their doors," Ben said.

"I knew you would," Lori replied. "I know it's a sacrifice for you, but I know you are loyal to your company." Lori could not figure out why that had happened to Ben until she was called into Mr. Walker's office.

"Lori, I have good news for you," Mr. Walker said. "The school board has decided to offer you another year's contract, if you promise to complete your Master's in three years," he said.

"Praise the Lord!" Lori exclaimed.

"Amen!" Mr. Walker replied. "I used to be a Methodist preacher," He said with a smile.

All the teachers seem happy that Lori was staying another year, especially Bobbi, and two single, divorced teachers who were Lori's close friends.

Ben helped his company with their final sale. The day the company closed their doors, Ben applied for unemployment checks for the first time in his thirty-seven years of working. He looked for work, but could not find anything.

Lori and Ben had promised each other before they were married that they would live in the place they could make the best living. "It looks like we meant to live in Wasco," Ben said when Lori told him her contract had been renewed for another year.

Lori decided to try to petition the university to reconsider giving her the degree that she had worked so hard for. The college was not agreeable to hear her side. As a last resort, Lori decided to sue the university in hopes of saving her college hours. She called the State's Teachers organization to ask for their help. They were the only lawyers that were familiar with teaching laws. And Lori could not afford to hire a lawyer anyway. She had spent all her money on her college hours and some of her mother's money too.

At first the Teacher's Organization thought they could help her. Lori learned that Dr. Coolie had stopped several students from getting graduate degrees. After the organization lawyers talked to the university, they changed their minds and would not take the case.

"I think it's the Lord's way of telling us He doesn't want us to sue anyone," Ben said.

"Then, I'll have to find a way to start working on my Master's all over again," Lori moaned. She could hardly think about it. It seemed like she had been taking college classes most of her life, and it was a terrible thought to start all over again.

Ben finally found a part time job working for a heating and air conditioning company in Concord. Lori was looking forward to going to Concord and living with Ben as soon as school was out for the summer. Ben was trying to finish the remodeling of his house so he could sell it and move to Wasco. Money was needed, so Lori signed up to teach in the Summer Migrant School. The school lasted six weeks and Lori was still driving to Concord on weekends.

Lori enjoyed working with the kids in summer school. They were mostly Hispanic and reminded her of Rosita. One fourteen year old was there because she had missed so much school. Lori talked her into signing a contract that Angel would not miss any more school "except for her own funeral".

Lori was chatting with four girls one afternoon. She made a startling discovery. The girls were all young teenagers and very pretty. Lori had always admired people with darker skin and brown eyes. The girls told Lori that they wish they were red headed and had white skin like she had. They said they hated their dark hair, skin, and eyes. "But, you are all pretty!" Lori exclaimed.

The girls did not see themselves as pretty. Lori decided they must have faced some difficult situations because they were "Mexicans".

Lori felt that the students accomplished a lot during the short school session. She went to Concord every weekend and helped Ben work on the house. She still smoked out of Ben's presence and out of the house. In the summer, she smoked on the front step hidden by a blue spruce so large that it took up half of the front yard. In cooler weather, she used the basement.

Lori earned an extra two-thousand dollars from summer school. She went back to Concord when school was out. Elaine and Lori traveled to a large Nebraska town where Lori used her extra money to buy wall paper and enough light beige, Kangaback carpet for most of Ben's house. Lori started papering the twelve foot ceilings and then the walls. She used white wall paper decorated with gold flowers. It was hard work but the beauty of the finished rooms gave her extra energy. The house began to look like a beautiful mansion, but it was only to be sold.

Lori painted the back parch, front porch, and the porch off the master bedroom with light colored enamel. She put white percilla curtains in all three bedrooms. Lori took two summer days to paint the complete basement, walls and floor, a light blue.

Joyce was home from college summer school and helped a little, but most of the work was left up to Lori.

Ben's new job terminated just in time for him to move to Wasco and look for another job. He found a job working at Alco and driving a school bus for Lori's school. The two jobs did not make half as much as what he was making at the furniture company. There was room enough for Ben, Lori, and Lady to live in the trailer, but Ben's dog, Bo, was too large to stay in the house. She had to be tied up behind the trailer.

The first weekend after Ben moved to Wasco, he and Lori left Friday as soon as Ben finished his bus route and traveled to Arkansas with Bo. Bo was given to Ben's step son Ronny.

Ben and Lori had traveled all night. It was about four hours before daylight when the lights on the Buick went out. Ben was able to pull the car off the highway without running into a hillside or dropping off into a creek. They tried sleeping until the sun came up. They discovered that the lights had gone out about the only place Ben could have pulled off the road safely. Not far from where they had pulled into a driveway, there was a deep ravine with a creek at the bottom, and on the other side was a rock wall where part of a hill had been blasted away to build the road.

"Praise the Lord for His protection!" Lori exclaimed when she saw the country in daylight.

It took another thirty minutes to get to Ronny's house. Ronny, his wife Betty, and their two high school age sons welcomed them. It was a fun Saturday with visiting and card playing. Ronny helped Ben find a mechanic to fix the lights on the Buick. It was easy to see that Ronny thought a lot of Ben.

"My family was so poor that we even had to put cardboard in our old worn out shoes to keep our feet warm when we walked to school. One of my grade school teachers took our class to an ice cream place for a last day of school fun time. I didn't keep up with the rest of the class, so she bought an ice cream cone for everyone but me. I had never had an ice cream cone before. I was so disappointed. But when mother married Ben, we lived like normal people," Ronny said, hugging Ben's neck.

Lori knew once again, that she had married a "Prince of a Man". Ben never wanted much for him self, but cared for other people. He had sacrificed for his four kids, and five step kids but he didn't seem to know it.

Ben told Lori once that he had not had many bad things happen in his life. Most people would think that having your father killed when you were a year old, having your mother and step father divorce when you were a senior in high school, and the only dad you knew disowned you, having your first spouse divorce you, and supporting your son but end up losing contact with him, marrying a lady with five children, having three more of your own, and losing contact with another two sons, tragedies. But, Ben always looked at things in a way that they could have been worse.

Lori knew she had loved Ben when they were married last march, but the more she got to know him, the more she loved him.

Ben and Lori had to leave for home after breakfast Sunday morning. It was almost sunup when they got back to the trailer. It had been a fun, but tiring weekend.

Ben was thankful for his two jobs. He found the bus driving very challenging. One first grader that caused trouble at school ended up thinking that Ben was his best friend. Ben had to correct Lambert often, but the kid just thought more of his bus driver after each confrontation.

Lori enjoyed the second year of school at Wasco even more than she did the first year. She enjoyed working with Mr. Walker and the other teachers. The second weekend, Ben had to work at Alco all weekend. Lori returned to Concord to start putting in the carpet. She started her work early Saturday morning. The carpet in the living room was not hard to install, but she had problems in the entrance and stairway. Lori had already painted the railing an off white to complement the carpets. She finally called a guy in town to come and help her. It took the rest of the day to complete the carpets in the two rooms.

Lori and Rick took the roll of light green carpet out in the back yard. They cut the carpet to fit in two of the bedrooms and hall upstairs. Lori called a carpet layer to install the carpet during the week. "We need it in by next Saturday so Ben and I can lay the new carpet in the dining room," Lori explained.

Lori felt very tired when she was getting ready to go home Sunday evening, but when she looked at the two finished rooms, it almost took her breathe away. The white ceiling and walls trimmed in gold, and the light colored carpet was so beautiful. The old house was beginning to look new again.

The next weekend, the two bedrooms upstairs were beautiful with the light green carpet and new wall paper. The guest bedroom had an oak floor that Lori had scrubbed and oiled. Lori papered the bathroom with a turn or the century pattern of dark maroon. This complemented the white fixtures and a maroon carpet was installed in the upstairs bathroom. Lori helped Ben hang two nice wooden cabinets on a bare wall of the kitchen. They finished laying the light colored carpet in the large dining room. The only thing left to do downstairs was the bath and kitchen.

Ben had to work the next weekend. Lori went back to Concord alone and put in a new kitchen cabinet and counter top. She stained the new cabinets with dark stain and painted the old cabinets white. Lori trimmed the old cabinets with strips of stained wood to match the new cabinets.

Lori finished the kitchen the next day by installing a kitchen carpet over the old, worn out tile. Ben had replaced the old worn out breakfast nook with an area for table and chairs. He hired a man to scrape the outside walls and paint the house white with gray trim. Lori thought she could do the painting, but Ben insisted on hiring someone because it was a two story house.

The next weekend the house was finished and Ben hired a Realtor to sell the house. He repaired the white picket fence in the back yard.

"Oh Ben, I wish this house was in Wasco, it's so beautiful," Lori sighed.

"You have worked very hard to make it that way," Ben said. He took Lori in his arms and kissed her. Lori could not help but imagine what living there would be like. They started back to Wasco.

"Ben, it looks like we are going to stay in Wasco. We need a larger place so we will have a place to put your furniture when your house sells. If we could just find a way to pay off what I owe on the trailer, and sell it too, maybe we can buy a house here," Lori said.

"I don't know of any houses for sale in Wasco. Do you?" Ben replied.

"I'm glad you asked me that," Lori answered, laughing. "Yes, I do. I've been driving around the city some evenings while you are working at Alco. I've found a brick house with a huge garage. I know it's been for sale for a long time because there are six foot weeds all around it," Lori said. "Would you mind if I checked on it?" she asked.

"Oh I guess it wouldn't hurt to ask around and see who owns it. But I doubt if it's anything we can afford even by selling both of our other houses," Ben answered.

The next week after school, Lori made enough telephone calls to find out who owned the house. The house had been for sale for over two years. The sign had finally been taken down. The contractor that built it had specialized in insulation. He had built the house and showed it as an example of his work. "The house is well insulated," the Realtor said. "When do you want to look at it?" she asked.

"Right now!" Lori exclaimed.

Lori met the lady and they entered through the garage door. The garage was almost large enough for three cars. Above the garage door was a worn out basket ball goal. The garage walls were finished, But not painted. The twenty four foot of shelving on the north side had been used as a work shop. Lori should have been disappointed when she stepped into the kitchen, but once again, she could see end results.

The cabinets were dark, dirty, and in need of a new stain. All the windows were made of heavy wood, but they had dog scratches all over them. They, too, needed new stain. The living room had a dirty, gold carpet, and the walls were painted light brown. There were no curtains on the windows. There were two full baths, and three bedrooms upstairs. One bedroom was painted a bright orange with orange carpet and one was painted a bright yellow with a yellow carpet. The master bedroom and bath was painted bright blue, with a bright blue carpet. All the window frames were badly scratched.

Lori followed the realtor downstairs. There was plumbing for another bath that was never completed. There was a large storage space under the stairs, two bedrooms and two large family rooms. The house had twenty-four hundered feet upstairs and a full basement. "It looks like these outside walls are at least two feet thick around the glass tiled windows," Lori commented.

"They are almost that thick," the lady said, "The contractor built the outside walls, went out eighteen inches and built another set of outside walls. The space was filled with insulation,"

"How much are you asking for the house?" Lori asked.

"The price is fifty-two thousand dollars, but you might bargain for fifty," the lady answered. "Let me show you the yard," she said.

The back yard was mostly weeds with a partly broken down fence facing the side street. The front yard was mostly weeds facing a busy street.

"Let me see if my husband wants to look at it," Lori said.

Ben looked at the house the next evening when he didn't have to work. "It might be something we can afford, if we sell both of our places, but it will take a lot of work," Ben said.

"The work is something that we can do. The house is expensively and solidly built," Lori said.

Lori talked to the Realtor and they brought the price down to fifty thousand dollars. "I don't' know how we can swing the deal until we sell our places, but we need to have a house ready for your furniture when your house in Concord sells," Lori said again.

Lori called Elizabeth. "Mother, could you loan us enough money for a down payment on a house until I sell my trailer and Ben sells his house?" Lori asked.

"No, but each of you three girls have twenty-five thousand dollars in the bank that your father put into savings accounts. He didn't want you to have it until I'm gone, but it might just be the time to give it all of you," Elizabeth answered.

"I didn't know that," Lori replied. "I guess this is as good a time for us as any."

Ben and Lori bought the brick home and put the trailer up for sale. Ben was asking thirty-five thousand for his house. It was less than he had paid for it, but he and Sue had bought the house during a time houses were selling for more. Lori decided she could take ten thousand for her trailer and still come out ahead.

The winter evenings were spent in another remodeling project. The ceilings did not need pained because they were made of sprayed on plaster with sparkles in it. Ben helped Lori pull the old carpets up and take them to the dump in his ancient Buick station wagon that Lori called Pinky. Lori oiled all the cabinets and window sills with Danish oil. She painted all the walls white on weekend and after school. Ben had to work most evening and weekends so Lori had plenty of time painting while she was waiting for Ben to get off work. It was usually around ten thirty when Ben came home.

One weekend they drove to Lincoln, Nebraska for Joyce's college graduation. It was scheduled the day before Christmas. They left early on Thursday evening and drove to Elaine's in order to get an earlier start Saturday morning. The temperature dropped to twenty-five degrees below zero that night. No vehicles would start the next morning. It was early afternoon before someone had time to come to Elaine's to jump start Lori's Buick.

Ben and Lori picked up Joyce and made it to Lincoln Friday night for another cold evening. The car started the next morning and they went on to the university.

Lori had a hard time taking pictures. There were nine hundred graduates and they had to sit so far away that they could not even see Joyce. Lori realized why Elaine's oldest son had done what he did at his graduation. When Tom graduated he had a sign under his gown. Right after he walked up on the stage and received his diploma, he held up the sign that said, "Mom, it's me."

Ben, Lori and Joyce and two of Joyce's close friends celebrated over a nice dinner that evening. It was a fun time of resting. They spent Christmas Eve with Sue's brother and his family. It was nice to spend Christmas with some family at least. Ben and Lori hurried back home to go back to work early the next morning.

It took three coats of paint to cover the hideous colors of the walls in the bedrooms. It took two months to paint the upstairs and downstairs white. It was a nice change from the dark walls of the trailer. In early spring, Ben and Lori laid light beige Kangaback carpets in every room except the kitchen and also put carpet on the basement stairs.

The realtor from Concord finally called. "Ben, I think I might have a buyer for you. They only want to pay twenty-five thousand for your house. I know that is a lot less than you were asking, but it's the only people that have the money that has looked at the house," she said.

"We really need to sell the house so maybe we can negotiate," Ben replied.

After several phone calls the house was sold for twenty-eight thousand, even after all the remodeling. "At least we won't have to make payments and utility expenses in Concord anymore," Ben said. He tried to hide his disappointment.

The weekend before the house closing, Joyce came by to stay a couple of days. Two convicts had escaped from a prison close to Wasco. They had hired a helicopter to land inside the prison and pick them up from the baseball diamond. The convicts had then made their escape in a yellow Ryder truck.

"I think I will watch the news on TV and see if they caught the convicts," Joyce said. Lori was busy with her work and Ben was reading the newspaper when they heard Joyce scream. They both ran into the living room just in time to catch most of the news.

"The two, dangerous convicts have been apprehended after a shoot out in Concord, Nebraska this evening. The police spotted the yellow truck and followed it, not wanting to stop it until it was out of town. The convicts spotted the police and started firing. Shooting took place in several streets in Concord before the convicts were arrested. The only injury was when one of the convicts shot him self in the foot," the announcer said.

The realtor that sold Ben's house made two funny comments during the closing. "This house has been so much fun to show, because it's the cleanest house I've ever tried to sell,' the lady said. The other comment was just as funny. "My husband is the superintendent for the schools here. He had just hired a new principal the day of the shooting. The principal called my husband that evening and said, 'Will you tell me one more time how quiet this little town of yours is,' the realtor said.

"We will have our furniture moved out in thirty days," Ben told the realtor. "We can't be out any earlier than that."

"A seller always has thirty days to move," the realtor replied.

The house in Wasco was about ready to move into when Mike called. "Mom, I wanted to tell you that I've found someone really special, and we're serious," Mike said. Her name is Libby and I'm anxious for you to meet her."

Ben and Lori went to Elizabeth's the next weekend. Mike brought Libby over. Libby was Hispanic and had dark eyes, skin, and black hair. She was slender and pretty. Libby had her hair pulled back in one large braid with pretty jewelry penned in her black braid. Lori thought she looked like an Indian Princess. She was almost eleven years younger than Mike. Libby had just graduated from high school.

Mike had told Lori once that he would have to marry a girl a lot younger, or marry someone his own age that had already been married and raise someone else's kids. "I want kids of my own," Mike had said.

Lori liked Libby's quiet personality and Mike seemed happy. It did break Lori's heart when she found out that Mike and Libby were living together.

Lori prayed about the situation. She finally wrote Mike a letter. "If Libby is good enough to live with, she is good enough to marry. You know better than to live that way, and I pray that you will soon do what you know is right," Lori wrote.

Mike called a month later. "Mom, I just wanted to tell you that Libby and I were married on Valentine's Day," he said. "We will bring wedding pictures for you to see the first time we come to see you."

"Congratulations!" Lori said. "Where were you married and who was there?" she asked.

We were married in Mitch and Staci's church. Mitch's family, dad, and his wife Karen, were the only ones there," Mike answered.

"Thank you for calling me and letting me know," Lori said and hung up. Lori fell back into a chair and sobbed. She remembered how she had made four western jackets and eighteen bulldogging ties for Mitch and Staci's wedding. She remembered how she had fixed a rehearsal dinner, and the fun the whole family had.

Lori couldn't help remembering all the thousands of nights she stayed home and took care of her two sons while Hollis ran around. She remembered the hurt when she had permanently lost Hollis to Karen. It was Hollis and Karen, not her, that had gone to Mike's wedding. Lori only had two children and had only gone to Mike's wedding. She felt that she had been replaced. She was still sobbing when Ben came home from work that night.

"Well, at least he did call you," Ben said, trying to make Lori feel better.

Lori had a battle with kidney stones the summer she was in Concord. Now it seemed that her bladder hurt continually. She felt like she had to urinate, but urinating did not relieve the pain. Lori had prayed about it and believed for the pain to go away. They were too busy, and she couldn't afford to go to the hospital. The pain became so severe that she finally went to the doctor. Dr. Remling did several on Lori. "Lori, I hate to tell you this, but you have cancer of the bladder," Dr. Remling said. "I have you lined up to be examined by an Urologist next week here in town. I'm sorry I'm such a bearer of bad news."

Lori felt like she had been slapped down again. This time she did not want to die. She was so happy being married to Ben, and she now had three grandchildren to enjoy, and Mike would be starting a family soon. When Lori entered the house, Ben was already home from work. Lori stumbled into the living room and said, "I have cancer of the bladder."

Ben looked shocked. He stood up and took Lori into his arms and held her tight. Ben started to sob. Lori had never seen him cry. Ben put is hand on Lori's head and prayed for her healing. Ben and Lori stayed in each others arms most of the evening. Lori decided not to tell her family, or co-workers about her health problem.

Dr. Remling put Lori on some medicine for pain that she was allergic to. She woke up early Saturday morning because her feet were burning. She jumped out of bed and shouted for Ben. "I'm burning up," she said. Lori watched the bright redness go from her feet to her legs and on up her body. It traveled until it reached the top of her head. Lori was terribly sick.

Ben put Lori in the car and rushed her to the hospital. While they were traveling across Wasco, Lori looked out the window. She saw an opossum trying to get in the door of the dentist's office. It looked so funny that Lori would have laughed if she had not been so sick.

The intern called Dr. Remling. The doctor rushed into the emergency room a few minutes later. "It's a medicine reaction," he said. He gave Lori a shot and told her to stay in bed for the day. Thank goodness it was Saturday.

On Sunday morning Lori's minister had just started his morning message. He stopped preaching and said, "Lori, come up here to the front. I have a feeling that we need to pray for you to be healed."

Lori was surprised, but obeyed. Many of the church people laid their hands on her shoulders while the minister put his hands on Lori's head and prayed. The pastor thanked the Lord for Lori's healing. Lori felt something go out of her bladder area, but the pain was till there.

The following week the urologist ran more tests. "Dr. Remling, I don't find anything wrong with this patient's bladder or kidneys," the specialist said.

"Are you sure?" Dr. Remling asked.

"Here are the results of the test; see for yourself," the specialist answered.

"Praise the Lord! Lori shouted.

The doctors looked startled, but they did not say anything. Lori couldn't wait for Ben to get home that evening so she called him at work. "I'm healed!" Lori shouted.

"Praise God!" Ben answered.

Two weeks later the pain in Lori's bladder was gone.

The house was ready by the time school was out for the summer. Ben and Lori rented a U-Haul truck and went to Concord after Ben's furniture. Ben drove the truck while Lori drove the old Pinto station wagon that had been Ben's Mother's. Mike and Libby met Ben and Lori at the house and helped them move in. Everyone went over to the trailer and loaded up Lori's furniture and unloaded it into the "new" brick home. Lori's furniture fit perfectly upstairs and there was room for all of Ben's furniture down stairs.

Libby was tiny, but stout and a hard worker. After all the furniture was in place, Lori covered up her hurt while she watched the video of Mike's wedding. Her heart hurt clear down into her feet when she saw

Karen taking her place in the wedding party. "Hurts from divorces never end," Lori told herself. She never wanted Mike to know how hurt she was.

The summer went quickly with much needed rest. Lori enjoyed working in the yard. There was so much trash raked from the yard that Lori had to get special permission from the city to burn. The city was willing to work with her just to see the place made nice again.

Ben fixed the back yard fence and Lori sprayed for weeds one week and then fertilized the grass the next week. She also painted the trim on the house, the inside of the huge garage, and painted the trimming on the screens.

Joyce worked in an Also store thirty miles from Wasco and stayed with Ben and Lori for part of the summer.

The school hired another Special Education teacher at the end of the summer. Bobbi was now the school counselor and Erin, the new teacher, was given Bobbi's nice room. Lori was disappointed to still be in the mobile unit, but she had spent a lot of time making large Disney posters to cover the ugly walls of the room. She tried to convince herself that she would be happier in the same classroom.

When Lori discovered that the Speech teacher was working in the basement of the Elementary gym, she was appalled. Lori went to talk to Mr. Walker. "Mr. Walker, I think it's terrible for the Speech teacher to have to teach speaking over the noise of the basketballs above the classroom. I know we are crowded, but I'm willing to share my large mobile unit with her. We can put up some things to divide our areas, and I think there will be enough room for both of us in there," Lori said.

"I think that's a great idea," Mr. Walker said. "I'll let her know so she can move her equipment. By the way, we have put you in charge of Title I Reading. You will be working with twenty-five first graders that are behind in reading. We have let the new teacher have most of the Special Education classes. You will be sharing part of your day with the other Title I teacher."

Lori didn't mind that. Lonnie, the other Title I teach, was one of Lori's closest friends. Lonnie's husband had left her after they had raised six kids. Lonnie still loved her wayward husband. She and Lori had spent many lonely evenings together and Lonny had traveled to Concord to take care of the guest book at Ben and Lori's wedding.

"Lori, there is a new program for Master's work in Special Education starting next week. The student will spend all day on Saturdays in the state capital going to the city's university. You can complete your program within a year by going to summer school both summers," Mr. Walker said. "I presume you will be going."

"That sounds great!" Lori exclaimed.

CHAPTER XIII

ANOTHER NEW HOME

Lori wanted to stay home and enjoy her "new" house and "new" husband, but she had to be gone sixteen hours every Saturday to the University. At least she did not have to travel alone like she had always done before. "It will be nice to have someone to talk to and study with, and to share expenses," Lori told Ben.

Mr. Walker, and Dr. Muriel from the University, obtained a scholarship for the four teachers and the tuition was only one-hundred, fifty dollars instead of three-hundred an hour. Even with the scholarship, it was hard for Lori and Ben to come up with the money.

Ben did not drive the bus the second year, but went to work at Safeway. Between Alco and Safeway, he was away from home most of the time. Many days he went to work at six o'clock in the morning and came home from work after eleven in the evenings.

Lori rode with three other Special Education teachers.

Rhonda taught in a small town twenty miles from Wasco. She had married a man old enough to be her father and had three grown step-sons and three sons in middle school and high school.

Mary taught Special Education in the middle school. It was her second year in Wasco. She had been so young and alone when she first came to Wasco that Mr. Wilson, the Middle school principal, almost became a step-father to her. Mary started dating a young man she planned to marry, but they were just living together at the time. Lori had heard that Mary bragged to her students about living with her boyfriend. She knew several parents had been angry about this and had protested at the principal's office.

Erin was the New Special Education teacher that had taken Bobbi's place and room. She was only twenty-two, and had just graduated from a university in North Dakota. Erin immediately told everyone, including the administrators, what a fantastic teacher she was, and how sharp she had been in college.

Lori had never met people as rude as these three teachers. Her two room mates in summer school had been "wild" but they had been nice to her. The three teachers only talked to each other, but when Lori tried to say something, she was told to "shut up" because "she didn't know anything." Lori decided to just be quiet, endure, and pray the trips would soon be over.

It was one-hundred, and sixty miles to the University, and the other ladies had a lot of time to make Lori miserable. She kept telling herself that things were not as bad as they seemed, but she had never felt so deflated by co-teachers.

Lori was nervous about going back to college after what Dr. Coolie, and the Valley University, had done to her. She wondered if she even dared to try again. She discussed her feelings with Dr. Muriel and told her what had happened.

We would never let a student leave our university a failure; we're here to help our students be successful," Dr. Sue Muriel said. "We will help you in any way we can, so don't worry and call any of us any time you need to."

Although school was only held all day on Saturdays, the students were taking five classes and were assigned twenty-five text books to read. Just class and study time could have been a full time job, not counting traveling the three-hundred miles to the capital and back ever week, and holding down a full time teaching job. The University had designed the graduate program for teachers that lived too far from the University to attend any other way.

Dr. Muriel was a pretty, slender lady who was about ready to retire. She was highly intelligent, understanding, and caring. The other teachers were just as helpful, but Lori was so frightened in class that she could hardly breathe. It was hard to forget Dr. Coolie telling her that she could never have a graduate degree. With her new professors' help, Lori gradually regained her confidence. The days it was not her turn to drive, she pretended to sleep all the way, or stare out the window to keep the other ladies from insulting her.

Mary was nice to Lori when she wasn't with Rhonda and Erin.

Lori was apprehensive about teaching first graders, but she soon enjoyed working with them. She made some funny flash cards to teach the students the alphabet, and some fun games on the two computers in her room. The rest of the time Lori used what she had learned with Language Experience. The students were enjoying writing stories. They were learning to read quickly. None of them were handicapped.

Lori was in the Title I room working with one class of first graders. Lonnie was behind a divider working with her older students when Erin walked into the room and shouted, "You have lost some of the records out of Special Ed. Students folders; don't you have enough sense to put them back where they belong when you're through with them?"

I haven't had the records since you had them last time," Lori answered quietly, trying not to upset her students.

"I know you lost them and I'm going to tell Mr. Walker that you did?" Erin shouted, stomping out of the room.

"Lori, Erin seems so nice that I can't believe she talked to you like that; I wouldn't have believed it if I had not heard it," Lonnie said, coming from her side of the room. "She acts so different around the rest of us."

A few days later Erin caught Lori in the hall. "I don't like you and I'm going to see to it that you don't come back to teach in this school next year!" Erin said.

Lori did not worry about what Erin said, but she noticed that Erin spent more and more time in Mr. Walker's office. "How does she find time to work with her student when she spends so much time in the office?" Lori asked herself and Lonnie.

Erin never spoke to Lori unless it was degrading. Lori grew tired of Erin's attitude and decided to talk to Mr. Walker about it. During her next planning period she found Mr. Walker in his office. "May I talk to you privately," Lori asked.

Mr. Walker nodded his head and motioned for Lori to come in before he shut the door.

"Mr. Walker could you please talk to Ms. Erin Brown; she won't speak to me unless she has something derogatory to say and she doesn't care if students are present or not," Lori tried to explain.

Lori knew there had been a terrific change in her warm and helpful principal but she never dreamed what her principal's answer would be. "Lori, it's hard for a perfect person like Ms. Brown to put up with un-perfect people like you," Mr. Walker answered.

"But, but," Lori tried to say.

"That's all I have to say about it," Mr. Walker said and held the door open for Lori to leave.

"What is going on?" Lori asked herself on her way back to her next class.

The first graders were now writing, and sharing their own stories, and Lori "printed" copies of each story for the students to read. By Christmas time, the kids even knew words like Zoologist. Mr. Walker seemed impressed when he visited Lori's room, but he remained unfriendly. Lori noticed that Mr. Walker was visiting her room more and more. Lori also noticed teachers talking quietly in small groups like they did not want to be heard. The faculty was no longer supportive. It no longer was a working together atmosphere.

The trips to the University became more unbearable. Lori told herself a hundred time, "Sticks and stones may break my bones, but words will never hurt me." Even that did not seem to work, and Lori prayed that spring would soon come and the weather would be warm enough for her to drive alone.

Ben was always loving and supporting. His love became more precious as the months passed by. He never mentioned Lori's smoking, but Lori knew he was praying for her to quit. The only place Lori smoked in the house was the smaller family room downstairs where she did her studying.

One week Mr. Walker and Erin missed three days of school to attend a Special Education Conference in the state capital. Lori did not think much about it except she was not asked to go. She had more fun working with her students anyway. When Mr. Walker and Erin returned, the young teacher seemed to be running the building. It was almost like she was black mailing Mr. Walker.

Mr. Walker had an attractive wife and two sons almost out of school. Lori knew he would never betray his family, but she knew that Erin had told so many lies about her that it would not be difficult for her to say something untrue about someone else. She found herself feeling sorry for her unfriendly principal.

Lori still had faith in Mr. Walker until he informed her that she was scheduled to meet with him, the superintendent, and Mr. Bono, the head of the Special Ed. Department in that part of the state. Lori dreaded the meeting.

"Lori, I feel like we need to let you know that we are not renewing your contract for next year. Mr. Walker feels that you have not progressed enough professionally. The school board will probably agree with him," Mr. Bloomingdale said.

"But, I'll be certified by the time school starts next fall?" Lori exclaimed. "I'm a full time student at the University right now, and I've made arrangement for summer school, and we have just bought a place here is Wasco," Lori tried to explain.

"Yes, I noticed that; the place really looks different since you bought it," Mr. Bloomingdale replied. "Maybe you can find a teaching job within driving distance of Wasco."

"Is there anything I can do to change your mind about my job?" Lori asked.

"It's up to the school board, but they usually go with the principal's recommendation," Mr. Bloomingdale answered.

Lori walked out of the office. She felt that she had been knocked down again. "Why am I constantly hurt by decisions made by men?" she asked herself.

Now, on top of everything else Lori had to do, she had to take time to update her transcripts, make copies, and send them to all the schools in the surrounding area. She called Mr. Bono. "Mr. Bono, I feel that I have done a good job with my Special Ed. Students, and I've worked hard on my degree, and I don't know why Wasco is not renewing my contract," Lori said.

"I don't know either; the only thing I can think of is they may not want to give you a tenure contract at your age," Mr. Bono said. "I'm sorry, but there is not much I, or you, can do about it."

"I can't help it that I'm in my fifties, and I have a lot of good years left," Lori replied. She hung up the phone and went back to class.

The ride to the University was more miserable than ever with other teachers laughing at her. They felt that their job were secure and they it was funny that Lori had lost her job.

Mary and Lori traded classes to do some teaching in another area for part of their field work for the University. It was such a relief to work with Mr. Wilson. He was so encouraging.

"I'm sorry that you won't be a part of our staff next year, Mr. Wilson said, "If I can help you in any way, please let me know. I'll give you a high recommendation to anyone, so put my name on your list of references on your applications for work; I'll write letter or answer telephone calls."

"Thanks. I appreciate that more than you'll ever know," Lori replied.

The six weeks at he Middle School passed too quickly. Lori soon had to return to the hostile environment of the Elementary School. The weather turned warm and Lori informed the other teachers that she would be going to the university in her own car. Erin was upset and shouted, "You'll be going with us whether you want to or not!"

Everyone in the office was shocked to hear the new teacher talking like that.

Lori was determined to make her last days at Wasco the best ever for her students. When Mr. Walker visited her classes for the last time, most of the students were reading on a high second grade level. "I don't think any of these students will need to be in Title I Reading next year," she said.

"Well, you've done a good job with them, but we don't want all the students in the regular classroom reading group!" Mr. Walker shouted. "You should know that!"

Before the school board meeting, Lori contacted all of her students' parents. They all signed a petition to keep her as their children's Sp. Ed. Teacher.

The night of the meeting, Ben stayed home to pray for Lori. Two sets of parents that had lived in Wasco for a long time went before the board and protested Lori's dismissal. Lori presented her case before the board while facing Mr. Wilson's confident smile. Lori and the parents were asked to leave the room while the board members and administrators discussed the matter.

Lori heard Mr. Walker talking in front of the board for about fifteen minutes. She could not hear what he was saying, but she could guess. When the six men and two women came out of the superintendent's office, Lori knew the board's decision by the smile on Mr. Walker's face. She thanked the parents for their help and went home to cry in Ben's loving arms.

Lori wrote a play for her first graders to give for their parents. Each group of students had to read their parts to show how well they could read. One of the most challenging boys was so nervous that he almost fainted. The kids did a super job and refreshments were served to each group of parents. It was fun and the parents seemed as proud as the students in their progress.

The last day of school, Lori put together a "Treasure Hunt". All the instructions had to be read and figured out. The hunt covered all the play ground and part of the school building.

One group was made up of three boys. The directions said to go west ten steps, then north. One of the boys forgot his directions and ran into another boy. The third boy said, "Who do you guys think we are? The three stooges?"

The treasure was gold colored boxes filled with prizes and candy. Each group found their treasure. It had been a fun day of reading.

Lori avoided telling the other teachers good-bye when she left the school for the last time. It was a sad time. She remembered how excited she had been to go to work here, and how nice Mr. Walker had been. Lori thought of the times she left Wasco to see Ben during the weekends, and how exciting it had been when she brought her new, loving husband to Wasco. She thought of the excitement of buying the brick home and making it beautiful.

The last year's memories were not good ones. Lori turned on the tape player and tried to forget the past, one more time, as she drove away from the school where she had spent three years of her life. "At least living here has given me Ben," Lori told herself as she looked at the old mobile classroom for the last time.

Lori left the next day to do more field work with a Sp. Ed. Teacher in a large high school close to the state capital. She kissed Ben good-bye and traveled to Gray Rock. Lori found the cheapest room in the expensive city and reported to the school the next day. There was one week of school left in Gray Rock.

Lori liked the teacher she was working with. Mrs. Dole was a slender, pretty woman, with dark hair. She had difficulty walking. She had two children in middle school. She told Lori she was raising her children alone. Her husband was a patrolman and had divorced her to marry one of the dispatchers.

"I understand your situation because that happened to one of my cousins," Lori said.

Lori was soon acquainted with all students. One young man was autistic. Mrs. Dole was surprised when the student let Lori help him with his work.

The day passed quickly and Lori returned to her tiny, cheap room to relax, smoke, eat, and write on her report for Dr. Muriel.

The second day Mrs. Dole came to school on crutches. "What happened to you?" Lori asked.

"I have MS and have to use crutches most of the time. It won't be long until I'll be in a wheel chair. It makes working with these kids more meaningful, since I'm handicapped myself," Mrs. Dole explained.

"Lord, it seems like life has been so unfair to Mrs. Dole, but she is a fighter," Lori prayed. "Please help her, Lord, and let her be able to raise her children."

Lori said good-bye to her new friends. She went home for a short weekend with Ben before starting to classes at the University the following Monday. It was nice to be working with Dr. Muriel and the other teachers, but Lori dreaded facing Erin, Mary, and Rhonda each day. Lori's prayers were answered. She did not have to work in any group where the other three teachers were working.

After the morning classes, Lori checked into the dorm. Again, her grain check from her father's estate had come through just in time to help her with more college.

Most of the dorms were filled with Orientals. Lori felt like she was staying in another country. She enjoyed her evenings alone. It was easier to concentrate on class work when she didn't have to spend so much time driving, teaching, and dodging hurtful words. The last full day of classes was held in a mountain town at an old restaurant. It was fun in spite of Lori's enemies. Dr. Muriel tried to write some notes on the chalk board, but her hand seemed to be twisted and her notes hard to read.

Dr. Muriel's last class meeting was in her expensive home in the suburbs. She had a huge dinner catered to her home. Everyone met Dr. Muriel's husband who looked like Phil Donahue.

"You are now certified as Special Education Teachers, and you will be taking your last four hours next summer to complete your Master's," Dr. Muriel explained. "Good luck."

"It will be so nice to spend a month with Ben before I go back to work," Lori told herself as she drove out of the state capital. Then the reality hit her. She had no job! Next month was her last check from Wasco. Ben was working for minimum wages, and there was no way they could live on what he made. Even with the crop check, Lori had a school debt to pay off. They would be paying one-hundred, fifty dollars a month for the next ten years to pay for her most resent schooling.

"Oh Lord, what are we going to do?" Lori asked.

There were no offers from schools in the mail. Lori did not know if they should put the house up for sale or not. She had sold the old trailer to Staci's younger brother a few months ago. Thank goodness it was taken care of. The only time Lori did not feel nervous about their situation was when she was in Ben's arms. He refused to worry. "The Lori will take care of us," Ben always said when Lori started to worry.

The next free day that Ben was off work, he and Lori took a drive down a river valley located three hours south. They prayed as they drove through a hundred miles of the pretty country. "Lord, show us where you want us to live," they prayed. They both felt drawn to a town called Sand Rock.

The second week Lori was home she received a telephone call. "Mrs. Fielding," the caller said, "this is Dr. Churchill of Rye County Schools. We need a Special Education teacher for high school. I called the state department and they don't have a record of your certification," the superintendent explained.

"I'm certified and my University was supposed to have me listed," Lori replied. "I'll call the state office and my school and find out what's wrong."

Lori made several long distance calls. She finally contacted Dr. Muriel. "I'm sorry about the mix up, Lori. I'll take care of it," Dr. Muriel said. "We have the states approval for certification with your amount of hours so it's just a matter of red tape."

Lori called Dr. Churchill and told him about the problem. "That's probably why I haven't been offered a job yet," Lori said. "I'm glad you found out and let me know."

"I thought it was something like that," Dr. Churchill replied. "Can you come for an interview next Tuesday morning?" he asked.

"I'll be there, and thank you," Lori answered.

Lori left early Tuesday morning to drive the three hours to Rye County School. "We haven't hired our new high school principal yet, so I'm the only one you'll talk to today," Dr. Churchill said.

"School will be starting in two weeks; Oh Lord, help me to get a job, moved, and ready to start teaching in this short amount of time," Lori prayed.

Lori drove around Rye County School looking at houses. She then drove twelve miles south to Sand Rock and looked at houses there. "I still want a place of our own, please Lord," Lori prayed.

"I think I have a place you might be interested in," a realtor said. "It's kind of unusual, but I think you'll like it, so let me show it to you."

The house was two blocks from Main Street. It was located on a quiet street with a lot of trees. There was a long, sandstone sidewalk and sheltered front entrance. The house was different enough that Lori wasn't sure which rooms were meant for what. The foyer had windows on each side of the front door, and five doors leading to different parts of the house.

The kitchen was long and narrow with an eating space at the end. It contained a new stove and dish washer, but no refrigerator. There were three large windows back of the eating space.

The next door off the foyer was an arch that led to a large living and dining room. There was a small fire place on the south wall. The beamed ceiling was raised with high windows facing east. The west wall was all glass facing a beautiful back yard and enclosed patio.

The first door to the left in the foyer was the master bedroom. It was large and had a large window facing north and two high windows facing south toward the entrance.

The next door was a bathroom with green fixtures. There was a built-in shower stall separate from the tub. The tile was green and reminded Lori of some old time Texaco gas station restrooms.

The next door from the foyer was a small bedroom that opened up to another room. This room had a narrow area that opened up to a large family room. There was another small bedroom leading off the family room.

The family room had sliding glass doors that opened up to a twenty-four by twenty-four foot patio. There was a laundry room and a three quarter bath beyond the family room. In the back was a carport and closed gate. The gate was covered with wild grapes. The walls were white and did not need painting.

"I love it, but I'll have to bring my husband to see it, and we have to sell our house before we can buy it," Lori said.

"The lady that owned this place borrowed against the house to help her sons in a new business. The business failed and she lost the house. When she moved, she took the curtains, air conditioning system unit, and even some roses from the back yard," the realtor said. "The bank that repossessed the house was bought by another bank and the house papers were lost for awhile, but it's ready to sell now."

Lori was happy as she drove back to Wasco. "Lord, I want that job and I want that house," she prayed. Then the thought hit her. Their brick house had been on the market two year before they bought it. They had to get enough money out of it to pay for the carpets and paint they had just bought. Lori was hit by fear again. "What if we can't sell our house?" she asked herself.

Lori told Ben about the job interview and the house. "If you like the house and get the job, we can do without curtains until we get back on our feet financially, and I find another job," Ben said.

Lori laughed and said, "Not this house."

Lori called the realtor that sold them the brick house. "We can't take less that fifty-six thousand since we have the expense of fixing it up," she explained.

"Well, I'll try, but houses aren't moving fast right now, and very few people can afford a house that expensive," the realtor said.

"Lori, I've been thinking. I need to have my teeth pulled, and I think I need to do it now while I still have dental insurance with my Safeway job," Ben said.

Lori agreed and Ben set up an appointment with one of the local dentists to have the rest of his teeth pulled.

"Joyce needs another car," Ben said. "I saw a 1976 one on a car lot downtown; it's like new and they don't want a lot for it."

Lori and Ben looked at the car and bought it for two-thousand dollars. Joyce came to Wasco that weekend. Lori had waxed the car and it looked new. Joyce left to go back to Nebraska on Sunday afternoon after church. She called two hours later. Lori answered the phone. "I have just been in an accident and the car is totaled," Joyce said with a sob.

"Are you all right?" Lori asked.

"I'm not hurt, but the car is totaled," Joyce said again.

"Oh, I'm sure it's not as bad as it looks," Lori replied, handing the phone to Ben.

Ben took a day off from work and they traveled to Nebraska to check on the car. It was badly damaged and it could not be fixed. Ben and Lori prayed that Joyce's old car would last her until she finished college.

The brick house sold. Lori did not have a job yet and they would have to move within thirty days. Ben and Lori received fifty-four thousand for the house. The man that bought it had two other homes on farms. He was looking for a place in town. The papers were signed and Ben and Lori promised they would be moved out in the allotted time.

"God will not let us leave Wasco without knowing where we are going," they told friends.

The new owner came to look at the house again. "I have other homes, but I've never had one this nice," he said, "If you can't find a place to move, I can give you more time."

Ben and Lori bought a 1983 Buick Century. It was as old as Lori' Buick, but it only had half the Miles. The car looked new. They were driving back to Sand Rock to look at houses when Lori found a book in the glove compartment. It was a manual where the previous owner had kept a record of all the repairs. She read where repairs had been made at 76,000 miles is what the car odometer read. Then she read of more repairs for 100,000 miles, and more at 150,000 miles.

"Ben, I can't figure this out," Lori said.

Ben was listening to a preacher on the radio. He always hated to miss church. "I'll listen when this is over," he replied. When Lori read the information, Ben knew what it meant. "This car has 176,000 miles on it and not just 76,000 miles," Ben explained.

"What can we do?" Lori asked.

"We'll just have to take the car back and hope they will refund our money." Ben answered.

It looked like the "unusual" house was the only house available that Ben and Lori both liked, if she got the job at Rye County schools.

Lori took the car back to the auto company and told them they did not want a car with that many miles. The salesman was shocked. "We bought that car from a guy I've known all my life. I can't imagine him lying abut the mileage. We'll make it right for you, but I wish you would call and talk to him; his name is Chuck Holcomb," the young salesman said.

Lori was shocked. Holcombs were an older couple that went to the same church that Ben and Lori went to. Lori dialed their number. Chuck's wife answered the phone.

"Oh Lori, I'm so glad you called. I haven't had a good night's sleep since we signed that odometer card. Chuck singed it first. What was I to do? Not sign it and make him a liar in front of some of his friends?" Mrs. Holcomb responded. "He won't talk to me about it, so will you please talk to him?"

"I guess," Lori answered. Lori waited until Chuck answered the phone. "Mr. Holcomb, we just bought your car and we paid too much for it considering all the miles it has on it. We don't want a car with this many miles. You lied and broke the law when you signed that odometer card," Lori explained. "What are you going to do about it?" she asked.

"Nothing! The car is worth whatever you paid for it, and I don't feel like I did anything wrong; we took very good care of the car." Mr. Holcomb replied.

"Mr. Holcomb, you broke the law, and you have broken God's law. The Bible says that all people that lie will end up in the wrong place for eternity. And, you need to make this situation right. What you did was not fair to us, or to the auto company," Lori said and hung up.

The auto company was ready to refund Ben's money when he and Lori found a Rivera Buick they liked. The trade was made and they never knew what became of the other car. The Rivera was eight years old, but it was pretty, low mileage, and had a sun roof.

That afternoon Dr. Churchill called. "We have decided to hire you for this next year; see you in a few days," he said. "Welcome to our staff."

"Praise the Lord!" Lori shouted. She called Ben at work.

"Thank you Lord," Ben responded.

The house in Sand Rock was bought by fax machine. Some friends let Ben and Lori borrow the U-Haul truck they had rented because no other trucks were available.

Ben and Lori gave Joyce Lori's Buick, and bought the newer car. Ben had all his teeth pulled and false ones put in. The brick house had sold. Lori had a new teaching job, and the house in Sand Rock was purchased, and they had moved, all within a week.

The Lord did not let them leave Wasco without knowing where they were going.

Two of Ben's friends from work had helped them load the furniture from the brick house. Mike had come and helped unload the furniture at the new house. "I like this house, mom," Mike said. "It's so unusual, and there's not much work for you to do."

Lori was determined to use her old ceramic top stove so the new one was put in the foyer for a couple of months before it sold. It took a week to find a refrigerator that would fit in the kitchen.

CHAPTER XIV

LORI'S LAST TEACHING JOB

Lori's job was similar to the one in Dannon. She had fewer students, fewer Hispanics, and no teacher's aid. It would be challenging, but fun.

Lori's classroom was the ugliest classroom she had ever had. The walls were painted a dark brown and the walls and floors were terribly cracked. Lori took a chance and covered the ugly walls with all the Walt Disney posters she had made and used in her classroom at Wasco. She thought her older students might laugh at them, or think they were too old for such things so Lori tired to make the posters fit by putting captions under the posters. Under the poster of the Three Little Pigs, Lori wrote, "I told the other pigs they should have finished school." Under another one she put "Don't surprise me, always finish you work!" Under Cinderella, she put, "Make your dreams come true, study."

One student, Ramon, had a Spanish last name but he looked enough Indian that Lori could picture him wearing a beautiful Indian headdress with feathers. He was tall, and usually without a smile. He had a sister in regular education classes. She was pretty and had just moved in with her boyfriend. Some people thought she was pregnant.

Angel was Hispanic. He was the youngest of twelve children. Angel was quiet and cooperative. "Mrs. Fielding, I just celebrated my sixteenth birthday and my folks told me that this is the best time of my life,"

Angel said. "I'm not having much fun and I wonder what's wrong and what my folks were talking about," he said.

"I think I know; they were telling you that you are close to becoming an independent adult, but yet you don't have all the responsibilities and worries of a family and children," Lori answered.

"Oh!" Angel exclaimed.

"Angel, just enjoy the age you are now because you will never be sixteen again; enjoy that age and make the most of it; enjoy your last years as a child and don't try to rush into adulthood," Lori said.

"I think I'll just take my time," Angel said.

Lori knew that Angel was a good enough kid that he was not thinking about doing anything dumb.

Charles was a tall guy, with muscles, was handsome, and a red head. His front teeth had been broken from the beatings he had suffered from his mother's boyfriends. During the year, the mother's present boyfriend had come home drunk, broke off a leg of the coffee table and beat Charles and his mother with it. Charles ran away for a few days. Lori talked to Charles's mother. She dearly loved her son but did not know how to live any differently and protect him. Charles quit school in the middle of the year.

Lori remembered the time Charles had a bad morning before he came to school. He had come into her room very angry and plopped his head down on his desk and stared at the wall for several minutes.

"Charles, get busy on your work," Lori said.

"Oh, get off my back!" Charles shouted.

"How ridiculous, I'm not tall enough to even get on your back," Lori replied.

The room was quiet for a few minutes, and then everyone started laughing. Charles finally laughed too and started working.

Jamin enrolled after school started. He had a sister that was married, and his mother was raising two sons alone. She was in bad health and the family was struggling on Welfare.

Jamin and his brother looked a lot alike and they were both six-foot, four-inches tall. Jamin had been put in Special Education because he had problems with some of his classroom teachers in his previous school. He started school with a terrible attitude, but was soon working for Lori.

Lori was visiting with Jamin's mother one day. "I loved my husband, the kids' dad, although he was out drinking most nights," she said. "I put up with his running around until the night he came home with a women and wanted me have an orgy with them; I thought it was time to leave with my kids and find a safe place for them."

"I know the Lord will take care of us," the woman continued "last year, me and my kids were living in the mountains; we had no income and we had just used the last of our fuel and eaten the last of our food. There was a terrible blizzard outside and the roads were closed. We finished supper, prayed for the Lord to take care of us and went to bed.

In the middle of the night someone pounded on our door. I answered the door. There stood two, tall men that I had never seen before. They said they had brought us some firewood. I looked behind them and saw two large sleds filled with firewood. The men unloaded the wood for us and stacked it next to the house. They brought in enough logs to last us through the week. Then they rode out of sight on the snow. We praised the Lord and went back to bed.

Early the next morning there was another knock on the door. I answered the door again. There were two more large men standing in the snow in the early rays of daylight. I did not recognize either one of them. The men said that they brought us some groceries. They also had two sleds filled with food and supplies. The men brought the food inside for us and left.

The food and wood lasted us until summer and we had a little income from the government by then. I tried to find out which church in town was responsible for the miracles, but no one seemed to know anything about it," Jamin's mother said.

Keith was Lori only senior. He had started Kindergarten with an ear problem and tubes in his ears. By the time Keith was over his ear problem, he was two years behind in Language. Lori helped Keith with his History classes and Writing. Keith and Lori tried also to cover the Math that Keith had not understood. He was so excited when he finally understood fractions that he thought they were a lot of fun. He was as much of a joy to teach as Lori's first graders in Wasco had been.

In October Ben found a job with a company that had just moved in from Minnesota. The company built and shipped steel lockers all over the world. Ben was working for minimum wages again and working at night.

Lori's days were filled with teaching her students subjects they had not been able to learn in other classes. She also worked with a Down—Syndrome boy, Trusty, that was twenty year old. Trusty was learning letters and numbers, and writing his name. He had quit running up and down the halls and was able to sit awhile in his desk.

The rest of the students were average, and most of them had been thrown out of other classes. A few were in trouble with the law.

Lori hated the evenings. She came home about an hour after Ben had left for work. She was sound asleep when Ben came in at four in the morning. He was asleep when Lori left for work. The only time they saw each other was on weekends. Ben and Lori looked forward to the weekends when they could enjoy being together. Their love grew strong and the weekend just flew by.

Ben and Lori hung sheets up to the windows until they found drapes to fit. The drapes in the living room measured 95" by 205". They found some drapes a person had ordered, then returned. They cost about half as much as ones already made which wouldn't have fit anyway.

Ben and Lori started attending a church that Staci's great aunt attended. It was not a Full gospel church like they had attended in Wasco, but it was friendly.

The first evaluation Lori's principal made of her teaching went great. "Woman, you are made of special material to get these big old boys to enjoy learning the way you do," Mr. Brown said.

"I do enjoy my work," Lori replied.

Most of the time, Mr. Brown was helpful. Lori went to talk to him once when he wasn't too cooperative. "Mr. Brown, is there any way that I can change my classes so that I won't have the four worst trouble makers in the whole school, in my class at the same time?" Lori asked.

"No! That's your problem," Mr. Brown answered.

Lori was disappointed, but determined to make things work. As usual, she had to administer tests to see if students needed to be in Special Ed. when they were referred by teachers or parents. The teacher Lori replaced, Mrs. Amy Anderson, had been hired as one of the officers on the staff of the area's Special Education Administration in that part of the state. Her position was next to the person that had the same status as Mr. Bono in the northern part of the state.

Lori had tested one student and put the test results in the student's folder in the office. A few days later, Mrs. Anderson came into her room. "I want to tell you that you should have put 'not referring to Special Education services' on the corner of the front page of the test!" she shouted. "The students has already been promoted out of Special Ed. And you have gotten us into trouble by not labeling the test that way!"

"I have never heard of such a thing!" Lori exclaimed. "I would have done that if I would have known, but I can't apologize for something I did not know to do."

"I think we need to talk to Mr. Brown about this," Mrs. Anderson said.

Lori followed Mrs. Anderson into the principal's office where she threw another fit before she left.

"If you don't do better, you'll get us both fired!" Mr. Brown shouted.

"Mr. Brown, I need to be informed what to do before I can do it," Lori said. "I can't apologize for something I didn't know about,"

"You just find out from now on!" Mr. Brown shouted.

Lori called Dr. Muriel at the university. "Dr. Muriel, I have just been reprimanded for not writing 'not to do with Special Education' on the front a test I was instructed to give. The Area Board and my principal are upset with me about it," Lori explained. "Did you know that was required?" she asked.

"I've never heard anything like that; all information needed on the tests should already be printed on the test," Dr. Muriel answered.

"Thank you for the information; and I wish people would tell me what they want before they get upset over what I do," Lori replied.

Lori was hoping that there would be some in-service meetings so she would know more about what the board wanted from the Sp. Ed. Teachers. Only two meetings were held and not much information was given at either one. The president of the board was soon fired and Mrs. Anderson took over as head of the board, making more money than most superintendents.

Lori also heard that Mr. Walker at Wasco had suffered a nervous breakdown and was now the high school Liberian. Lori sent Mr. Walker a letter and told him she forgave him for ruining her life for awhile, but she knew now that it was the Lord's will for them to move to the valley where they now lived. She also asked Mr. Walker to forgive her for her anger against him. She never received an answer.

Lori invited all her students to the house in Sand Rock for a Christmas party. Ben enjoyed the young men as much as Steve had enjoyed her students, and Ben was as much help.

Ben loved to play Pac Man on the small computer Lori had bought with her last grain check. It was the same CD she used on her computer at school to help her students in Reading and History, and to play games after the students finished their work and homework. When Ben made a high score on Pac Man, Lori would take it to school to challenge her students during their reward time.

"I'm getting tired of putting my name all the time on this game," Ben said one evening.

"Why don't you use Trusty's name; since Trusty has Down Syndrome, he will never be able to get a high score or play the game; I think it would look great to see his name on a high score," Lori said.

"That's a great idea!" Ben exclaimed. He put Trusty's name in and made the highest score he had ever made.

Lori took the disk to school with her the next day. Angel worked extra hard that morning and earned the right to use the computer. He looked at the score Lori had brought in. Angel proceeded to try and beat the score.

Lori was busy with her other students when the bell rang for the next class. She looked up and saw that Angel had a score almost as high as Ben's. "Just keep going and I'll tell your Art teacher why you will be a little late," Lori said.

While Lori was hurrying down the hall, she told the other students that the game was really Ben's but Ben had Trusty's name on it. By the time Lori returned to her room, Angel had won his game. "Oh, Angel, that's your highest score, Lori exclaimed.

"Yeah, but I just barely beat Trusty's score!" Angel sighed.

Lori was laughing so hard that she could hardly explain to Angel that is was really Ben's score he had just beaten. The other students were laughing harder than Lori.

Lori only had two girls in her classes during the year. One did not stay long, and the other one had a baby about the time school was out and missed a lot of school.

It was time for Lori's second evaluation. The other one had been so pleasant that she was relaxed for this one. Mr. Brown was more quiet and wrote down notes. Lori thought it had gone basically like the first evaluation. The next day Mr. Brown came into Lori's room and shut the door. He sat down at one of the work tables and looked at her. "I want you to know that we are not renewing your contact," Mr. Brown said.

Lori was too shocked to speak. Mr. Brown walked out of the room leaving her speechless.

Several parents wanted to go before the school board on her behalf. "No thank you; it won't do any good, but I appreciate your support," Lori told them.

One of the seniors came into Lori's room. "Mrs. Fielding, we want to invite you to our Senior Banquet next week," the young man said.

"I feel funny about coming since I'm not going to be here next year," Lori replied.

"Oh that all right; we're not going to be here either," he replied, bouncing out of the room.

Ben and Lori attended the banquet and had a good time. The cook that was slicing a large piece of meat told Lori, "Let me know when you have enough slices." Lori thought he said, "Let me know when you see the slice you want." Before Lori realized it, he had piled several pieces of meat on her plate. The students saw it and thought it was funny and teased her about it.

Mr. Brown was always friendly and supportive. He told Lori several times that she was a good teacher. "Then why don't I have a job anymore?" Lori wanted to scream. But, instead, she just smiled and said, "Thank you."

One morning the students were called into the gym. "Our nation has gone to war in the Middle East," Mr. Brown announced. "This is the first time that any of you have seen our nation at war; I can remember when the United States went into World War II after Pearl Harbor was bombed. I was young, upset, and wanted to ask a lot of questions. We're not having classes today, but we want you to meet with your teachers and talk over our world situation and ask any questions you want, and any of you can come in here and pray for our nation any time you want today."

Lori had students in her class room all day talking about the war. Most of them had no concept of war. Lori found a play written about some soldiers in Vietnam and had the kids to read it. They did a good job and Lori taped it the second time they read it. The day passed quickly with no news from the front lines. Classes were resumed the next day.

Some students had been coming into Lori's room to work on their Math assignments. Lori became suspicious because they finished too quickly. She checked with some of her own students and found they had no idea of how to do problems they had just made and A on. There was no doubt that answer sheets were being passed around. Lori went to talk to the Math teacher.

"Mr. Tipton, if you would just require your students to show their work, it would stop them from cheating," Lori said.

"Mrs. Fielding, if the students are getting answers, they are getting them from you, and I'm not going to change the way I do things," Mr. Tipton snapped.

Lori was disappointed. She went back to her room and talked to her two students that took Math under Mr. Tipton. "Promise me you won't use the answer sheets anymore; if you have any problems, I'll help you work them out," she said.

When finals came up, Jamin came into the room. He was laughing so hard he could hardly sit down at the table. His tall, large body was bouncing.

"What's so funny?" Lori asked.

"Mr. Tipton gave a test today, and I was the only student that knew how to do the problems," Jamin said.

"I'm proud of you," Lori replied, "Just remember that honesty always pays whether it looks like it at the time or not."

Lori gave several awards at the Award Assembly. There was an award for "The most improved student", "Mr. Personality", "The most improved attitude", as well as academic awards. Keith made the Honor Roll for the first time in all his twelve years of school. Lori was proud of all her students.

"Mom, we have just brought Libby to the hospital, and she is in labor," Mike said over the phone, "I'll call you when the baby arrives."

Lori hated to go to school that day, but she gave Mike her work number. She expected a phone call all day at work. Lori called the hospital when she came in from work, but Libby was still in labor. Lori went to school the next day, still waiting for the phone call. Things did not look good. Lori was ready to go home when the office called her to come to the phone.

"Lori?" Elizabeth asked, "I'm so sorry Lori."

"Oh no, not bad news," Lori was thinking.

"I'm sorry we haven't been able to call you until now. Libby was in hard labor for thirty-six hours. You have a new granddaughter and she weighs eight pounds and ten ounces," Elizabeth said.

It's amazing how quickly terror can turn into joy. "Praise the Lord!" Lori managed to say.

During the last few weeks of school, Lori noticed that she was not feeling well. She was also passing blood from her bowls. Lori did not tell Ben about it and thought it was just from the stress of losing her job. She thought she would feel better when she found another job.

The last day of school, Lori received another call. It was bad new this time. Vera Lee's fourteen year old son had been killed in an auto accident. Jason was the baby Vera Lee had been afraid to bring back to the old farm to visit Lori because she had seen a vision of Jason being killed in an accident on the old farm. Jason and his little sister had been the kids that rode on the back of the bicycles when Vera Lee and Lori took long rides together. Lori decided she had to hold back the tears until she got home.

On her way to Mr. Brown's office Lori saw a table with food. There was a decorated cake in the middle of the table. Lori thought it was someone's birthday until she read what was written on the cake. It said, "Good-bye, and Good luck." There was a pretty card next to the cake addressed to her. Lori read the nice verses and the signatures of all the teachers in the school.

Lori was so surprised, and touched, that she begin to cry. Trusty put his short, fat arms around her a patted her on the back. "It's all right," he tried to say in his unusual language.

"Trusty, would you like to walk downtown with me and we'll buy some donuts for our afternoon classes?" Lori asked.

Trusty nodded his head yes. He took Lori by the hand and together they walked the four blocks to the Bakery. Lori watched the young man, swinging her hand and bouncing happily around. He was like a small child. "I wonder what it would be like to live in his world?" Lori asked herself, remembering all of the things that were making her unhappy.

Lori finished her last class and left the building by the side door. She did not want the sadness of telling so many great teachers good-bye. She lit up a cigarette as she backed away from Rye Country School for the last time. "Will this be my last day of teaching, or will I get well and find another teaching job?" Lori was wondering as she watched the old building disappear.

The next day, Ben and Lori went back to Lori's home town and to Jason's funeral. One of the funeral wreaths was made from the young man's football that he had left at Bryan's, house the day before. Lori's oldest grandson and Jason had been close friends.

Ben was working days now. He and Lori were able to spend more time together after Lori's job terminated. Lori was so devastated over losing another job that she did not want to be around anyone but Ben. She did not want to drive anywhere and she did not want to talk to anyone. Lori was feeling worse physically and decided to go into the hospital for tests before her school insurance ran out. She had to put on a hospital gown and was taken to the x-ray room. A heart monitor was fastened to her chest. The doctor was in the process of x-raying Lori's intestines when she heard a nurse ask, "Did someone unplug the heart monitor?" Everything went black for Lori.

"We aren't going to do anymore test," the doctor said, "her heart has completely stopped!" More help was on the way when Lori's heart started working again. She regained consciousness within a few minutes. The only place Lori was hurting was where the x-ray machine had been in her intestines, but she felt terribly weak.

Lori had to stay in the hospital the rest of the day for observation. By early afternoon she was able to eat two pieces of toast. Ben was called at work to pick up Lori and take her home.

There was time to spend with her computer, writing, music, and new home. She gained enough strength for Ben to take an extra day off so they could attend Lori's mother's family reunion in Texas. They took Lady Dog with them.

The reunion was a time of fun and laughter. There was a gift exchange and most of the gifts were silly ones. Lori took a picture of her aunt from Washington wearing a large nose and glasses and one of cousins covered with stringy stuff. Funny games were played.

During the morning worship service, Lori played the piano for the singing, and then she took the microphone and told Aunt June's family about the time she and Aunt June had spent a lot of time together. It had been between Lori's first and second marriages.

Aunt June had asked Lori to go with her to Lori's Uncle Sam's house. Lori waited in the car while Aunt June talked to her brother who was living in the basement of their home. She told him that he needed to quit fighting with his wife and move back upstairs. She asked Sam to forgive her for anything she had ever done to upset him, and she told him that he needed to accept Jesus as his Savior and get ready to go to heaven.

Aunt June came back to Lori's car and hour later. "For once he didn't argue with me, and he did listen," Aunt June had said. She had told Lori that she had gone to everyone she could think of to ask for forgiveness, even to the church that had asked Aunt June to leave because she was always praising the Lord and they thought she was too loud. "I'm not mad at anyone and I've made things right as far as I know," Aunt June has said before she went home.

The next day, at home, Aunt June stretched out on the sofa and "moved to heaven". Cousin Betty had come by and asked Lori to go with her to Utleville, and help take care of the arrangements. Lori's folks were vacationing on the Texas coast and the rest of the family was not close enough to help. Lori went with Betty.

"I know mother had a heart attack and died after she read my letter telling her that I have just left my husband, Carl," Betty said, crying. "She thought a lot of Carl."

"You can't blame yourself. Your mother was ready to go," Lori replied.

"I have never picked up such a relaxed corpse," the undertaken said, "It looked like she had no pain at all; her arms were still resting behind her head."

Betty and Lori checked the mail box. Betty's letter was still there, unopened. "See, it's not your fault," Lori said again.

After Lori had told her story, Aunt June's family thanked her for sharing what happened. Betty had still been blaming herself for her mother's death fifteen years later.

The reunion was soon over and Ben and Lori started home and decided to eat dinner before they left the city. It was cloudy and cool when they went into the restaurant where they visited with relatives that had decided to eat there too. By the time they returned to the car, the sun had come out and it was hot. Lady Dog was laying in the front seat, unconscious.

Lori tried to get lady to respond and put cold water on her head. Lady batted her eyes and started moving. She recovered, but was sick on the way home. "We're never going to take her with us again when it's hot!" Ben exclaimed, petting Lady.

They were home in time for Ben to get a good night's rest before returning to work. Ben was getting ready for bed while Lori was in the back bathroom. She was smoking and had the door closed and the window open. "I'm never going to be able to go back to teaching, so there's no more excuse for stress; there is no more excuse to smoke," Lori told herself. She tossed her cigarette into the stool and put the rest of the carton in the trash.

This time Lori did not dig out the horrible things or buy more. She did not tell Ben that she had quit smoking until she was sure she was finished with the nasty habit that had enslaved her for eight more years. "I'm going to trust the Lord to help me get my health back," she told Ben.

Lori looked through a large box of tapes that she had taken with her each time she had moved. She had not played them for at least ten years. It was of her former pastor. "He knew the Bible better then anyone else I ever know," Lori said aloud, "I'm going to get into God's Word to get my health, mentally and physically, back."

Lori's health gradually improved. She discovered that it takes seven years for lungs to recover from smoking.

Lori's biggest battle was the worry over finances. She had to retire on a reduced teacher's retirement because she had only taught twenty years and was not old enough to retire with the full amount. It took six months for the retirement checks to start coming in. The second month that Lori had to pay her own insurance, it went up ninety dollars a month. Ben was working for little more than minimum wages. The house payment was one hundred, fifty dollars a month and so was the payment on her recent education that she would never use. There had not been enough money for Lori to finish her four hours of Master's degree in Special Education. She had gone through another twenty-six hours of graduate work, and never obtained the degree.

Ben refused to worry. He kept on giving twenty percent of his income to the Lord's work and believing that everything would turn out all right.

Lori forced herself to go to a large Bible study in order to keep in contact with people. She was soon teaching the twenty-five preschoolers and loving it. She used her keyboard and lots of music with the stories. She ended up writing her own lessons and using a puppet to tell the Bible stories. She was asked to play music and sing at a Nursing Home. The music took a lot of practice and time. After singing at the Home, Lori walked home feeling that she didn't have any problems after visiting with the people at the Home.

Lori had another battle with kidney stones. The pain was so severe that she thought he was going to die. She put on some healing tapes and four hours later the pain left, and she was able to fix Ben's dinner.

When Lori's doctor learned about the sacrifice Ben and Lori were making on her Education payments, she said, "Lori, when you take out a student loan, you pay for insurance that covers the loan in the event that you are unable to work full time. With your health problems, you will never be able to work full time; I can help you fill out the right papers to get the loan paid off."

Lori was almost afraid to believe, but the papers were filled out and Lori and Ben received a letter showing that the loan had been paid, in full, by the insurance. It was wonderful not to have to make payments on education that would never be used.

It was amazing how busy Lori stayed even though she wasn't working. She planted roses and other flowers in the pretty yard, and painted the outside of the house. She even found time to start writing again. Lori had the time to have hot coffee and a snack waiting for Ben when he came in from work.

Lori and Ben never took each other for granite, Ben was so honest that he became more precious to Lori as time went by.

One event showed Ben's honesty. They had visiting relatives in Nebraska. Ben went to see the lawyer that had taken care of the legal work when Sue died. Ben had called the office several times through the years to pay what he owed them. Ben explained that they the firm had never sent him a bill.

"I've looked through all our files and can't find that you were ever one of our clients," the secretary said. "What shall I do?" she asked the attorney.

"Well, if Mr. Fielding insists that he owes us something, make out a bill for one-thousand dollars," the attorney replied.

Ben and Lori had been so broke at the time that they had to pay the attorney weekly until the money had been paid. "Everything was pretty much in order when Sue died, and not much money was involved, and I know Mr. Lauden didn't spend much time on us. I know that I shouldn't have owed them any more than two-hundred dollars," Ben had said.

Ben started getting a lot of overtime at the plant as the company became busier.

The Buick Rivera turbo engine started giving problems. Ben was passing a slower vehicle when the turbo quit and they were almost hit by an oncoming car. The second time it happened they knew it was time to look for a different vehicle. Ben and Lori stopped by an auto place to look at the new Dodge that had just come out. They ended up buying a year old low mileage Cougar.

"I can' believe we did this!" Lori exclaimed.

"I can't either," Ben replied, laughing. "They just kept making us a better offer until we were signing the papers."

Ben was soon working sixty hours a week. This extra overtime made it possible for them to take their first vacation since they had been married. Ben took off the last week in April and the first week in May. Counting weekends, they had eighteen days to go to California.

The weekend before they left they took Lady Dog to Elizabeth's and borrowed her camcorder. Ben and Lori left as soon as Ben came home from work Friday evening.

Ben drove all night. He and Lori held hands during the trip the way she and Steve had done. Lori was too excited to sleep so Ben would not let her drive when he stopped to take a short nap on the Arizona and California border. They stopped by an Air Force base in California and picked up Ben's thirteen year old granddaughter, Holly.

Holly was a tall, slender blonde, with dark eye lashes. It was instant love between Lori and Holly. Holly lived with her mother and step father, not Ben's son. "When are we going to eat?" Holly said a block away from her home. It seemed like she was always hungry.

They traveled to Ben's step daughter's home in the mountains in northern California. Mandy and Ted were glad to see the Fielding family and so were their twin granddaughters they were raising. The twins were a year younger that Holly.

Ted and Mandy had lost everything in a fire the year before. The fire started in the clothes dryer. Everything was destroyed except for a pictures album that Ben had made in memory of Sue. Ted had taken earlier videos of the property and valuables and the insurance company had replaced everything and built a new home just like the one that was destroyed. The house had a large deck facing the dense, beautiful forest.

Ben's other step daughter, Rita, and husband Ken, lived in a two story, round house a short distance away. The family hosted a large family dinner in honor of Ben and Lori. There were about twenty-five family members present, including Ben's son, Roland from Seattle.

Ben and Lori felt so honored and enjoyed their visit. Lori, once again, saw how much Ben's step kids and their families loved him.

"I've always admired Ben for marrying into this mixed up family and helping all of us," Mandy said. "You see, my real dad was in prison most of the time, and he abused Rita and me. Ben has always been more of a friend than a father to me since Ted and I were married about the same time as mom and Ben."

Ben and Lori had to take Holly back home to go to school two days later. Roland had not seen his daughter for five years, so he rode along on the four hour trip to the Air Force Base with them.

"Thanks for letting us take Holly this weekend," Ben said.

"I'm glad you wanted to spend time her; she doesn't have much chance to be around her relatives, especially Roland's," Holly mother said.

Ben and Lori stayed at Mandy's for a few days. When they drove to Sacramento, Roland returned to Seattle. They stayed a few days with Ben's oldest step son, Royce and Maggie his wife. Their home was located in an expensive area in the east part of the city. There was an oak tree as large as the house in the front yard. The balconies overlooked the area's beautiful golf course.

Royce was a family counselor and had to go to work every day. Maggie did typing for the California State School Department. She worked on the computer at home and faxed the material into the main office. It was a pilot program of people working at home instead of in a office.

"You sure have a beautiful home, and you sure know how to make your guests feel comfortable," Lori said.

"Royce and I have enjoyed having you here; I don't think we have ever enjoyed company this much," Maggie replied.

While Royce and Maggie were working, Ben showed Lori "his city." He showed her different places he had lived, the schools he attended, where his mother used to live, and where he and Sue had lived. They visited Sue's grave. "Sue left you quite a legacy with all these great children and their families," Lori said.

Ben agreed. He drove across the levee and showed Lori the place where he had grown up. "This really looks nice!" Ben exclaimed, "That spot over there," he said pointing his finger, "now looks like a park of trees and flowers. It used to be where we grew broomcorn. The buildings look great and the house looks almost new." He parked the car next to the house.

A young man came out and asked, "May I help you?"

"I grew up here a long time ago, and I just wanted to see what the place looks like now," Ben explained.

"We bought it three years ago and are very proud of it. I don't work as steady as my wife so I've had time to do a lot of work around here," the young man said. "Would you like to see the inside?" he asked.

"Sure, if you don't mind," Ben answered.

The owner showed Ben and Lori through the house. It was refinished and clean. "I remember when my dad built on these two rooms and what a large home I though we had," Ben said showing Lori where the add-on had taken place. "Let me have your address and I'll send you some pictures to show you what the place looked like fifty years ago, if you are interested," Ben said.

"That would be great!" the man exclaimed.

Lori wrote down the man's address.

Ben took Lori to visit Old Sacramento, and a museum located at an old Fort. He wanted to show the things that came from the Donner Party when so many people perished in the mountains above the city, but they had been moved to a museum closer to where the tragedy had taken place.

On the following weekend, at Ben's Aunt Fanny's family reunion, Lori took videos of all her new relatives. Ben had one cousin that flew in from San Francisco to ride back to his home with him. "I live in Pacifica which is a part of San Francisco," Cousin Rob explained. He seemed hyper and troubled. "You guys seem happy, Rob said.

"It's because we know Jesus as Lord and that makes us happy," Lori replied.

"I don't want to hear anything about your religion," Rob exclaimed, "I don't believe in God!"

"All right," Lori replied.

"I want to take you out to San Quentin Island and show you around before we go to my place," Rob said. He bought the tickets and took Lori and Ben on a large boat to the island that had once been the nations top security prison. Lori interviewed a man that was selling his book. He had been a prisoner during the fifties. Rob video taped the interview.

"What do you think of prisons today?" Lori asked.

"Well, some people live better on the inside than some people live on the outside now days. When I was a prisoner here, we didn't have enough heat to keep us warm, no hot water to shower with, and no contact with the outside world," the man explained, "We could hear people having fun in San Francisco, but it just made us feel worse."

It was late afternoon when Rob directed Ben to his townhouse. Lori and Ben were surprised when they entered the townhouse. Rob had no furniture. He slept and ate on the floor, Oriental style. What surprised and embarrassed Lori was Rob had nude pictures of Oriental woman in sexual positions on several walls of his house and Rob talked liked he hated Orientals.

The feeling that overtook Ben and Lori when they entered Rob's house made them thankful they had each other.

Rob talked about his ex wife. They had been divorced for twenty-five years and he was still having nightmares every night about her sleeping with different guys. It sounded like it was driving him crazy.

"Oh Lord, please release Rob from, this torment," Lori prayed quietly.

Ben and Lori sat on the floor with Rob and watched a video movie called "What about Bob?" It was so funny they laughed all the way through it.

"I work for TWA Air Lines," Rob said. "I make around sixty thousand dollars a year. Right now, I'm teaching English full time at one of the high schools here in the city, making around forty grand a year; and I don't have enough money to take you guys out for dinner."

Ben and Lori looked at each other. "Boy, what we couldn't do with a hundred thousand dollars a year!" they were thinking.

The next morning they followed Rob to the air port. Rob showed them around before he reported for work. Lori took videos of the huge planes coming and taking off. Ben and Lori did not know the street back to Rob's place had four different names. They thought they had gotten on the wrong street and became lost. It took most of the day to find their way back to the townhouse. They walked along the beach and Lori picked up interesting sea shells. Rob joined them on the beach when he came in from work.

"I've lived here two years and this is the first time I've walked along the beach," Rob said.

The last night Ben and Lori spent with Rob, he told them about the property he owned in Thailand. "It's called a hotel, but it's really a whore house," Rob said, "The girl's come with the rooms. When the women get to be in their mid-twenties, they are too old and worn out to be any good to anyone. The girls start working when they're about twelve."

"How sad!" Lori exclaimed.

All in all it had been a enjoyable two days with Cousin Rob. He was different, but Ben and Lori liked him. They traveled back to Royce's for a couple more days before they started home. They saw so many pretty places that it was hard to start home. "I have decided that I really like vacations," Lori said, squeezing Ben's hand as he drove east.

"Me too!" Ben replied.

Ben and Lori stayed one night in Nevada and one night with Lori's sister in the mountains. "The mountains are so pretty that I dread going home to the plains," Lori commented. She looked in every direction from the house. There were beautiful mountain ranges going north, south, east, and west.

They visited Lori's sisters until noon and started the last part of their journey. A few hours later, Ben drove down the alley leading to their unusual house. "This is the prettiest place we've seen yet; I think we need to stay here awhile," Lori said looking at all the beautiful iris blooming in their back yard.

Ben agreed.

That fall Lori and Ben were invited to a pancake supper in a little town sixteen miles from Sand Rock. The town was about the size Lori had grown up close to. "I'd like to live here; Sand Rock is too large for me," Lori remarked.

The next week she drove back to Drover and looked around. Most of the houses were small and older, and not many places were for sale. Lori found a property next to a small lake that had several trees and an old deteriorating house on it. She called around until she found the owner. The owner would not sell at any price.

Lori found some empty acreage behind a church. It has few smaller trees and was right next to the lake. Lori asked around until she found the owner of that property. The owner decided that he might sell enough of the property for a house.

Lori talked it over with Ben and they put the unusual house up for sale. Lori put an ad in the local paper and a sign in front of the house. She felt that she could sell without a realtor's help. The house sold within two weeks for sixty thousand dollars.

Lori and Ben found a two year old double wide mobile home for sale. The home was twenty-eight by sixty-six feet. It had two and a half bathrooms, three bedroom, living /dining room with sliding glass doors, large kitchen, and a family room with a nice fireplace. They negotiated a price and were ready to buy the home. Lori called the land owner to finish buying the land.

"I have changed my mind about the land; I think I can put my land to better use than that," the owner said.

Lori was terribly disappointed. "I guess the Lord has something better for us," she said.

One of Lori's close friends rented Ben and Lori a nice sized house that they had bought for their daughter and were now trying to sell. Lori still wanted to move to Drover but she worked on the rented house to make it easier for her friend to sell. Meanwhile she found some property in Drover that had once been for sale. She went to talk to the people that lived there, a Hispanic family.

The property had a small double wide mobile home with a detached double, metal garage. "We couldn't sell our place so we took it off the market," the lady said.

"If we can help you sell your house from off the land, will you sell us the land?" Lori asked.

"Yes, if you'll handle all the phone calls; we have an unlisted number," the lady answered.

Lori listed the house for sale in the local paper. She had several people interested on the telephone until they looked at the home. It hadn't sold when the ads ran out.

"Why don't you just buy the whole place?" the owner suggested.

"I don't think we could afford it, and still be able to move a larger house onto the property," Lori answered. "What is the bottom dollar you can take for it?" she asked.

"Twenty-five thousand," the owner answered.

Lori and Ben talked it over and bought the small house and property. Lori's friend bought them a new carpet for the double wide in return for all the work Lori had one on the rented house. The new property was twice as close to Ben's work.

"Lori, guess what?" Ben said, smiling when he came in from work.

"I have no idea what," Lori replied.

"I was promoted to a lead position at work with a good increase in wages," Ben said. "I didn't even ask for it."

"Praise the Lord!" Lori said, hugging her hard working husband.

As soon as the former owners moved out, Lori went to the double wide to work. She took down all the broken Venetian blinds and replaced them with drapes, sheers, and Pricilla curtain. Ben rented another U-Haul truck for moving and Lori hired a construction company to install the living room carpet. "I'm getting too old to put anymore carpet down," she told Ben.

Ben agreed.

Two days before the move, Lori met with two carpenters and a carpet layer early in the morning. She told the three men how she wanted the Kangaback carpet laid, and the small piece of tile she wanted laid at the front door. "I'm sorry Mam, but it can't be done," the head contractor said.

I guess I'll just have to do it myself," Lori said, disappointed. She picked up on end of the large roll of carpet and started to drag it outside. "Let me help you with that; it's heavy," one of the men said

"If I'm going to have to lay this carpet by myself, I'll have to move it by myself," Lori said. The men left and Lori pulled the carpet out on the front grass. She measured and started cutting. Lori was tried, but the carpet was half in by the time Ben came by after work. Ben took the next day off and they finished installing the carpet.

The next morning the two guys Lori had hired to help move were late showing up. They finally came with hangovers. Lori administered medicine for their headaches and the men worked well. Ben knew how to arrange the furniture and what wasn't used or sold was stored in the garage. Most of the furniture from the living room and family room in the old house was placed in the large living room of the mobile home. The third bedroom was used for Lori's "playroom". It contained the new computer, electric piano, musical instruments, and a table for painting.

The house was not much larger than the trailer house Lori and Steve had remodeled. It was right next to the lake and the sunsets were beautiful as they reflected on the water. There were mud hens, muskrats, beavers, different kinds of ducks, and Canadian and snow geese during different times of the year. The Rocky Mountains could be seen in the distance. Lori missed her unusual house, but she enjoyed the quietness of Drover and the busy lake.

Lori painted the home and metal garage white. It took three coats of paint for the garage. Ben helped Lori build a six foot, privacy fence between their property and the old, tumbled down house next door. Lori planted flowers, trees, and a large garden.

Within a period of two years, the student loan had been paid, Lori had quit smoking and felt great, Ben had been promoted, and they were living in a place that was paid for. Lori, not Ben, was amazed at what the Lord had done for them.

Lori no longer went to the Bible Study group but had time for private Bible study each day. She still practiced one day a week with her music and spent the next day at the Nursing Home several miles away trying to give the residents a little happiness.

"I said to get out of here and I meant now!" one of the Nursing Home supervisors was saying.

Lori turned around and looked behind her to see who the lady was talking to. She suddenly realized that the lady was talking to her. The supervisor had told Lori once that the workers at the Home had complained about her being there because they thought she was too religious. The one supervisor had not been friendly for a long time, but Lori never though she would be thrown out.

"I can't believe she talked to you like that," Gladis said. Gladis had become one of Lori's close friends. Her husband, Daniel, was one of the residents at the Home. He had two brain surgeries. Gladis spent every day at the Home with Daniel.

Lori remembered the time she had gone into Daniel's room to play music for him. He had told her some things that weren't true. "I'm going to starve myself to death," Daniel told Lori.

The next week the Lord gave Lori a message for Daniel. The next time she went into his room, she said, "Daniel, the Lord told me something to say to you, but I don't' want to tell you unless you want hear it," Lori said. "Would you like to hear the message?" she asked.

"Yes, I would," Daniel answered.

"Daniel, the Lord told me that you have been a person that likes to control everything that is going on around you. I don't know you very well, but this is what the Lord said. The Lord said that it is time to let Him take control of everything around you," Lori explained.

Daniel nodded his head yes. "Gladis and I were taking about that the other day," he replied.

"Daniel, leave it up to God when you are supposed to leave this old earth; it's something you don't need to worry about," Lori said. She prayed with Daniel before she left the room. Daniel accepted the Lord as his Savior a few days later and did not worry about taking his own life.

Now, Lori had been kicked out. Lori felt like she had been knocked down again. She wept as she drove back home. She heard the Lord talking deep inside her. "Daughter, don't cry; they don't want Me there either. I did not call you to sing there but I have called you to write. I want you to write your experiences to encourage others when times are tough to keep believing in Me," the Lord said.

Lori begin writing again. She was in the school library one day talking to the librarian. "Lori, this school is always looking for subs. Why don't you bring in your transcripts and sign up?" the lady said.

Lori was soon called to sub in everything from preschool to high school Math and English. She was shocked over the changes that had taken place in the schools the four years she had been away. The children seemed to do as they pleased, and they were terribly behind in academics. Lori wasn't sure if it was just because she was only a sub, or the world had changed that much. The older students lied about their names and sassed her when she tried to get them to work.

Lori had to throw one student out of class several times because of his filthy language. One day the student walked up to Lori and quietly said, "You have no right to throw me out of class by the way I talk. I'm not breaking any law, and by what the government says, you have no right to kick me out of class. Besides, some teachers use the same language as I do."

"I don't use that kind of language, and no one in my classes are allowed to talk that way either," Lori replied.

"Has the government gone so far in protecting children that teachers are afraid to discipline, and even parents are afraid to discipline too?" Lori asked herself. Lori heard that the school in Drover had three cases in court brought by parents against teachers disciplining their children. It seemed so unfair to the students involved.

Lori had the high school students write sentences using simple instructions. This way she could check their spelling and grammar knowledge. What the students handed in were mostly very simple sentences, very poor handwriting and grammar, and one paper even threatened her life. "You kids are at least three years behind in English; we have to do something!" Lori exclaimed, forgetting that she was just a sub.

Lori was not popular with the students and she spent so much time sending kids to the office and complaining that she was not called to sub the next year of school. Two of the teachers suffered nervous breakdowns that year. One of them lived close to Lori. Lori took her some Christian tapes and tried to encourage her. "We can't be bitter; we have to let the Lord handle it," Lori tried to explain.

"You have never had any trouble in your life so don't tell me how to handle mine!" the lady shouted. "Get out of my house!" she screamed.

Lori did not try to argue, but she did continue to check on the lady to see how she was doing. The lady finally apologized and said, "It was your tapes and encouragement that started me back on the road to recovery."

Lori decided to try subbing again to help with expenses. She found a larger school where subbing was easier. She was subbing in the Middle school one day when the principal called her into his office.

"Mrs. Fielding, I want to talk to you about a special assignment we have. It might be something that you would be interested in. We have a seventh grade student that is in Home Bound teaching. We are looking for a Home Bound teacher," Mr. Warren said.

"I might be interested," Lori replied.

"Good, I'll have the mother and student come here before you leave today, and see if it might work out," Mr. Warren said. "The district is looking for someone to work with this student two hours each day."

'I have to drive nine miles or more to teach here, so it would cost too much to drive in for just two hours work each day," Lori replied.

"We might be able to change it to more time and less days, if you are interested," the principal said.

Lori was busy working with some students when she looked up and saw a woman with white hair. The woman did not look old enough to have white hair. "Can I help you?" Lori asked.

"Are you Mrs. Fielding?" the lady asked.

"Yes," Lori answered.

"I'm Mrs. Bonner, and this is my son, Kris. We need to talk to you about Home Schooling," the lady said.

The other teacher motioned that is was all right for Lori to leave the room with Kris and his mother. They followed Lori upstairs to the empty Teacher's Lounge. Lori motioned for them to sit down, and waited for Mrs. Bonner to talk.

Lori learned that the teaching would take place in the Bonner home. Kris was restless while the two ladies talked. He continually annoyed his mother. He was small for his age and hyper. Lori thought it might be something she could do. Mrs. Bonner seemed impressed with Lori because she been a Special Education teacher. She went back to talk to the principal. She ended up working with Kris three days a week for a total of twelve hours and making twelve dollars and hour.

Lori was impressed with the Bonner home. It was a lovely home with a swimming pool in the back. Kris had an older brother that was a senior in high school and a reporter for the local newspaper. Kay Bonner ran a collection agency for several doctors from an office in her home.

Kris was a challenge. It took Lori and Kris several months to learn to understand each other and become friends. It was hard for Kris to have friends because he often lost his temper and insulted people. It was easy for him to get into fights. Lori went with Kris several times when he danced Indian dances with other young men in the Kiva. She watched the dancers come off the stage in a trance. Kris often ended up trying to fight another dancer. Lori had to watch him constantly.

Lori taught Kris seventh and eighth grade. They took field trips and Kris loved to visit Lori's little house on the lake.

The third year Kay Bonner wanted Kris to be put in the local high school. There he would be with six-hundred other students.

One day they would never forget was September 11, 2001. Lori was getting ready for work when Ben called. "Lori, you might need to listen to the news before you leave," he said.

Lori was in a hurry but she turned on the TV and watched in horror as she saw a large air plane hit the second World Trade Center tower, and watched it tumble to the ground. The news was telling about the destruction of the building while Lori had visions of destructed lives. She listened to the news on the way to school and prayed for the people and not the buildings.

There were no lessons being taught in the school. Everyone was watching the news on TV. They saw the trade tower falling over and over.

"I bet it's the Russians," Kris commented.

"No Kris, I think it is the work of an Eastern thinking mind to do something like this. The Russians are too much like us to kill like this," Lori tried to explain.

"This is an emergency!" someone shouted over the intercom, "Please evacuate the building and take all the students to the south parking lot past the gym as quickly as possible."

Lori and Kris joined the other hundreds of students and teachers making their way to the south parking lot and found out it had nothing to do with what was happening in New York City. There had been a bomb threat at the school and some other schools in the area.

Lori watched two large planes crossing the sky and knew it had to be military planes since all other planes had been grounded by then.

The day had been such a disaster that the administrators decided to just send the kids home. Parents were coming to pick up many of the students anyway.

The teachers watched the parking lot slowly empty of teenagers and their vehicles. Lori had left her purse in the room with the car keys in her purse. One administrator took a chance and ran into the building a grabbed her purse and gave it to her. Lori was embarrassed over the situation.

The phone was ringing when Lori came into the house. It was a step daughter in California afraid that they had not heard the news since they lived so far from any large cities. As the death reports climbed, and there was such sadness everywhere, Lori was thankful to fall into Ben's arms that evening.

Kris did well in Algebra, Language, and Science. He was still having trouble with writing. One of the teachers started Kris on a great

Grammar program on the computer. Lori worked with Kris three days a week. Sometimes when she came in at nine, Kris would be upset over something that had taken place in the other room before she got there. Lori had to take time to calm him down. Somehow, Kris didn't see Lori as a threat like the other teachers. They usually had fun working together.

Lori and Kris went on monthly field trips with the other Sp. Ed. Students. They were fun and gave Kris a change to get along with other students. On one if the frield trips Lori was overseeing three older boys at an arcade in a shopping mall. Her group returned to the bus but the rest of the party was gone.

"I think they went to a store across the street," the bus driver said.

Robin and Earl ran ahead of Lori toward the other store. Kris and Lori followed them. They were crossing the parking lot when Lori saw a commotion in the area Kris was standing.

"That guy carrying the coats almost ran over me!" Kris explained.

Lori and Kris walked into the nearest store to be told that the guy had grabbed a rack of coats and ran out the door. Kris gave a good description of the guy. The cops showed up and Kris described the guy again. All the attention made Kris excited. "I think it was that guy coming in the door right there," he said pointing.

The policeman quickly realized they were talking to a "special" person and went to talk to someone else.

Marty was a tall, three-hundred pound young man in the group. He had difficulty walking. "You remind me of my grandmother," Mary told Lori. He stayed close to Lori and Kris all day.

"It's time to start back to school; who wants to go with me through the pet shop to see the animals first?" Lori asked.

Kris and Marty followed Lori through the pet quarters. They were walking back down the mall toward the bus when Marty fell. Lori and Kris tried to pick him up, but couldn't budge him. A man came running over to help, then another man, and then another man. Together, the five of them were able to get Marty back on his feet. Lori was sore for days but it had been a fun trip. The kids were well behaved and thoughtful of each other.

It was a wonderful part time job and Lori was saving a little each month. Air conditioning and gutters were put on the little house, and there was almost enough money to send in her manuscripts.

"Mrs. Fielding, did you know that your student punched two other students with a sharp object when they came into the room?" one of the other teachers in the Special Ed. Room said.

Lori ran to Kris. "All right Kris, give me your weapon!" Lori shouted.

Kris handed Lori a piece of plastic that had once been a ruler. It measured about two by three inches. Teachers and administrators came running into the room. Kris went into a panic and made threats trying to protect himself. Mrs. Bonner was called to take Kris home.

The principal asked Lori to write down what Kris had said. She hated to but thought maybe it would help him in some way. "I know you are not dangerous, and your mother knows it, but the other people may not know it," she told Kris.

Lori went to check on the two hurt students after the Bonners left. The young man said it was no big deal, and the young lady would not show Lori where she had been punctured on the arm.

Kris was expelled from school for a week. At the end of the week a special meeting was held at the high school principal's office.

"Parents are calling and wanting to know if their kids are safe with Kris in school. He will have to go through counseling before he can return to school," the principal explained.

The Bonners were disappointed when Kris was put in an Alternative school for thirty days to receive counseling. Another meeting was called. Mrs. Bonner wanted Kris back in the high school, but Mr. Bonner and Kris had decided that he should stay in the Alternative school.

Lori walked out of the meeting to let them decide whether she would be working with Kris anymore of not. She called Mrs. Bonner the next morning and found out that was no longer employed.

Lori thought about subbing but it was hard work and Elizabeth was having health problems. Lori needed to be available in case Elizabeth needed her. The Lord would provide for them although their monthly income dropped six-hundred dollars a month.

Although Lori had eight piano students, she missed the teaching that had been such a big part of her life. Maybe it would not be so hard when Ben retired and was around all the time.

Lori wrote and worked outside as the days flew by. There were no more tests, criticism, or stress over trying to be a great teacher and getting along with administrators. Lori enjoyed taking tomatoes, pepper, cantaloupe, watermelons, and squash to many people from her garden.

Mike now had two sons and Lori had seven grandchildren, counting Holly, to enjoy.

Ben's youngest son came for ten days one summer. He hitched-hiked into town. Ben had not seen him for five years and hardly recognized him. When Lori met Don he reminded her so much of Ben with his cherry personality. He had hitchhiked all over the world with his belongings on his back. Don had to keep busy. He scrubbed road oil off the white Cougar, painted the trim on the doublewide, fixed a rocking chair, and many other things that needed done. "I have never been any place and rested as well as I have here," Don said. "These ten days have gone awfully fast, but it's time for me to go on."

"Would it help if I drove you to Marktown on the interstate highway?" Lori asked.

"That would help; I'm supposed to meet a buddy there," Don said, "you probably won't see me again for three years; and then I might settle down close to you and dad."

Lori drove Don the hour and a half trip to Marktown, a city of two hundred thousand.

"I think it's on this corner," Don said, "No, It's the next corner."

Lori parked the car and unfastening her seat belt when Don kissed her on the cheek and stepped out of the car. Lori looked up and didn't see her step son again. "He really was here wasn't he?" she asked Ben that evening.

Ben laughed and said yes.

Lori was not feeling well again. She had another battle with kidney stones. Again she felt the Lord was specking to her.

"The American diet is not good for the body," the Lord seemed to say. "To feel better, you need to stop eating white flour, white sugar, and chocolate, and you need to stop drinking coffee and tea, and you need to eat a lot of fresh fruit and vegetables, and drink plenty of water."

The first few days Lori changed her diet, her body rebelled like a spoiled child. Lori couldn't visualize breakfast, or visiting with someone without a cup of coffee. She had drunk coffee since she had been in grade school. Some of her relatives had told her that drinking coffee would turn her hair black. Lori did not enjoy being a red head and was disappointed that her hair didn't change color. It was hard to not make birthday cakes for her grandchildren or the rest of the family. Ben still loved his coffee, sweets, and Cokes. It made cooking the right way harder. Eventually Lori did not care for sweets as much as she did at one time.

CHAPTER XV

ANOTHER HOME

By the time Ben turned sixty-five, the president had signed a new law where a person could continue to work and draw Social Security at the same time. Elizabeth and Arthur were no longer able to take care of themselves so Lori and her sisters had to put them into assisted living in the same town where Mike and Mitch lived. Lori and her two sisters worked a week getting everything ready for an auction sale and the house empty for the new owners.

Lori and Ben traveled to where Lori's parents were every other weekend and for all holidays so Lori's parents would not be alone. They found a small, old, home across the street from Lori's parents. About that time they received a letter from one of their credit card companies that they could borrow cash without any interest for a year. Lori called the number. She was able to borrow twenty thousand dollars on the card without signing any papers. The amount was deposited in their checking account. They made the monthly payment out of Ben's Social Security check.

"I can't retire until we sell this place in Dover because we can't afford two homes on my Social Security and your retirement," Ben said.

The trailer by the lake was put up for sale. Lori advertised in the papers and put a sign in front. Many people came to look and wanted the place but the double wide was not on a foundation and would not pass for a loan. The only way they could sell the house was to find someone that had the cash.

Ben and Lori started remodeling the old house as well as visiting Lori's parents during any extra time they had.

Lori was watching TV with Ben one evening when the room started spinning. She did not tell Ben but rushed to bed and lay still until she went to sleep. She felt better the next two days and then she had the spinning sensation again. This time she became terribly ill. It was Saturday and Ben was home. He took Lori to the hospital. She was very sick for four days.

Elizabeth asked Mike to bring her to see Lori because she knew Lori was seriously ill.

At first the doctors thought that Lori had a heart attack. Lori finally realized that she had a heart monitor under her gown. The doctors thought that maybe it had been a stroke when they ruled out heart problems. An amorism was even mentioned. Lori and Ben's minister came to visit. "I think God is healing you of what is wrong and it has the doctors confused," he said.

"I didn't even know you believed in healing, but I think you are right," Lori replied.

The doctors let Lori go home after an appointment with an eye specialist. Lori saw double for three months. Lori was pretty sick for several days. Ben did not miss any work but called Lori at 9 a.m. and at noon to check on her.

There were so many things Lori could not do and driving was one of them. The long days passed. Lori spent a lot of time in prayer and watching TV with one eye. One day Ben called home and Lori was crying. "You are worse?" he asked.

"No! The Lord has healed my eyes and I can see only one thing of everything now," Lori said.

"Praise the Lord!" Ben shouted.

Lori had gone so long without driving that she only drove into town once a week for groceries. This short distance even made her nervous.

They met many interesting people while showing their home for sale. There were two guys that seemed interested, but Lori didn't feel right talking to them. She and Ben figured out what was wrong after they had left. Another time Lori received a call from a man that said he was coming to look at the house. The Lord warned Lori not to answer the door. The Lord also impressed upon her that it was dangerous to show a guy, or guys, her home alone, and especially the bedrooms.

It was on a Friday that the Spencers came to look at the property. They were about the same age as Ben and Lori, and owned other property in the mountains. "My husband has many health problems and the doctors have told him that he has to move to a lower elevation to feel better," Mrs. Spencer explained.

"Do you want to look through the house again?" Lori asked.

"No, that's not necessary," Mr. Spencer replied and begin to tell Lori about his many health problems.

Lori was thankful for the shade trees to stand under but she felt tried when the Spencers finally left. "They seem the least interested of anyone," Lori said to herself as she watched them drive away.

Ben was at work when Lori received a call the next Tuesday morning. "We want your house and we will send you a check in the mail today," Mrs. Spencer said.

"Why don't we all meet downtown tomorrow at the title office and we can get everything done there," Lori suggested.

"That sounds like a better idea," Mrs. Spencer replied.

Ben used his noon break to come to town and help Lori sign papers. He gave his company two week notice that he would be retiring. The home that took so long to sell had sold in less than a week.

"We are going to give a retirement party for Ben and another worker," Ms. Kingly said. She was the daughter of the family that owned the company and worked in one of the offices. "Do you have some pictures of Ben that we can use as a power point at the party?" she asked.

Lori took Ben's picture albums to the plant. She had only been there during Christmas parties, so Ben did not know Lori was working with Ms. Kingly.

The night of the party, both of Lori's sons were busy with basketball games and were not able to be there. Ben was surprised when Joyce came in, but did not suspect anything until pictures were shown on the wall. Ben was called up to the front to be "roasted". One of the supervisors had Ben put on his old bowling shirt from California that Lori had brought in.

The M.C. told how Ben had managed two lumber companies in California and had lost his job when he tried to weld two pieces of wood together and burned the place down. Everyone laughed. The company gave Ben a fifteen year ring for the time he had worked for the company.

"My, how times flies when you are having fun," Lori said and Ben agreed.

Ben and Lori had to work fast to make the old house livable. New cabinets were installed that matched the old ones. The holes in the walls were repaired, two new bathrooms put in along with new carpet. The main level of the house was beautiful with its old molding around the doors and windows etc. The basement was almost as large as the upstairs but not finished.

By the time Ben and Lori were able to move, Lori's parents had to be put in a Nursing Home twenty miles away. Mike and his family had built a new home in Dannon and were seventy miles away. Mitch and family had moved to Mike's old place. Ben was now adjusting not going to work and finding things at home to do like mowing the grass.

The following September Ben and Lori planned a five thousand mile vacation. "It will be nice not to have to hurry back to go to work. I don't ever remember going anywhere and not having to hurry back," Ben said when they started their journey.

They traveled to Nebraska to visit relatives and on to Minnesota to visit Lori cousin. None of the family had visited Lori's cousin in thirty years. Devin and Karen were excited to have Ben and Lori and showed them their part of the world. This included traveling four hours to their cabin in northern Minnesota. Everyone was surprised when they had a tornado come within sixty miles of where they were staying.

Devin's cabin did not have an indoor bathroom but a toilet instead. He had told Lori that they had a motion light there. When Lori used the toilet before she and Ben went to bed, she tried to wave her arms around to turn on the light. It didn't work so she used the flashlight that she had brought with her. The next morning she felt foolish when she saw the light fixture on the wall. The toilet also had carpet.

After leaving Minnesota, Ben drove on to North Dakota and they spent four days visiting Holly, and her family. Holly had a wonderful husband, and had given Ben and Lori two great grandchildren who were two and four. They had a great time playing with the children and taking videos. The children cried when it was time for their great grandparents to leave.

It took a day to cross Montana but they saw a lot of beautiful country. They had lunch with an old friend in Stevensville. Their next stop was to visit Lori's first husband's uncle in Yakima, WA. Uncle Willard was in his nineties, but seemed much younger. He drove Ben and Lori around his city and gave them a history lesson as well as the present state of the city: annexing etc.

The next morning Ben and Lori had a large breakfast at a Perkins Restaurant and headed for the western part of the state. Ben was amazed how different Spokane was from the costal region as they drove toward the Pacific Ocean.

"Whidbey Island has quiet a history for our family,' Lori said. "I had two uncles that moved here after World War II. One had been stationed on the island while he was in the Navy. We used to come here ever few years to visit. In 1949, and I was a freshman in high school, we came to visit. My mother gave birth to my only brother. He was still born. Daddy didn't know what to do so he took his only son into the forest and buried him. He could never find the place again.

My uncle was always proud of Deception Pass Bridge that links the island with the mainland. He collected pictures of the bridge. When Daddy moved to heaven in 1979, my uncle sent mother a picture of the bridge. There was a man sitting below the bridge watching the fishing boats. There was no doubt that the man was my dad. The picture was taken in 1967," Lori said. "We are almost there."

Ben stopped the car on the mainland side of the bridge. He and Lori took several pictures before they crossed over. The bridge was high and the land was beautiful. "What a beautiful world!" Lori exclaimed.

Two miles down the road Ben pulled the car off the road. "What's the matter?" Lori asked.

"I'm too dizzy to drive," Ben replied, before he became deathly sick.

"I don't think I can drive in this traffic," Lori replied. She helped Ben to the passenger side of the car. "Oh Lord, please help me," Lori sobbed. She tried to see through tears and steady her shaking hands. Ben was vomiting and clutching his chest. Lori pulled off the road and took out her cell phone and called a few people to pray. She called her aunt to get direction to her home and told her aunt that Ben was very sick. Lori pulled behind some buildings to steady her nerves. Ben was vomiting so much they used a whole box of facial tissue before they traveled further.

Lori had never been more frightened. She realized that she had gone too far down the island and had to turn back and look for road sign through tears. She called her aunt again. She was supposed to turn on Scenic Road and not Phoenix Road. She finally saw the right sign and soon came to a place she recognized.

Aunt Tina and one of her sons came out to meet them. "Since your Uncle Ray had his stroke ten years ago, I have to be careful not expose him to anything," she explained. "We will put you and Ben in the bedroom that was once our family room away from the rest of the house until Ben gets better."

Ben stopped vomiting long enough to tell Aunt Tina that he was having a bad reaction to some cold medicine he had taken. It took all three of them to get Ben into the house and on the bed because he was so sick. He seemed to feel a little better but grew worse in the night. Lori called 911 at one o'clock that morning.

Two ambulances showed up. Several people helped load Ben and put an IV in him. Lori did not wake up Aunt Tina but crawled into the front of the ambulance with the driver. The driver knew Lori's relatives. Ben was rushed to ER where a young doctor examined him. Ben told the doctor the same story about the cold medicine. "You can go home if you can go to the restroom by yourself," the doctor said with lots of authority.

Ben somehow gained enough strength to go to the restroom and back alone, although he was very dizzy. He was released and Cousin Shawn came to take them back to Aunt Tina's.

Lori didn't visit with her relatives much because Ben was too sick in bed for her to leave him. During the night he grew worse and had to use the bathroom several times. He had no sense of balance or direction and kept slamming Lori against the wall as she tried to help him. Lori had to call 911 again about one o'clock in the morning again. Although Ben was very sick, he never lost consciousness.

It looked like the same ambulance that showed up that took Ben the first night. This time tests were run and the doctors discovered brain damage which meant a stroke. He was admitted to the hospital. Lori was busy trying to find all the information from their Medicare and insurance: papers one does not usually take on vacation. She also called Kenneth Copeland Ministry for prayer.

The doctors worked with Ben for a week. Lori slept in an uncomfortable, straight backed, hard chair that week. Ben was too sick to appreciate her being there. One doctor wanted to send him to a rehabilitation hospital but the other doctor didn't think Ben's heart was strong enough to leave the hospital.

Aunt Tina had called her youngest son's wife to drive Ben and Lori to the other hospital and she was waiting for them while the two doctors argued.

Ben's roommate's wife worked at the hospital. She was in the room and demanded that something be done for what they were putting Ben and Lori through. Ben was finally put in a wheel chair and taken to their car where Cousin Bonnie was waiting. Lori still didn't feel like she could drive well enough through the heavy traffic to take him. It took three hours to transport Ben to the rehabilitation hospital in Bellingham, WA: fifty miles from Canada.

The countryside was beautiful but Lori was busy watching Ben to be sure that Ben was handling the ride all right. Cousin Bonnie was on the cell phone all the way teaching a younger lady how to barrel race for a rodeo.

The first parking lot they drove into was in front of the wrong hospital. Lori went in and was given instructions how to get to the right hospital. Bonnie pulled up to the back of an older hospital and two women came out with a wheel chair. Ben was taken inside what was once the main hospital many years ago. It had been remodeled into a rehab hospital when the new one was built. The inside was old, but neat and clean and the nurses were very caring.

Ben was taken to his room and put to bed.

"You look like a person that never thinks about herself," one nurse said. "I'm going to get you a folding cot and set it up next to your husband's bed. The nurse soon had a bed set up for Lori. Lori had never remembered how well it felt to lay down and stretch out again.

The nurses started immediately with Ben's therapy and Lori's training. Lori was shown how to give Ben a bath, etc. and she learned how to push his wheelchair.

Ben's personality changed drastically. As hard as Lori tried, she could not please Ben with anything she tried to do for him. No matter what she said, he would criticize her with no mercy. Lori found it hard to make even the simplest choices. She wanted to be close to Ben, but the stress was almost unbearable.

Ben slowly regained strength. Lori pushed the wheelchair from place to place for his therapy. One therapist was teaching him how to take care of himself, and others in how to get around in a wheelchair.

After two weeks, the staff decided that Ben was strong enough to be dismissed. Their case worker set up Ben's therapy sessions on Whidbey Island.

A senior volunteer driver drove them back to Aunt Tina's. The driver had just won a battle with cancer. The woman was nice and pleasant to visit with. They had to stop in town for Lori to have several prescriptions filled. Lori felt like she was walking in a vacuum tube. She checked her blood pressure while she was waiting for the medicine. It was 200/100.

"You're going to the doctor," Aunt Tina said when Lori told her about her blood pressure. She made an appointment for Lori to see a doctor she knew in town. Lori stopped by after she took Ben to therapy the next day and started on new medicine. Aunt Tina found a military supply house where they could pick up a wheelchair with no expense. But, the chair was so heavy that Lori could not get it in and out of the trunk of the car. Ben was able to get around with the large walker with lots of help, but tired easily.

Lori drove Ben to therapy several times a week. Aunt Tina could not help because she was almost blind and her cousins were all working. Ben hollered at Lori constantly while she was driving. He did not trust her driving and Lori was doing the best she could. She would be sobbing each time they back to Aunt Tina's.

Lori and Ben were not satisfied with the therapy Ben received in the first place and decided to try another therapist that was several miles further away. She would never forget the day that Ben turned loose and took a few steps alone between two monkey bars at the workout center. It gave him courage to know that he would walk again.

"You have to get rid of that walker. It makes you look like a grandpa," the new therapist said.

"But, I'm a great grandpa," Ben replied.

"But you don't have to look like one," Greg responded. He worked with Ben three times a week. Greg was so positive that it helped make up for his pushing Ben so hard.

That November the island received the most moisture, the most snow, the lowest temperatures, and the high winds in its recorded history. Many of the utility poles blew over causing many homes to be without electricity. Aunt Tina's home was all electric. One night she started a fire in the fireplace in Ben and Lori's room to warm up the house. The smell of the smoke made Ben sick.

Uncle Ray, who was handicapped from his stroke, moved from room to room by holding onto furniture and walls. He could not talk but was able to make a few noises. Aunt Tina got him up every morning, dressed him in western clothes, fixed his breakfast, and turned on the Western channel on TV. Their four kids that lived on the Island came by frequently to take them places or see if they had everything they needed.

Lori would have liked to help Aunt Tina clean her house and do other things since Aunt Tina could not see very well, but Lori's back started hurting. She went to the chiropractor and found that she had some disks out of place. "I haven't done anything to put my back out of place," Lori told the doctor.

Sometimes just stress can throw your back out of place," the doctor explained. Many times Lori would wake up in the morning after a short nights rest and remember that Ben was very sick, she hurt badly, and they were seventeen hundred miles from home.

It took a treatment a week for four weeks before Lori started feeling better. The pain had gotten so bad that she had ended up sleeping in a chair again.

Ben and Lori's kids were good to call and check up on them. Lori tried to talk Joyce into coming after them when her dad was strong enough, but she was too busy with her job and didn't feel comfortable making the trip in winter.

Lori was talking to Mitch. "Son, would it be possible for you to come to Washington after us when Ben is strong enough?" Lori asked.

"I guess I could," Mitch replied. He was used to driving school buses in all kinds of weather.

"When could you come after us?" Lori asked.

"My Christmas vacation starts next week. That would be the best time for me," Mitch answered.

Greg had Ben walking with a cane up and down steps and even steps outside. He worked Ben hard the last day they were together.

Mitch took a flight from Denver to Seattle where he caught a shuttle bus to the island. Uncle Ray was having trouble settling down so Lori decided to take Ben to a motel the last night.

One cousin came by to visit that afternoon.

"Mom cried after you left today," she said.

"I guess that means we didn't wear out our welcome," Lori said trying to laugh. "We had planned to stay three days and it turned out to three months. She took very good care of us. It was hard telling her good-bye today. I told your mom today that she has seen the good, the bad, and the ugly with us these three months."

"She will miss you guys and you reading the mail to her etc." the cousin said.

It was about time for Mitch to come into Pine Harbor. Lori wasn't sure she could drive across town after dark to pick him up. She knew where the station was but she was not comfortable driving in traffic or at night. Lori was relieved when another cousin knocked on their motel door. It was Cousin Shawn checking to see if they needed anything. He gladly drove them to the bus station and then they all ate out together.

Mitch left with Ben and Lori early the next morning. Lori had made Ben a bed in the back seat. Mitch had no trouble finding his way through Seattle. The further they drove away from the coastal area, the more the weather was like winter. Mitch stopped every two hours for Ben to get out and walk as to cut down the chances of another stroke as Staci had ordered him to do.

They left Idaho just before one storm and came into Wyoming right after another storm. Mitch had run the buses so long that he knew how to watch the weather reports on TV for the safest travel. They spent the last night with Lori's sister and made it home the next day. There were several inches of snow in the yard when they drove in. 'I guess we have already had our big snow," Lori commented.

Two days later Ben, Lori, Elizabeth and Arthur were invited to Staci's sister's place for Christmas dinner. It had been a different kind of Christmas season and they had to leave early because Ben tired easily.

Two days later it started snowing again. It snowed heavy for two days. The Assisted Living Quarters across the street was almost covered with snow. Ben could not keep his doctor's appointments and the National Guard had to bring him his medicine because the town was snow bound. They were house bound for a week. It was a good time for recuperation for both of them.

"Oh Lord, I can't stand all the stress from Ben hollering at me all the time since his stroke," Lori told the Lord. From deep inside her she heard a still small voice, "Love Ben in every way possible. Make him happy in every way you can, and leave the rest up to me."

"Yes, Lord," Lori said.

Little by little Ben stopped hollering at Lori. He even became comfortable with her driving which helped her gain more confidence. Instead of criticizing her, he would try to make her feel better about herself if she made a mistake. He became kind, understanding, and thankful for her help.

"Thank you Lord. I guess I have found out how to change a man," Lori said with a grateful heart.

Ben received more therapy and was eventually able to walk with a cane but he would never drive again. He and Lori took Elizabeth to a cousin's wedding that summer. By the time they loaded Elizabeth's wheelchair into the trunk, they were both so tired that Ben left his cane in the parking lot. It was never returned. Ben now walked holding onto Lori instead.

"The reason I like to use a cane is because when you stumble and have a cane, people are considerate. Without a cane they look at you like you must be drunk," Ben explained.

Ben and Lori spent all their "free" time at the Nursing Home with Elizabeth and Arthur.

One day there was a call from the Home. "Would you be able to sit up with Arthur tonight?" the lady asked. "He is in the hospital again."

Arthur didn't sleep much but they watched the movie Giant on TV. "That's a nice looking woman," Arthur said about Elizabeth Taylor. "That's a nice looking man," he said when Rock Hudson appeared.

The next time Arthur was in the hospital the doctor had to jump start his heart. The family decided that they would not have that done again. Lori was sitting up with him when he opened his eyes, squeezed her hand, and smiled. She thought he was going to move to heaven right then but the nurses came in and put something into his IV. Arthur moved to heaven the next day after Lori had gone home to rest.

Elizabeth just couldn't get over loosing Arthur. Although handicapped herself, her hobby had been to see that Arthur had the best of care. She was disappointed when she couldn't move into a home of her own when Arthur was no longer there.

It was a year and a half later when Lori heard the doctor say, "I'm sorry Lori, but this is the last days for your mother. She has pneumonia and her lungs are worn out along with her heart and kidneys."

Lori called the rest of the family. Her sister came in from Arizona to take turns sitting up with Elizabeth before she moved to heaven the last of August, three and a half months later.

Elizabeth had been so handicapped that she had to be lifted to the bathroom with a large machine. Ben sit it the back of the room to offer support while Lori tried to feed her mother and see that her needs were taken care of. Elaine and Gary sit up with Elizabeth eight hours in the morning and past noon, while Ben and Lori sit up until eight or nine o'clock in the evening. Lori played the key board each evening until she thought her mother was asleep. A few times when she finished playing, Elizabeth would clap her two fingers together and Lori would play a few more songs.

There was not much time to eat so Lori thought it would be a good time to lose some weight. She went on a candida diet, which eliminated dairy, white sugar and flour, and yiest products. She used almond milk, crackers instead of bread, and fruit instead of desert. She could even eat yogurt. Lori was able to lose thirty-five pounds before Elizabeth moved to heaven.

Preacher Sally was with the family a lot of the time and Lori and her sisters were holding Elizabeth's hands when her life left her old body. Elaine did most of the arrangements and Elizabeth looked beautiful in a silk lined casket trimmed in red roses. There was a golden rose on each corner of the casket and Lori and her sisters each took one rose for a keepsake before the casket was gently lowered into the ground. There were not so many things to be taken care of as when Arthur and Elizabeth had been moved out of the large yellow house south of town.

Ben was sick the night Elizabeth moved to heaven. Lori thought he had pneumonia. She called Kenneth Copeland Ministries again and asked for prayer. Staci came by early the next morning and examined Ben. "He has a bad case of bronchitis," Staci said.

"Ben," Lori said one evening, "I would feel safer if we had a larger vehicle to drive." "Do you think we could find one on the internet that we could order?" she asked. "We don't travel many places where we can look at car lots,"

Ben looked on the internet and ended up on E-Bay. They looked at several Pacificas and ordered a gold one. "I know a lighter color will be easier to keep clean that our red Buick has been," Lori said.

Ben kept feeling worse. On the night of December 12, Ben took a shower. He was so weak he could not dress himself. The next morning he started shaking uncontrollably. It was Sunday and Lori called the hospital and told them she was bringing Ben in. Dr. Jacob was at the hospital when they arrived. Ben was put into the hospital and Dr. Jacob ordered several tests to find out what was wrong with him.

A few days later Lori received word that the Pacifica was coming in by truck late one evening. She did not want to sign the papers for it until she had someone else look at it and Ben was still in the hospital. Lori asked a close friend and her pastor to come to the park where the Pacifica was to be delivered. Everything looked pretty good so Lori signed the papers. She drove the "new" vehicle to the hospital that night; getting to know it in the dark was quite an experience.

A farmer bought the Buick. When he came to pick it up from the house, Lori tried to have all the papers in order and make sure everything was removed from out under the seats, etc. "I guess that's everything," Lori sighed.

"Do you want me to pay you?" the farmer asked, laughing.

"I guess so," Lori replied, "You have to forgive me because I'm not thinking straight with my husband in the hospital and all. Thanks."

Lori was given the empty bed in Ben's room along with pajamas. Ben was so sick that the only way Lori could go to sleep was to imagine that she was a little girl crawling up in the Lord's lap for comfort.

A few nights later Ben was terribly sick when the night nurse said, "I hate to do this but I have to." She put a casitor in Ben and within minutes had drained two sacks of fluid from his kidneys.

"I think I know what is wrong now," Dr. Jacob said after he received the report and ordered new tests.

It was Christmas time and Lori drove an hour to pick up Ben's two sons from the bus station. Roy came in from Oregon. Lori had decided to pay bus fare for Roy to come home for Christmas as Ben's Christmas present. Don came in from Texas.

Lori took Roy and Don to the hospital to see Ben. She later checked them into a motel across the street from the hospital. Joyce was driving an hour each day to sit up with Ben. Now Roy and Don could help Lori and Joyce sit up with him.

Lori and Roy were in the hospital when Dr. Jacob came in. "We have some test results. I need to talk to you for a minute," he said and went on to explain, "Ben has congestive heart failure, pneumonia in each lung, and a blood clot in his heart. I have called the heart hospital in Denver but I'm not sure any one will take him since it is Christmas."

Lori called the rest of the family with the news, trying not to cry.

Dr. Jacob received notice that the hospital had an empty bed. Christmas Eve morning Lori was told that she could fly with Ben by Flight for Life to Denver. Ben was loaded on a stretcher with two E.M.T s working with him.

The freezing wind was blowing so hard that Lori had difficulty closing the ambulance door. The plane did not look very large for such weather. Lori crawled beside Ben holding Ben's hand with one hand and she had the other hand in back of his head. Ben was so "out of it" that he thought Lori was riding in the front with the pilot.

The flight was smooth and they soon could see the Rocky Mountains. Pikes Peak looked like a beautiful lady in a white dress.

"I love to fly but not under these circumstances," Lori told the others.

Ben was quickly taken off the plane, put in an ambulance, and hurried off to Aurora South, a huge hospital in east Denver. It was easy to get lost in all the long halls in the hospital. Ben was given blood thinners and other medicine to drain the extra liquid from his lungs and heart. This made him have to urinate frequently. He did not want to use a bed pan and it took two people to get him to the bathroom.

Joyce brought Roy and Don to Denver Christmas Day. They were stranded for a short time in a white out blizzard, but finally made it to the hospital. Roy and Don sit up with Ben at night while Joyce drove Lori to a motel to rest. Lori and Joyce sit with Ben the twelve hours of day while the boys tried to get some rest.

A week later the pneumonia and the fluid from Ben's heart was gone. The blood clot was still there but Ben was taken by ambulance back to the local hospital in Kansas on New Years Eve.

Lori thought she would be driving Ben back to the local hospital so she had Mitch and Mike to bring the Pacifica to Lori's sister's place close to Denver. She had to take the vehicle home alone and become more acquainted with their new car.

Roy went back to Oregon. Don stayed in Denver and Joyce returned to Kansas and work. Lori was able to take Ben home January 7th. Again, Ben was getting around with a walker.

Joyce and Lori had bought Ben a Wii game for Father's Day. They played six games of bowling and two of golf for part of Ben's therapy. Ben started playing the games sitting in a chair but was eventually able to go through the motions standing. There were many trips for therapy. Ben had to have his blood checked every week because he was on blood thinners. Lori and Ben felt like the blood clot left Ben's heart through prayer. As Ben became stronger, he no longer needed a walker. Lori had helped him keep his balance for so long that she felt off balance when not holding Ben's hand.

"Since your folks no longer need us, how about moving to Dannon where we can watch the two youngest grandsons play ball and hopefully get Mike and his family in church," Lori said one day, "I'm tired of driving the seventy miles every time they have a game."

"I have been thinking the same thing," Ben replied. They put the old, remodeled house up for sale and started looking at homes in Dannon.

"I'm glad we had the basement finished last year," Lori said, "It should make it easier to sell, and gives the place a lot more living space.

Lori showed the house to an amazing number of times for the country to be in hard times. Almost everyone liked the house but few people had much money. Lori showed it to everyone as though they might buy it.

A retired nurse from down the street came to look at the house. She called back that evening. "I don't know if I made myself clear or not . . ." Sherry said.

"Oh no," Lori thought as she listened.

"I don't know if I made myself clear or not but I'm very interested in your home," Sherry said. A few days later she made an offer good enough for Ben and Lori to accept.

The houses in Dannon seemed quite expensive. Lori found one she liked. It had started out as a trailer and had been added on several times. Ben didn't like some things about the house and he didn't like the neighborhood of which it was located.

One day they traveled to Dannon and started driving up and down each street looking for "For Sale" signs. Lori drove down the last street on the west side of town. She made a couple of left turns and ended up in a section of town that had several modular homes. As she drove the length of the street and turn on the co-a-sac, there was a log looking house with a partly finished double garage. It had a For Sale sign in front.

Lori walked around the house. There were several trees growing out of a mountain of sand. The fence was partly broken down. The windows were without curtains or blinds and Lori could look inside. The house was quite large and Lori could see a fire place in the family room. Lori was excited because, once again, she could see the place the way it could look, not the way it did look.

Ben didn't feel like getting out.

Lori dialed the realtor's number.

"I think I have the property sold but it's not final yet," the realtor said, "Would you like to look at it."

"When can you show it to us," Lori asked.

"I live thirty miles away so it will take me at least forty minutes to get there," the realtor answered.

"We'll be waiting for you," Lori responded.

Lori was excited when she looked at the house. It had four nice-sized bedrooms, including the large master bedroom, and two and a half baths. The island kitchen, and the dining room were small but the front living room and back family room were large enough. The realtor gave them the ads on the house. "The roof has been fixed and the two air conditioners work," she said.

Lori thought the price was reasonable.

"If you think you are interested, you need to work fast. I have another party that wants it and they are trying to get a little more on their loan to buy it," the realtor said.

"Can we buy it?" Lori begged.

"The Lord told me not to pay over $72,000 for it and I will not go a penny higher," Ben answered.

Later, Lori regretted many times that she had talked Ben into buying the house. The roof leaked and they ended up putting on a steel roof. Most of the "garage" had to be rebuilt and garage doors installed. The air conditioners did not work and it took six thousand dollars to have new ones put in. The carpet and part of the walls were soaked with pet pee. Somehow, Ben and Lori had not noticed the terrible order when they look at the house and bought it.

The old carpet had to be taken out, walls were repaired, and new modeling put in before the new carpets could be installed. They used everything they could think of to get rid of the smell.

The driveway had to be shoveled out to be lower than the house so water would not go under the house when it rained. Trees had to be removed, relocated, gravel put in the double driveway and the visitor parking space. Sod had to be put in along with a sprinkling system.

To make matters worse, the contractor they hired to do the work, or get the work done, was a talker and not a worker. Ben kept faith in him to the very end. He didn't finish the job and did poor work on everything he tried to do. He even messed up the new tile in the master bath and all the carpets were installed without stretching and the seams coming together.

Lori and Ben had to live with the "boo boos" or pay someone else to redo the work. Paint was still setting out the day they moved in. Lori ended up calling the contractor every morning, begging him to come to work. They traveled the seventy miles every day in hopes of seeing the contractor and talking him into working. One day there were four young boys playing around the place with no adults for quite too long of time. They had their house closing the day before they moved to Dannon.

Mike and his family were out of town for a football game the day Ben and Lori moved but Mitch, who was a football coach in another town, brought two of his football players to help. Staci and granddaughter, Jenny, also helped in the move. It was September 11th. Everyone talked about what they remembered the other September 11 ten years earlier.

There had been a lot of disappointments but the house was pretty, comfortable, and close enough to the high school for the two grandsons, Jacob and Jerry, to come over for lunch on school days. Jacob was sophomore and Jerry was a freshman. The boys were there for thirty minutes to eat and read the local newspaper. Both grandsons lettered in football. Ben was strong enough to go to all the home games.

When Dannon's team was finished with their season, Ben and Lori traveled with Staci and Jenny four-hundred miles to see the play-off game that Mitch's team was playing. Ben was very tired when they reached their destination and rested. He felt good enough later to take a cousin and husband out to dinner that lived in that area.

The football field was covered with wet grass and Canadian Geese dung. It was slippery. Mitch's team was thirty-five pounds lighter per player than the other team. They were used to running zigzag while the other larger team could just march straight through. It was a good game but Mitch's team ended up losing.

Jerry and Jacob went right into basketball. Jerry played on the freshman team and was third in scoring and first in rebounds. Jacob played on the Junior Varity team. Ben and Lori were able to see all the home games.

At Christmas time Ben helped Lori put together one-hundred and forty Christmas letters with pictures. They had a lot of news to share: Ben's near death experience the Christmas before and his gaining from 135 pounds to 165 pounds. He was now able to walk too fast for Lori to keep up. They also told about their new home in Dannon and the family they were able to enjoy. God had been good.

Lori received a Christmas letter from a mother of two boys she had tutored. They were both now in the Navy and had been to Iraq twice. One was now a Navy Seal. It made the war seem more real when two of Lori's precious students were involved.

"What this about you and Christmas time?" Lori asked Ben when she had to take him to ER in Dannon on Christmas Eve day. With more medicine, Ben did not develop pneumonia again. A late, very cold spell killed some new plants they had planted the fall before.

Basketball turned into baseball. Jerry played on the JVs again and Jacob lettered for the second time on the varsity. They both played third base.

Dannon made the State play offs that were held in the northern part of the state. They won two games before losing enough to be out. Lori was able to drive Ben to the games. The first night they stayed with Lori's younger sister. The second night they stayed with the oldest grandson and his wife, and the third night they stayed in a Motel so Ben could rest. They slept all afternoon. Dannon lost the next day so they drove home. It had been fun.

Later that week Lori's cousin, who had just lost her youngest son, came with the older son to visit. Lori arranged for LaTricia's nephew to be there with his new wife and baby. They had not seen each other for a long time. They had a great time together.

The next week Lori's sister and husband from Arizona came to spend a night. Elaine and Gary left the next morning to join friends in the mountains.

Lori had not remembered being so happy. Ben needed a lot of rest but seemed to feel better and enjoy things they were able to do. He was even able to mow the lawn by taking frequent rest breaks. It was one of their happiest times.

CHAPTER XVI

BEN'S MOVE TO HEAVEN

"Lori, we need to drive downtown and pick up some supplies at the lumber yard and then have the tires rotated on the car," Ben said.

"It is unusual for me to have a headache, but I have one this morning and I don't feel like driving right now," Lori said.

"That's all right. There is no hurry," Ben replied.

Lori was feeling better by mid afternoon so they went down to the lumber company and then to the tire company. Lori and Ben were sitting in the waiting room. The car was almost ready. Ben stood up.

"Where are you going, Babe?" Lori asked.

"I don't feel well," Ben answered. He fell back into his chair. His eyes rolled up in his head and he quit breathing.

Lori grabbed Ben's head and started praying the healing scriptures they went over every day. "Ben, you are not going to leave me," Lori shouted, "I'm not going to live in our new place alone, do you hear me!"

Ben started breathing again. Nine, one, one was called. Six guys rushed in, put a patch on Ben's arm and an IV in his veins. The ambulance rushed Ben to the Dannon hospital and Lori called Libby. "Ben has had a heart attack and they are taking him to the hospital," she shouted. Libby was at the hospital before Lori got there because Lori felt upset and confused and couldn't think of the quickest way to get to the hospital.

Ben' heart rate was 200 with very little blood pressure. "We are going to have shock your heart, Mr. Fielding and we don't have time to put you to sleep for the procedure. It is going to hurt," an intern said.

Lori and Libby waited in the waiting room. Libby heard Ben said ouch, but Lori didn't hear it. Ben came out of it and was coherent. He was able to respond to Libby's teasing.

Again Ben was loaded into a Flight for Life plane and Lori was allowed to go with him. There were smoke clouds from the large fires in New Mexico so it wasn't a pretty day for a flight. Ben was again taken by ambulance to the large heart hospital in Denver. His vitals were checked every hour all night. Lori tried to get some sleep in the small chair at his bedside. She was so uncomfortable that she ended up sleeping a couple of hours on the hard, cold floor.

The next morning the heart doctor said, "I will not let Ben leave the hospital without a pace maker sybulator in his heart. He will not be able to live through another cardiac arrest," he explained. He explained to Lori that a heart attack is plugged arteries and Ben's heart had stopped which was cardiac arrest. "We will have to do exploratory surgery this morning to see that he doesn't have any blockage in his arteries before we can put in the pace maker," the doctor said.

Lori waited in a small waiting room and prayed while Ben was in surgery. Two hours later he was brought back. "I can't believe I didn't have any discomfort and they didn't even put me to sleep. I feel pretty good now," Ben said. He was scheduled for the pace maker the next morning.

That evening Don and a friend came by to visit. Ben and Lori ate a large hospital meal because Ben would have to fast after midnight to be ready for the morning surgery. They laughed together and played a game that Lori had in her purse. Ben won as usual.

"Mr. Fielding, here is a pamphlet on the pace maker. We would like for you and your wife to read it so you will be able to ask questions," the nurse said.

Ben started reading. Lori put on her night gown and lay down in a large chair that had been brought in. She was soon asleep. A few minutes later, she heard a terrible noise that woke her up. She saw the pamphlet fall to the floor. She looked at Ben. His head and body were weaving and he couldn't talk. Lori knew it was a stroke. She called the nurse. "I need help in here!" she shouted.

The nurse came running into the room, took one look and called a stroke alert. Within minutes, several men and a few women were in the room.

Lori scooted into a far corner and watched them rush Ben to the ICU part of the hospital. She suddenly realized that this was no longer Ben's room. She had to get out before another patient was brought in. Lori quickly dressed and gathered up her things, but she didn't know where to go.

A nurse came in and said, "You come with me. We will let you sit at the nurse's station until we know where you need to go."

Lori's hands were shaking so badly that she could hardly dial Joyce's number on her cell phone.

"I'll be there tomorrow," Joyce said in a daze.

Lori was taken to Ben's ICU room where several people were working with him. He managed to call to Lori, "Pray for me. I'm just too much trouble."

"Oh Lord, I never wanted him to feel that he was every any trouble," Lori said to herself. She could see Ben losing everything from the toll the stroke was taking.

Ben was taken to the lab for an MRI. The report was that both sides of Ben's brain were heavily damaged. "We found a lot of old brain damage from his first stroke. He is now brain dead and I can't explain why his body is able to keep moving," a male nurse said.

A minister friend called Lori and said, "Lori, you must get out of the way and let the Lord call Ben home if it's his time."

Lori felt in her heart that Ben had asked the Lord to take him home immediately and she had gotten in the way by praying scriptures over him in faith. Ben had not really felt good for five years. He had been concerned about ending up in a Nursing Home and leaving Lori without enough money to live on. "Oh Lord, help me to be strong and make the right decisions," she prayed.

Lori realized that they had put a respirator on Ben. She remembered the conversation they had not too many weeks ago. "I don't want any life support, and I want cremation, and no funeral," Ben had said. Nothing had been put in writing.

"I want no life support, cremation, but I want a service because I want the people I love to hear the Gospel message one more time," Lori had said, laughing.

Lori explained the conversation to one of nurses in charge and requested that the respirator be removed from Ben's precious, helpless body.

For the next six days Ben's body flopped around. Hospital sitters were assigned to help keep Ben on the bed along with the family's help. The sitters were Christians and very supportive. Don sat up with the sitters at night while Joyce took Lori to a motel where they could rest. Lori felt like crying all the time. She spent her time with Ben rubbing his head, arms, and legs and trying to keep him covered. He was not able to swallow. A few times Lori thought he had squeezed her hand, but she couldn't be quite sure. She could see some expressions when she called relatives and put the phone on Ben's ear.

"Go on home and be with the Lord. I'll be all right. Just turn loose my love," Lori said over and over, kissing Ben's precious head.

Mitch brought Staci and Libby the three-hundred miles to see Ben. Libby was sure Ben opened eyes and looked at her.

Don had bought Ben a softball and mitt for Father's day. Lori was shocked when she walked into the room one morning and saw them on Ben's hands. "Don has his own way of mourning, and I guess it doesn't matter," Lori said to herself.

Lori's youngest sister stopped by several times and Elaine and Gary stopped by on their way back to Arizona.

"All we can do is to keep him comfortable," one nurse said. The heart doctor stopped by to tell Lori how sorry he was that things turned out the way they did.

"If that is all they can do, then why don't we take dad home," Joyce suggested.

"That sounds like a good idea," Lori agreed.

A case worker was assigned to them to make arrangement for an ambulance, dismissal, etc. "We have found a Nursing Home in Dannon but they have not said whether they will take him or not," the case worker explained.

Lori's cell phone rang. "We can't take your husband until you come in and pay us four-thousand, four-hundred dollars for the rest of the month a woman said.

"I can't do that since I'm in Denver, but I will pay you as soon as get my husband there," Lori explained.

"Since you live in Dannon, I guess that will have to do," the lady said before hanging up.

The case worker found an available ambulance from near Dannon that happened to be in the area. Lori followed the EMT people as they tried to take Ben out of the hospital. No one was helping and they kept getting lost in the endless halls. Ben had to be taken the long route home because they did not think he would make it and they did not want to have a corpse in their ambulance while they were out in the middle of nowhere and there were not many towns along the shortest route.

Since Ben was so near gone, there seemed to be no hurry and the lights and sirens were not used. They lifted Ben out of one ambulance an hour from Dannon and he was put into a Dannon ambulance for the rest of the way.

Joyce had driven the shortest way and was at the Nursing Home long before they arrived with Ben. Don stayed in Denver to wait for Roy to come in from Oregon that evening. The family was turned over to hospice. A prayer shawl was thrown over Lori as soon as she came into Ben's room.

There seemed to be several capable people, nurses and hospice workers and Lori felt comfortable to rush home for a little rest. Joyce went with her. "I can't believe I left my baby with strangers," Lori said before she went to bed.

Lori was back to the Nursing Home early the next morning. She again rubbed Ben's body and kissed his head. She kept telling him that she could make it alone and for Ben to just turn loose and go to be with the Lord.

The hospices doctor came in about mid morning to check on Ben and said, "He is already in heaven although his body is still lingering."

Joyce didn't think there was much she could do so she started back to Kansas and her work.

Mitch brought Jacob and Jerry. Ben was lying still by then. Don and Roy came in a little later and there was no response from Ben's body.

"Lori, Ben is not getting much oxygen, so do you want us to pull it?" a nurse asked.

"Oh Lord, I don't want to make this decision," Lori cried. She had her hand on Ben's chest when she realized that he was not breathing. "I guess I don't have to make that decision now," she said.

Everyone was helpful in calling family members. Lori had lost her love, her best friend, her rock, her bookkeeper, her baby and her soul mate. She had to think about all there was to be done and not her feelings of devastation. Joyce had just gotten home when she received the death message. "I think I will stay home a couple of days before I come back," she told Lori.

Lori called a former student who was now running one of the local funeral homes. Jack and his wife left immediately to pick up Ben's body. Don and Mike helped load the body. It didn't matter to Lori since Ben was not in it anymore but with the Lord instead.

The next day they returned with Ben's body to have papers signed for the cremation. They could not find anyone available to sign the paper and had to take Ben's body back. Lori had to change the day of the memorial service for two days later and she had to pay two-hundred, fifty dollars a day to have the body in cold storage. Lori did not want to have Ben's body embalmed since cremation was planned.

Lori started to write Ben's obituary. It was not easy to write. Ben was not even sure of the correct spelling of his real father's name and thought the stone on his grave was spelled wrong. His father had been killed by a hit and run driver when Ben was only a year old. Lori had only known Ben twenty-four years of his seventy four years. No one wanted to help her but agreed with what she wrote. Roy added that Ben would be greatly missed. Lori wrote a poem in honor of Ben and called it The Quiet Man of God.

There he is sitting in a large chair with Bible and notebook . . . . The quiet man of God.

Bible, glasses, white hair, taking notes to better know his Lord . . . The quiet man of God.

There he is with a check book in his hand, giving to people in need near and far . . . The quiet man of God.

Always there for people that needed him . . . The quiet man of God.

Finding value in each person whether great or not . . . The quiet man of God.

Head bowed praying for others when he was struggling . . . . The quiet man of God.

Now made perfect in the presence of the Lord . . . The quiet man of God.

"Roy and Don, would you help me pick out some pictures for the power point at the funeral," Lori asked.

"You just pick out what you want," they both said. They didn't seem interested in helping but agreed with what Lori picked out.

Ben's oldest step son and wife drove all the way from California to be with the family. Ray and Marie came in with a lot of groceries and Marie took over Lori's kitchen and cooked a lot of food. Lori did not mind turning the kitchen over to Marie. She could now think about everything else. It was hard to not forget something important. Holly and her family could not come from North Dakota, but some relatives traveled a long way to be there.

Lori had their former pastor open the service and read the obituary. Her lady pastor friend brought a good message about Ben not being dead but more alive since moving to heaven. Rick, their present pastor, brought a great message on one of Ben's favorite scriptures that there is a time and place for everything.

Roy drove Don, Joyce and Lori to the church. Lori's heart felt like it was going to break as she patted the wooden urn that contained Ben's ashes. She read his name at the top and the Prayer of St. Francis of Assisi on the side. She thought she wanted scriptures until she read the prayer that sounded so much like Ben prayer for is life. About twenty pictures were shown on the screen. Two close friends sang "In the Garden" which was one of Ben's favorite songs. They sang two other songs. The music was beautiful.

The service was more like a celebration than a funeral. People met at the cemetery for a short encouraging message, then back to the community building for a large dinner. Lori was disappointed that many people could not stay for the dinner and to visit. The church ladies had a lot of food left over which they put in freezer bags and labeled to send home with Lori.

Joyce left the next day but Roy and Don stayed a few days. Roy helped Don rebuild the old broken fence around the Lori's place and put a new one on the north side. Don stayed a couple more weeks, to build a large shade in the back. Jacob and Jerry helped. The next door neighbor loaned them his tools and pickup.

The week after the service Lori went with a close friend to a Bible Camp. She cried a lot but enjoyed the four girls that had been put in her charge. The children were mostly Hispanic and Navahos. It was hard to come back home even with Roy and Don there.

Lori put Ben's obituary in three local papers, collected Ben's small life insurance and paid off most of the bills, and contacted the Social Security office. It would be impossible to keep their place on just what she made on her teacher's retirement. She invested some of her inheritance form Elizabeth for more monthly income, and papers. So she could have monthly income from Ben's 401 K investments.

Lori spent hours on the phone to find out what the automatic withdraws were from Ben's account he still had in Nebraska. She was finally able to close that account and have everything in one bank. "I can screw up one checking book easily enough and I sure don't need two to keep up with," she told herself.

Lori had to pay the ambulance company that had taken Ben the nine miles from the Denver air port to the hospital. The bill was nine-hundred dollars. When Lori sent the money she also sent insurance information hoping it would eventually be covered. The expensive flight and the rest of the other ambulances were paid off as well as his hospital stay by insurance. Lori was thankful that she had enough left over to live on.

The house was so empty when Don finally left. Lori cried so much that she started to have nose bleeds, begin to lose her voice, and her eyesight became worse. She would think that she was doing better, then the thought would hit her that Ben would never be there again and she would start crying all over again.

It was always hard to come back into the empty house. Lori spent most of her time out in the back. The awning was new and the only place where there were not a million memories. Lori was so grateful that Ben had moved to heaven in the summer time and she could be outside. She was soon walking about five miles a day. Lori was walking one evening when a storm hit. There was lightening all around. Lori heard herself say, "Lord, let the lightening hit me and take me to be in heaven to be with you and Ben but please don't let it hurt." She could not understand why she was still here and Ben was gone.

Lori bought new throw rugs and pictures to try to make the house look a little different, but nothing seemed to keep her from Ben's memory.

The kids were good to call and Jacob and Jerry did the mowing every Thursday. Mike would come by to check on their work. Lori sat between two, large widow ladies at church and tried to make new friendships. She tried to fill her time with music, writing, and reading. TV always made her miss Ben more. No matter how hard she tried, Lori always had too much time to think about Ben. She had a herb she took at bedtime that was supposed to help her sleep.

I will be glad when I enjoy living alone as much as you seem to," Lori told Joyce. There were many times Lori wished she could have left with Ben. At her age was there any future for her?

Lori had two very close friends. Suzy and her husband had gone into mission work many years ago. Suzy had been a widow for over two years. She had twenty-eight grandchildren that kept her busy. Lori felt free to call her at any time of night or day. They spent many hours on the phone.

Harvey and Lori had grown up together, gone through school together, and graduated together. Lori had gotten married immediately and Harvey married four years later. Harvey's father was killed in a tractor accident when they were eleven and Harvey had to go to work young to help support the family. Both Lori and Harvey had two sons. Harvey's oldest son moved to heaven when he was only nineteen. His wife moved to heaven when she was in her sixties. Harvey knew what losing loved ones can be like. Both Harvey and Suzy helped Lori through some very tough times.

Lori gradually begain to see life differently. She learned to be thankful that Ben was not suffering in a Nursing Home. She seemed to find people that needed encouraged. Maybe that is why God didn't take her with Ben.

Lori took a vacation back to Whidbey Island to visit Aunt Tina. She did not like to drive in the cities so she asked cousin LaTricia and her son, Luke to go alone so Luke could do the driving. They visited other relatives along the way and spent four days with Aunt Tina. Lori still felt embarrassed about the way Ben had treated her the three months they had been there five years earlier. "But, he was so sick," Aunt Tina said.

"The bowling alley has a good deal today," Aunt Tina said. "Would you like to go bowling?" she asked. Luke was excited about it, and Lori thought it would be fun since she had bowled in a league for several years. LaTricia said she would try it. They met Aunt Tina's friend there. Aunt Tina was still a good bowler although she was blind.

Everyone one had thrown their ball by the time Lori had put on her shoes and found a ball that felt comfortable. She stepped up to throw the ball when it felt like she had stepped on ice and someone was pushing her. She could not stop and slid down half way to the pins. The family heard Lori's head hit the hard floor. Lori was unconscious for a few minutes. When she tried to get up she fainted again.

The next time she knew anything, the EMT people had put a collar around her neck that was hurting her jaw. She realized they had her hooked up to a heart monitor and had jabbed her wrist twice to put in an IV. Lori was put on a stretcher and into an ambulance. The ambulance looked familiar. "What is this thing about Whidbey Island?" Lori sobbed while they were rushing her to the hospital.

The ER room looked familiar. Lori was crying again. The nurses and doctor checked Lori and could not find anything wrong with her. She was afraid to raise her head up again, but this time she was fine. She was given a pill for the pain that she "was going to have."

"Thank you Lord for healing me," Lori whispered. The family took Lori back to Aunt Tina's a watched her close for a couple of days. Lori's cousin did her hair two days later and there was not one sore spot on Lori's head. She was so thankful.

Lori had a memorial stone with her and Ben's names put up next to his buried ashes. It showed an open Bible and said, "Together forever with the Lord." Lori and Ben had drawn something similar a few years ago because Ben wanted to put a stone on his folks' grave in Tempe, AZ. They were not able to obtain enough information to have the stone made because Arizona would not cooperate. Lori was able to get the information because some laws had been changed. She had a similar stone put up in Tempe on Ben's parents grave. She honored Ben in every way she knew how.

Lori flew to Phoenix with a friend to see the stone. It was beautiful. They were able to spend a few days with Lori's sister and husband and see "their part of the world" for the first time.

At Christmas time Lori volunteered her house for an open house tour to help the organization for battered women. It gave her inspiration to decorate for her first Christmas without Ben. She continually had

Jacob and Jerry over for lunch on school days. It was hard at first without Ben.

Mike and Libby took Lori to all the football games and both boys lettered again. They were also able to go to the basketball games and baseball games. Lori bowled and made many new friends. She found that there were many people that needed her encouragement. It gave her purpose.

The main thing was that Lori had many hours available to spend in prayer and Bible study and just time with her Lord. The Lord even impressed upon her when to have the car serviced and other things that Ben had taken care of. The joy of the Lord filled Lori again and several people said they loved to hear her laughter.

Jacob called one Sunday morning. "Grandma, can I go to church with you?" the teenager asked. "I'll tell you as soon as I come down out of orbit," Lori answered, laughing. "Lord, can you please tell Ben and mother," she prayed. "That is the real reason we moved to Dannon."

Lori lived as long as Elizabeth had lived. She enjoyed trying to be a blessing to many people and help them to find the joy of the Lord. The Lord had blessed Ben and Lori with so much happiness, that the hard years were forgotten. Now the scriptures that the Lord gave Lori when she was divorced from Hollis made sense. Isaiah 52:1. Enlarge your tent for the number of your children shall be more than the children of the married woman. She had two children, three step children, and five step-step children.

Lori saw Jess ready to usher her into the beautiful city ahead. "The Father has just commanded me to come and bring His children home before the great tribulation," Jess explained. "You will soon be reunited with your family. It was because of you and Ben's prayers that all the family will be brought into this wonderful place."

"Why would anyone live a life without the Lord?" Lori asked. "There was so much to be gained in this life as well as the exciting life ahead."

"I guess they just don't know any better, or they just think they are too busy," Jess answered. "And they never knew how much our Father God loved them until it's too late."

Suddenly, Lori felt a joy like she had never felt before. What more could she ask than to spend eternity upon eternity with her Lord and her family" "I'm so glad the Lord never gave up on me," "She said. "Oh thank You, Jesus, for making all this possible," Lori whispered as she walked through the gold trimmed pearl gate. "Thank you for helping me get up again and win."

THE END